VIOLENCE IN THE NAME OF HONOUR
THEORETICAL AND POLITICAL CHALLENGES

EDITED BY SHAHRZAD MOJAB AND NAHLA ABDO

İSTANBUL BİLGİ ÜNİVERSİTESİ YAYINLARI

VIOLENCE IN THE NAME OF HONOUR
THEORETICAL AND POLITICAL CHALLENGES
EDITED BY
SHAHRZAD MOJAB AND NAHLA ABDO

© COPYRIGHT FOR INDIVIDUAL TEXTS RESTS WITH THE AUTHORS
ALL THE AUTHORS ARE RESPONSIBLE FOR THE CONTENT OF THEIR INDIVIDUAL TEXTS

İSTANBUL BİLGİ UNIVERSITY PRESS 86
SOCIOLOGY 3

ISBN 975-6857-98-6

FIRST EDITION, İSTANBUL, NOVEMBER 2004

BİLGİ İLETİŞİM GRUBU YAYINCILIK MÜZİK YAPIM VE HABER AJANSI LTD. ŞTİ.
ADDRESS: İNÖNÜ CADDESİ, NO: 28 KUŞTEPE ŞİŞLİ 34387 İSTANBUL/TURKEY
PHONE: 0212 311 60 00 - 217 28 62 / FAX: 0212 347 10 11

www.bilgiyay.com
E-MAIL yayin@bilgiyay.com
DISTRIBUTION dagitim@bilgiyay.com

EDITING BY CAN CEMGİL - STEPHAN DOBSON
DESIGN MEHMET ULUSEL
ELECTRONIC PAGE MAKEUP MARATON DİZGİEVİ
PRINTER AND BINDER SENA OFSET AMBALAJ VE MATBAACILIK SAN. TİC. LTD. ŞTİ.
LİTROS YOLU 2. MATBAACILAR SİTESİ B BLOK KAT 6 NO: 4 NB 7-9-11 TOPKAPI İSTANBUL/TURKEY
PHONE: 0212 613 03 21 - 613 38 46 / FAX: 0212 613 38 46

İstanbul Bilgi University Library Cataloging-in-Publication Data
A catalog record for this book is available from the İstanbul Bilgi University Library

 Violence in the name of Honour: Theoretical and Political Challenges
 Edited by Shahrzad Mojab, Nahla Abdo
  p. cm.
  Includes bibliographical references and index.
 ISBN 975-6857-98-6 (pbk.)

 1. Honor killings—Turkey. 2. Honor killings-Sweden. 3. Honor killings–Israel.
 4. Victims of family violence. 5. Patriarchy. 6. Women—Violence against.
 I. Mojab, Shahrzad. II. Abdo, Nahla.
  HV6191.V56   2004

VIOLENCE IN THE NAME OF HONOUR
THEORETICAL AND POLITICAL CHALLENGES

EDITED BY SHAHRZAD MOJAB AND NAHLA ABDO

Contents

vii Contributors

1 Introduction
SHAHRZAD MOJAB – NAHLA ABDO

13 SECTION 1 Theoretical Explorations of Honour Killing

    15 The Particularity of "Honour" and the Universality of "Killing"
    SHAHRZAD MOJAB

    39 Kinship, Politics, and Love: Honour in Post-Colonial Contexts – The Case of Turkey
    NÜKHET SİRMAN

    57 Honour Killing, Patriarchy, and the State: Women in Israel
    NAHLA ABDO

    91 Life-and-Death Honour: Young Women's Violent Stories About Reputation, Virginity and Honour – In a Swedish Context
    ÅSA ELDÉN

    101 Honour Killings: Instruments of Patriarchal Control
    NICOLE POPE

111 SECTION 2 Community Struggle Against Honour Killing

    113 The Cultural Basis of Violence in the Name of Honour
    NEBAHAT AKKOÇ

    127 The Story of Ayşe
    KA-MER

    137 In the Name of Honour
    LEYLÂ PERVİZAT

    143 Gendering Multiculturalism
    DILSA DEMIRBAG-STEN

149 Long-Term Measures to Combat Honour-Related Violence in Patriarchal Families
RIYADH AL-BALDAWI

157 The Dialogue Project to Prevent Violence: Discussions with Fathers and Sons
NIKLAS KELEMEN

163 SECTION 3 State Responses to Honour Killing

165 Violence in the Name of Honour Within the Context of International Regimes
YAKIN ERTÜRK

177 Acting With Honour: Justice Not Excuses in Crimes of So-Called 'Honour'
CHRISTINA CURRY

193 Swedish Government Initiatives to Help Young People at Risk of Honour-Related Violence
LISE BERGH

203 Confronting Honour Violence: The Swedish Police at Work
KICKIS ÅHRÉ ÄLGAMO

211 Violence in the Name of Honour in Swedish Society: What Lessons can be Learnt from the Swedish Experience
JAVERIA RIZVI

225 SECTION 4 Appendices

227 Recommended Resources on Women and Violence
SHAHRZAD MOJAB

231 Programme for the Seminar on Violence in the Name of Honour, 4–6 December, 2003

235 Bibliography
241 Index

Contributors

NAHLA ABDO
is a professor of sociology at Carleton University, Ottawa.

NEBAHAT AKKOÇ
is the founder and director of the women's organization KA-MER in Diyarbakır.

KICKIS ÅHRÉ ÄLGAMO
is a Swedish Detective Inspector with the National Criminal Investigation department.

RIYADH AL-BALDAWI
is a Swedish psychiatrist and Director of the multicultural clinic Orienthälsan. He is a member of the Swedish government's Reference Group for Women at Risk in Patriarchal Environments.

LISE BERGH
is State Secretary, Swedish Ministry of Justice.

CHRISTINA CURRY
is a project consultant for Amnesty International. She has completed two projects for Amnesty International: one investigating sexual violence in custody, and the other investigating violence in the family in Turkey.

DILSA DEMIRBAG-STEN
is a Swedish writer and journalist.

ÅSA ELDÉN
is a researcher at Uppsala University's Feminist Studies in Social Sciences department.

YAKIN ERTÜRK
is the UN Special Rapporteur on Violence Against Women, Ankara, and professor of sociology at the Middle East Technical University, Ankara.

NIKLAS KELEMEN
is a Swedish social worker and freelance journalist who works with the The Dialogue Project of the non-governmental organization Save the Children.

SHAHRZAD MOJAB
is an associate professor, Department of Adult Education and Counselling Psychology, Ontario Institute for Studies in Education at the University of Toronto, and Director, The Institute for Women's Studies and Gender Studies, University of Toronto.

LEYLÂ PERVİZAT
is a human rights activist and a programme co-ordinator with KA-MER, Istanbul.

NICOLE POPE
is a Swiss journalist and author based in Istanbul. For the past 15 years, she has been Turkey correspondent for *Le Monde* newspaper.

JAVERIA RIZVI
is a Project Manager with Terrafem, a support network for immigrant women, Stockholm.

NÜKHET SİRMAN
is professor of anthropology at Boğaziçi University, Istanbul.

Introduction
SHAHRZAD MOJAB - NAHLA ABDO

News about violence against women at local, national, and international levels is increasing at an alarming and deeply disturbing rate. Recent reports by Amnesty International and Human Rights Watch, among others, depict an appalling picture of the situation of women in Afghanistan and Iraq under conditions of war and occupation (Human Rights Watch 2003a and 2003b). There is a report about the execution of a sixteen year old Iranian girl whose crime was an extra-marrital relation; in Turkey, domestic violence is on the rise, and sexual violence against women in custody is well documented (Amnesty International 2003). We also read and hear daily about the violence of 'Wall' building by the state of Israel, which has made life especially difficult for women (see Ministry of Women's Affairs 2004).

Also, as we are writing this piece, we hear news about two French journalists taken hostage in Iraq with the demand that France abolish the ban on the wearing of the veil in public schools. The reports on violence against women in Africa, Latin America, and Asia provide a broader spectrum of sources and forms of violence, from the spread of poverty, starvation, and HIV/AIDS, to trafficking and trading young girls and women. Even under conditions of peace, such as in India and southeast Asia, femicide is now practiced widely (Russell and Harmes 2001; Shalhoub-Kevorkian 2002).

If violence against women is on the rise, our knowledge about the conditions that generate this violence is also advancing visibly. Academic research has made great strides in documenting, theorizing, and interpreting this social phenomenon. There is, at the same time, increasing grass-roots activism against male violence. Women's shelters, as well as hotline services, for instance, are set up in many countries throughout the world. Many states are committed to combating male violence. Some states such as Canada offer refugee status to women who are oppressed in their countries. On the international level, too, there is considerable progress in the struggle against violence against women. For instance, the United Nations and the European Union have launched major initiatives including:

1. *Declaration on the Elimination of Violence Against Women*, UN Document Series Symbol: ST/H/, UN Issuing Body: Secretariat Centre for Human Rights, Proclaimed by the General Assembly Resolution 48/104 of 20 December 1993;[1]

2. *Working Towards the Elimination of Crimes Against Women Committed in the Name of Honour*, United Nations S/57/179 General Assembly Distr.: General 30 January 2003 Fifty-Seventh session Agenda item 102 02 54997 Resolution adopted by the General Assembly;[2]

3. Security Council Resolution 1325 on *Women, Peace and Security*;

4. *Convention on the Elimination of All Forms of Discrimination Against Women* (CEDAW); and

5. *So-Called 'Honour Crimes'*, Council of Europe, Parliamentary Assembly, Resolution 1327, 2003.[3]

---

1 See <http://www.hri.ca/uninfo/treaties/ViolWom.shtml>.
2 See <http://www.soros.org/women/files/honor_english.pdg>.
3 See <http://assembly.coe.int/Documents/AdoptedText/ta03/ERES1327.htm>.

In civil society, individuals and organizations are more aware than ever before about the gender war on women. The *Convention on the Elimination of All Forms of Discrimination Against Women* (CEDAW) has been translated into many languages by lawyers, activists, and concerned citizens, and this declaration has been used for reforming oppressive gender relations.

If our knowledge is relatively adequate, if the state and the citizen are more conscious than ever before, and if there is action on the international level, why then is violence on the rise? The situation is a complex web of contradictions between consciousness and reality, knowledge and practice, the individual and the state, the agency and the institution, nationalism and feminism, religion and politics, and culture and politics.

Resistance to change is, undoubtedly, made up of multiple factors and forces. First, the entrenched nature of patriarchy in all contemporary societies is underestimated. Patriarchy is often reduced to a 'wrong', uninformed, uneducated, or deviationist male attitude. A more complex approach would see it not as a psychological or individual problem, but rather a social and historical institution. It is the *system* or *regime* of the exercise of male gender power. The exercise of power is critical if only because gender relations are unequal, hierarchical, and conflictual; women resist domination, and this resistance has to be managed if the institution is to survive. Equally crucial is the complex intertwining of male gender power to the unequal divisions of class power, race power, and ethnic power. Male power is, thus, produced and reproduced by other social forces and institutions such as language, law, religion, education, family, popular culture, and media.

A second factor: male power, much like class and state power, is reproduced by both consent and force. Patriarchal violence, as such, involves much more than a simple recognition of it as a problem of the individual, his mindset, or his ignorance. It is *systemic*. In fact, in the case of honour killing, women and even relatives often participate in the murder of a mother, daughter, sister or other female members of the family or kin.

Third, if symbolic, physical, and sexual violence is embedded in androcentric gender relations, if it threatens the safety of half of the population, and if its costs are, economically, high, how does the institution of the state respond? Marxist and feminist theories, in contrast to liberal and post-structuralist positions, question the neutrality of the state and law in the regulation of class, gender, or racial conflicts. The state and its juridico-political structure tend to reproduce economic, social, and cultural relations that are embedded in patriarchy. It took two centuries of women's and feminist struggle to reform the legal frameworks of some Western states along the lines of gender equality. The granting of universal suffrage rights, for instance, involved much more than a 'negotiation' between the state and suffragists. In the course of a century of resistance, suffragists had to take to the streets only to be beaten, jailed, and suppressed by other violent means.

Fourth, while considerable progress has been made in some Western states in instituting gender equality in conventions, charters of rights, constitutions, and legal frameworks, inequality in the extra-legal world continues to constrain this equality. This contradiction between formal equality and extra-legal inequality cannot be resolved under the present status quo, although it can be alleviated. Violence against women has not yet been uprooted in countries where legal equality has already been, more or less, achieved (for example, in the Scandinavian countries, or Britain and Canada). The norms of female propriety are still tied to property relations, in both capitalist and pre-capitalist formations. Untying the bond between the two is a formidable task not possible through legal reform alone.

Fifth, legal equality, a goal yet to be achieved in many states, does not automatically translate into mechanisms (courts, law enforcement, shelters, early warning systems, etc.) to uproot or constrain male violence. In Sweden, the murder of Fadime Şahindal by her father (in 2001) could probably have been averted if the government had known about the seriousness of the threat. The murder of Heshu Yones Abdalla in Britain (in 2002) also could have been be prevented.

Sixth, the state, even if willing to uproot patriarchal violence, is constrained by the fact that males engage in violence in spite of its consequences. While in many countries the citizen's right to life is not yet recognized by the state, men also feel free to take the life of women on charges of impropriety. This implies that both the state and the citizen need to be educated. Women, in the absence of feminist consciousness, fail to resist violence effectively, and eventually contribute to its perpetuation (production and reproduction). Education, in the form of spreading feminist consciousness by all means possible, is crucial for a serious encounter with patriarchal violence. The formal educational system from kindergarten to the university, and informal education through popular culture, media, literature, arts, and other venues, needs to be mobilized.

Seventh, patriarchal violence is universal. It is both Eastern and Western. In the West, where feminist knowledge emerged, anti-feminism continues to be dominant in popular culture. While identifying male violence as a problem of non-Western societies is a racist claim, it is true that there is an unleashing of male violence in certain parts of the world, especially in North Africa, the Middle East, and South Asia. Women of Iran, Afghanistan, and Saudi Arabia, to list only a few, have suffered under theocratic regimes. The civil wars (Iraq since 1961, Turkey 1984–2000, Iran 1979–1980s, Afghanistan since 1978), regional wars (Iran–Iraq in 1980–1988, Iraq–Kuwait 1990–1991, Afghanistan since 1979), and neo-colonialist wars (the U.S. against Iraq 1991 and since 2003, Afghanistan since 2001; Israel in Lebanon and in the Occupied Territories) have unleashed terror on the population, and have allowed patriarchal violence a free reign.

Eight, while patriarchy and its violence cannot be reduced to religion, the Islamic theocracies of Iran and Afghanistan codified misogynist legal–political orders, which subjected women to violence enshrined in Islamic *shari'a* or 'canonical law'. These theocracies, for example, conduct legal stoning to death of married adulterers and allow men to engage in honour killing. They also commit violence such as beating, insulting, detaining, and fining women for violating dress codes. The state justifies these atrocities by appealing to the Koran and *shari'a*. In the wake of the coming to power of the Islamic Republic of Iran in 1979, many secular states from North Africa to South Asia islamized their laws in order to appease Islamist political movements. The United States and other Western powers trained, financed, and led Islamists in their fight against the secular pro-Soviet regime in Afghanistan in 1980–1991.

Ninth, in their quest for changing their destinies, people in North Africa, the Ottoman Empire, and Iran pursued a politics for women's rights, modern justice systems, separation of state and religion, socialism, independence, and other democratic gains. This is part of a rich history of struggle that dates back to the late nineteenth century. However, many Islamists deny the people of the region this period of their history. Equally significant, the mainstream media and Western states also share the Islamist politics of setting up a great divide between the peoples of the region and those in the West. Western Orientalist knowledge, as noted by Edward Said (1979), Ella Shohat (2002), and others, has regularly engaged in treating the peoples of the Orient as backward, ignorant, and irrational.

In the last few decades, a host of theoretical positions ranging from the politics of identity to post-structuralism to post-modernism to cultural relativism have joined the chorus of Orientalists, mainstream media, and Western states in setting up a great divide between the East and the West. Paved with good intentions such as respect for cultural *difference*, these theoretical positions deny the peoples of the region their history of struggle against religious obscurantism and oppressive ethnic and cultural traditions. They fail to see that the main targets of the Taliban or Iran's Islamic regimes were and are the women of Afghanistan rather than Western states or Western capital. These theoretical positions, emanating from Western academe, have shaped the policies of the members of the European Union and other Western countries, some of which have by now substantial populations practising Islam.

While, as stated earlier, our knowledge about gender violence has advanced substantially, we have yet to learn more in order to move against oppressive gender relations in this complex historical moment. This colossal task requires the co-ordinated work of women activists, feminists, governments, media, educators, political parties, religious leaders, and everyone else. No serious progress can be made without the spread of feminist knowledge, feminist organizing, and grass-roots mobilization on the local, national, and international levels.

Finally, feminism and feminist epistemology and knowledge as advocated here is critical and anti-racist and capable of seeing and understanding the global context while simultaneously operating at the local and national levels. The critical feminist knowledge required is one capable of going beyond all boundaries constructed on racial, national, class, gender, and ethnic grounds. It is a type of knowledge that defies ideological chauvinism of all types. This is a mammoth task and challenge which faces all women and feminists concerned with improving women's conditions and ameliorating violence against women.

It is in this context that a unique seminar was organized by the Consulate General of Sweden in İstanbul called the *International Seminar on Violence in the Name of Honour*, held in İstanbul on 4–6 December of 2003. The organizers brought together a diverse group of activists, policy makers, documentary makers, and academics in order to engage in a re-thinking of honour killing and to strategize towards global action in combating violence against women. Readers of this book will see the contributions of this diverse group to an understanding of violence and ways to challenge it. As with other seminars and conferences, participants learned a great deal through interacting, debating, and talking with each other. This experience shows that with modest support from a state, it is possible to contribute to the struggle against violence.

This book is organized into four sections. The first section, 'Theoretical Explorations of Honour Killing', provides methodological and theoretical attention to the issue of honour violence. Shahrzad Mojab's 'The Particularity of "Honour" and the Universality of "Killing"' offers ideas for the prevention of the crime of honour killings and discusses both short-term and long-term interventions in the regime of gender relations that perpetuates violence against women. Nükhet Sirman analyses the social conditions in Turkey that produce honour-related crimes in her article 'Kinship, Politics, and Love: Honour in Post-Colonial Contexts—The Case of Turkey', paying particular attention to anthropological kinship categories and gender. She shows how the issue of 'customary crimes' plays out within the post-colonial nation-state of Turkey, which claims to be a modern state institution, and the important role of the notion of love and the family in the project of state building. 'Honour Killing, Patriarchy, and the State: Women in Israel' by Nahla Abdo analyses sexual violence and honour-killing at the local, national, and global levels and argues that a proper understanding of the phenomenon of honour-killing must be contextualized: First, historically, in order to see and recognize changes over time; and second, structurally and institutionally, allowing for a proper comprehension of the socio-economic, political, legal, and juridical forces of the state, particularly the colonial state.

Åsa Eldén writes 'Life-and-Death Honour: Young Women's Violent Stories About Reputation, Virginity, and Honour—In a Swedish Context', which provides a feminist perspective on male honour-related violence, using case studies, legal cases, and interviews with Arab and Kurdish women. Nicole Pope in her chapter 'Honour Killings: Instruments of Patriarchal Control' compares and contrasts violence against women in so-called 'Western' and Islamic societies. Pope reflects on the problem of culture versus the social in relation to such violence, and argues that no matter where violence against women occurs, whether in the West or not, such violence ultimately revolves around the issue of control over women. She concludes by stressing the importance of support for local initiatives to combat this violence.

The second section focuses on the theme of 'Community Struggle Against Honour Killing' within both Turkey and Sweden. Nebahat Akkoç of the women's organization KA-MER presents 'The Cultural Basis of Violence in the Name of Honour', giving a brief overview of the history of this organization which provides support to women faced with violence. She relates the stories of two murdered women, Şemse Allak and Kadriye Demirel, and outlines the progress made by this organization in the space of a year. In addition, she details twenty-one applications for assistance. The article concludes with KA-MER's ground-level advice for dealing with the issue of honour violence against women, with important comments on the ownership of language and on advocacy through practice, and specifies seven areas requiring improvement within the context of the Turkish state and civil society. The second piece in this section is KA-MER's 'The Story of Ayşe', which tells of one of the concrete successes of KA-MER in action—but while the life of Ayşe was saved, new problems arise as she and her husband must adapt to life in a new city. The contribution of Leylâ Pervizat is entitled 'In the Name of Honour', and is reprinted from the journal *Human Rights Dialogue*. Her article emphasizes the importance of redefining the concept of honour within the community as an important preventative step in combating violence against women in Turkey.

Turning to Sweden, Dilşa Demirbag-Sten's 'Gendering Multiculturalism' addresses the growing problem of racism in Sweden, and the debate around honour violence in that country. She argues for the need to allow minorities within Sweden to formulate the problem and its solutions, as these people are the ones who are affected by it. Riyadh Al-Baldawi's article, 'Long-Term Measures to Combat Honour-Related Violence in Patriarchal Families', after recognizing some Swedish government initiatives around violence in families, outlines four steps to be taken, ranging from short-term measures to long-term interventions. Finally, Niklas Kelemen's chapter, 'The Dialogue Project to Prevent Violence: Discussions with Fathers and Sons', gives an account of a large seminar with men from the immigrant community as an example of the kind of fieldwork undertaken by that Project to combat chauvinistic attitudes towards women.

The third section of our book focuses on 'State Responses to Honour Killing', and begins with a key-note address by Yakın Ertürk, UN Special Rapporteur on Violence Against Women, entitled 'Violence in the Name of Honour Within the Context of International Regimes.' She provides a synopsis of the international agenda to combat this violence, and includes an annex giving a chronology of the evolving United Nations actions towards women's human rights and gender equality. Christina Curry argues for the reappropriation of the term 'honour' in her 'Acting with Honour: Justice Not Excuses'. After outlining core human rights contained within international treaties, she addresses the issue of making rights a reality, with particular attention to the Turkish penal code.

The last three articles in our book return to the Swedish context. Lise Bergh, State Secretary, Swedish Ministry of Justice, presents us with 'Swedish Government Initiatives to Help Young People at Risk of Honour-Related Violence', which briefly introduces us to the history of how the Swedish government came to see honour violence against women as an important issue needing to be addressed; she indicates some of the ways in which the Swedish government has set out to change attitudes and address women's safety. Kickis Åhré Älgamo contributes 'Confronting Honour Violence: The Swedish Police at Work', which provides a perspective from the National Criminal Investigation department. Here we are presented with the initiatives of this police force as they overcome various obstacles to their work, including immigrant fear of security forces in general; the article also describes 'double liability to penalty' provisions within Swedish jurisprudence, which allows Sweden to set a higher penalty for a serious crime punished by a disproportionately low sentence in a foreign country. Our final chapter comes from Javeria Rizvi who reflects on 'Violence in the Name of Honour in Swedish Society.' She analyses cases of honour killing in terms of how Swedish courts tried the cases, and also in terms of how the media covered these events, and closes with lessons to be drawn.

Since the seminar from which the chapters presented here was held, there have been numerous progressive developments in the struggle against honour violence. In Turkey, amendments to the Penal Code opens doors for the possibility of fully punishing perpetrators of these crimes; it remains to be seen how effective these new laws are in action. The establishment of a Ministry of Women's Affairs in Palestine is a step in the right direction, and a promising venue for carrying through women's voices and their quest for rights and gender equality. Yet, similar to other political changes, such as in the Turkish case, the challenge for Arab and particularly Palestinian critical feminists is to see the extent to which this ministry can survive under internal (national) pressures, such as the economic, political, religious fundamentalist movements and so on, as well as the external (regional and international) pressures, particularly of continuous Israeli occupation and colonial policies. In another development, European police met in the summer of 2004 in The Hague to strategize ways to combat honour killings; such violence is now becoming widely recognized by states as an issue requiring urgent attention.

The final section, our Appendices, contains a short list of recommended resources on the theme of women and violence, and also the original Programme for the Seminar on Violence in the Name of Honour, 4–6 December 2003.

The original seminar on which this book is based, and indeed the book itself, would not have been possible without the generous support of the Consulate General of Sweden. In particular, the hospitality of Consul-General Ingmar Karlsson and Mrs Margareta Karlsson was generous beyond everyone's expectations and was greatly appreciated by all seminar participants. Annika Svahnström,

Consul at the Consulate General of Sweden, hosted all the participants of the seminar and graciously offered her time during the production of this book. Finally, we are grateful to Stephan Dobson for his superb editorial work in bringing this international volume to completion.

SECTION 1

Theoretical Explorations of Honour Killing

The Particularity of 'Honour' and the Universality of 'Killing': From Early Warning Signs to Feminist Pedagogy[1]

SHAHRZAD MOJAB

INTRODUCTION

The increasing violence against women and our inability to curb it pose a serious challenge to every individual, but especially to activists and institutions such as academia, governments, media, and schools. Male violence is of ancient origins and is deeply rooted in the very fabric of social, economic, and political organization. It is rather obvious that this violence cannot be *eliminated* without a radical rupture with the regime of gender relations known as *patriarchy*.

This paper offers ideas for the short-term, immediate, prevention of the crime of honour killing, and discusses long-term intervention in the regime of gender relations that perpetrates the killing of women. This study is based on case studies of honour killing in Iraqi Kurdistan, and in the Kurdish Diasporas in Europe.

---

1 This study is, in part, based on my previous and ongoing research on honour killing.

CONTAINING HONOUR KILLING: EARLY WARNING SYSTEMS

Honour killing is of ancient origins. In many patriarchal societies, 'adultery' has been punished by killing, often without allowing the accused any benefit of doubt. In parts of Kurdistan (especially in Iraq and Turkey) where war has led to the destruction of thousands of villages and major relocations of the population, the social and economic fabric of Kurdish life has been seriously disrupted. This has unleashed extensive tension, especially in gender relations. War has set off extreme male violence in the form of honour killing.[2]

Although there are no longitudinal studies of honour killing in the region, there is a consensus that the crime has increased exponentially since the 1990s. At the same time, there has been, in recent years, a sharp increase in female suicides, especially in the form of self-immolation. Some of these self-immolations in Iraqi Kurdistan are apparently nothing more than the burning of bodies in order to disguise killing in the name of honour. This is probably because, since 1999, honour killing has been criminalized in Iraqi Kurdistan. Killers have, thus, re-adjusted to legal reform.

According to a survey of 'self-immolation of women in the Kurdistan Region', there were, in the first six months of 2001, sixty-six cases of self-immolation in the city of Irbil and its surrounding region in Iraqi Kurdistan. Of these 66, nine lost their lives (13.6%). Most of them were young women: Nineteen were 12 to 17 years old, twenty-three were 18 to 25 years old, fourteen were 26 to 33 years old, and ten were 35 to 55 years old. In the first six months of 2002, the number of recorded cases of self-immolation increased to 80, of which 29 lost their lives (36.25%) (Bustanî 2003: 20–2). According to this survey,

> in many cases a woman's self-immolation has not been her own wish and consent when her family pressures her to self-immolate if she has done a bad deed (*karî xirap*) or if she is under suspicion, or

---

2   For Turkey, see especially Amnesty International, 'Turkey: Women Confronting Family Violence.' <http://web.amnesty.org/library/print/ENGEUR440132004>. (Accessed: 27 July, 2004.)

the family kill her but in order not to be sent to court, they burn her and pretend that she has self-immolated. (2003: 20–2)

In the other major city of Iraqi Kurdistan, Silemani, the Teaching Hospital of Silemani (Nexoşxney Fêrkarî Silêmanî) recorded 155 cases of self-immolation of women in 2001. Of these, 45 lived in the city of Silemani and 59 were from the surrounding region (Emîn 2002: 6). Dr. Luqman 'Ebdul-Qadir, from the burn injuries section of the hospital, said in an interview:

> This phenomenon [self-immolation] has tormented us, and is incessantly increasing; it is a very regrettable situation, and it hurts the conscience of all of us that the other gender is subjected to this fate and loses its life in pain and torture. To tell you the truth, we cannot do anything; we are calling for help, and ask responsible authorities and organizations to take adequate and serious action.... (Emîn 2002: 6)

We learn from genocide studies that genocide is not a jack-in-the-box that props up all of a sudden. There are early warning sings that are not difficult to detect.[3] For instance, when a group is dehumanized or denigrated verbally and openly, it should be taken as a warning about a possibly impending crime. This is also the case in honour killing. In Europe, where the killing of Fadime Şahindal (Sweden) and Heshu Abdalla (Britain) made international news, the crimes could have been prevented if any member of the family, the government, the community, and advocacy groups had taken the warning signs seriously. The case of Ayşe, as reported by KA-MER and distributed to conference participants (see 'The Story of Ayşe' in this volume), also shows how consciousness about the criminality of honour killing, attention to the warning systems, and the existence of the women's advocacy group, KA-MER, saved a woman's life.

---

3   Rudy Doom and Koen Vlassenroot, 'Early Warning and Conflict Prevention: Minerva's Wisdom.' *The Journal of Humanitarian Assistance*. <http://www.jha.ac/articles/a022.htm>. (Posted 3 June, 2000.)

As the case of Ayşe and many others indicate, honour killing is usually not an individual act. It is a crime in which the family and the community participate. Much like genocide, the group nature of honour crimes makes them easier to anticipate and prevent.

The concept of early warning (EW) was first used in the prediction of natural disasters and stock market crashes. Recently, EW systems were developed for the purpose of detecting and signalling various conflicts so that preventive action could be initiated. However, the gender dimension was absent in the development of early warning indicators that would identify areas at risk of violent conflicts.[4] Based on the cases of 'honour' killing which I have studied closely (Mojab 2004; Mojab and Hassanpour 2000a; Mojab 2000; Mojab and Hassanpour 2000b), here are three cases that exemplify how EW can work:

The Case of Heshu. I was in London when Yones Abdalla killed her sixteen-year-old daughter, Heshu, on 12 October, 2002. I found out through friends in the Kurdish community, including those in the Kurdish Women's Organization and in Kurdish Women Action Against Honour Killing. Some knew the family, and had heard that Heshu had told her friends that her father had threatened her. We have found out, after the sentencing of the killer on 29 September, 2003, that he had been beating her daughter repeatedly before she killed her.

In spite of this knowledge, nothing had been done to prevent the murder. Even when Heshu was killed, a major Kurdish political organization, the Patriotic Union of Kurdistan (PUK), which has offices in London, and where the murderer had worked as a member, lied about the crime, and declared it a racist attack on the father and the daughter. Two days later, in a public lecture on honour killing, which had been scheduled by Kurdish Women's Organization months before the crime, PUK supporters told the audience not to jump to the conclusion that this was an honour killing, and that they should rather

---

4   Susan Schmeidl and Eugenia Piza-Lopez, 'Gender and Conflict Early Warning: A Framework for Action.' London and Bern: International Alert. June 2002. <www.internationalalert.org/women/Ewgender.pdf>.

wait for the results of police and court investigations. The notice for commemoration of Heshu's death, issued by *kesûkar* (family/relatives), also claimed that 'a black and evil hand' had 'taken the butterfly Heshu away from the garden of life'. Even the Kurdish Women Action Against Honour Killing (KWAHK), while suspecting that this was honour murder, issued a statement in which it decided to avoid 'hearsay', and to wait for the results of official investigation:

> The tragic events of October 12th have shocked all members of the Kurdish community. We are all deeply touched by this news and are following the case closely. Although there is a great deal of pressure on us to act and take a position, we have decided not to add to the hearsay circulating in the community and to wait until the Metropolitan police finishes its investigation.
> As our campaign has proven since its launch in March 2000, we rely on verifiable evidence in our campaign against violence against women. Not only do we refuse to follow the rumours inside the community, we also believe that rumours damage Kurdish people in general and Kurdish women in particular. So much so, that it should not be forgotten that some of the honour related killings, which we have documented, have happened as a consequence of hearsay. We want to be rational and independent in our action. This is why we have decided to wait for the result of the investigation being carried out by the Metropolitan police.
> Luckily, in this country, it is the widespread belief that the law is an impartial instrument for justice. We rely on British law to resist the weight of any group or force and to deliver justice on the basis of truth.[5]

While it is important not to jump to conclusions anywhere and in any case without adequate evidence, the approach of KWAHK is least helpful in so far as it ignores the evidence that was available when Heshu was killed. Had the 'hearsay' about Heshu been taken seriously, she could have survived. When a young woman in a patri-

---

5 'Statement by Kurdish Women Against Honour Killing in Relation to Heshu Yunis's Murder.' Dated 18 October, 2004. <www.kwahk.org/index.asp?id=11>.

archal family tells her friends that her father has threatened her, this should be taken as a warning sign. Had Heshu been aware of the seriousness of honour crimes, and had she had access to advocacy groups, she would not have lived with her parents, especially after the first beating, and after she wrote a letter to her father.

In October 2002, after she was murdered, and when the 'hearsay' included her complaints about her father's threats, an advocacy group should not have waited for police and court investigations. 'Hearsay', defined as 'information which cannot be adequately substantiated' (*Oxford English Dictionary*, online), should be treated by women advocacy groups as hard fact unless it is proven to be false. Hearsay is a source for depicting warning signs of an impending honour crime.

The Case of Fadime Şahindal. Fadime, killed by her father in Uppsala, had already taken the case to the court and had been separated from her father and brother who had been convicted in court. She apparently relied on the power of the rule of law, and underestimated the power of patriarchal violence. She was killed while visiting her sister. Here the court and law enforcement powers of an advanced civic nation tried but failed to prevent the loss of life of a woman under protection. This is, in part, the failure of victims to take patriotic violence seriously even when state support is available.

The Case of Ayşe. The case reported by KA-MER shows that Ahmet, a male relative of Ayşe and her husband, had depicted the warning signs of an impending killing, and acted to prevent it. Here the consciousness of Ahmet, his knowledge of the existence of KA-MER, and his determination to help the target, prevented the killing.

THE STRUGGLE AGAINST HONOUR KILLING: OBSTACLES
The three cases examined above call for a radical re-thinking of the struggle to eliminate crimes of honour. We need multi-dimensional, multi-disciplinary, and radical approaches. There is a thread that runs through the different cases of Fadime, Heshu, and Ayşe: consciousness

about the seriousness of this crime lags behind the frequency and brutality of its occurrence. In spite of the rather advanced support system in Sweden, the victim, a university student and already separated from her family through court action, lost her life. In Turkey, where such support systems are non-existent or minimal, Ayşe survived because of the intervention of a family member and the response of an advocacy group. In Britain, Heshu lost her life in part because she received no help and did not know about how far male violence could go.

The case of Ayşe highlights the community nature of most honour killing. According to KA-MER's report,

> Her [Ayşe's] husband said that, he knew his wife was innocent and trusted her. But he also knew that life is difficult for a man if he can not get rid of his dishonour in the eyes of the family and society. But he accepted his wife back. He told that he did not know how much he could stand against pressures of villagers, brothers and family.

Finally, Aşye and her husband were sent out of their village to live in the city. According to KA-MER,

> We are used to the expulsion of the guilty one. But this time the victim was a woman and the guilty was a man. Thus the practice changed. The guilty one is staying in the village and the victim is trying to continue her life in the city, with worry and depression.

While this intervention has saved the life of Ayşe, it is far from satisfactory. While we need to take immediate action as KA-MER has ably done, to save lives, the everyday struggle against honour killing should aim at overcoming the feudal-patriarchal regime that sanctions the crime. The goal should be to promote the idea that state and non-state actors, that is, all citizens should accept that *women should enjoy the right to life and the right to security and safety*. This is not a struggle in stages. The short-term and the long-term projects are part of an overall single project. I will outline here some of the obstacles to projects for eliminating honour killing which I have encountered in various contexts in recent years.

It is important to note that the struggle for gender equality in the Middle East dates back to the late nineteenth century when Middle Eastern women and men began to denounce patriarchal oppression and violence including honour killing (e.g., the male Turkish poet Tevfik Fikret [1867–1915]). Today, the struggle against honour killing is internationalized, and informed by major breakthroughs in feminist theory. This struggle is, at the same time, constrained by religion, nationalism, the interests of the nation-state, media and popular culture, globalization, and academic theorizing.

Two major UN documents call for the *elimination* of honour killing. The concept of 'elimination' appears in the 1993 'Declaration on the Elimination of Violence Against Women'[6] and 'Working Towards the Elimination of Crimes Against Women Committed in the Name of Honour' issued earlier this year (2003).[7] But the elimination of any social and historical phenomenon like violence requires a serious intervention in the status quo. This intervention is necessarily a planned or conscious undertaking. It implies the replacement of one system of gender relations with another system, which does not exist yet. It means nothing less than building a new outlook, a new society, and a new world. This is the case because male violence is not simply a problem of the individual male's psychological make-up. In the words of the UN 'Declaration on the Elimination of Violence Against Women',

---

6 'Declaration on the Elimination of Violence Against Women.' UN Document Series Symbol: ST/H/, UN Issuing Body: Secretariat Centre for Human Rights, Proclaimed by the General Assembly Resolution 48/104 of 20 December 1993. <http://www.hri.ca/uninfo/treaties/Viol Wom.shtml>.

7 'Working Towards the Elimination of Crimes against Women Committed in the Name of Honour.' United Nations S/57/179 General Assembly Distr.: General 30 January 2003. Fifty-Seventh Session Agenda item 102 02 54997. Resolution adopted by the General Assembly [*On the Report of the Third Committee (A/57/549)* 57/179]. <http://www.unhchr.ch/Huridocda/ Huridoca.nsf/0/d71daccfe833c9a3c1256a7700542307?Opendocument>.

> violence against women is a manifestation of historically unequal power relations between men and women, which have led to domination over and discrimination against women by men and to the prevention of the full advancement of women, and that violence against women is one of the crucial social mechanisms by which women are forced into a subordinate position compared with men.

This 'historically unequal power relations between men and women', which generates violence and is reproduced by it, is anchored in all aspects of life, modern and pre-modern. The unequal division of gender power is (re-) produced by language, arts, culture, law, class, nation, religion, knowledge and all other social formations.

Legalism, the Rule of Law, and Legal Education

Feminism provides much of the theoretical and political framework to account for this rupture. We already know, on the strength of evidence from two centuries of feminist and women's movements, that we cannot readily eliminate the patriarchal regime of gender relations, which is incessantly produced and reproduced by tradition, culture, religion, folklore, law, attitude, and force of habit. Today, in many Western countries constitutional and legal equality between the two genders has been, to a great extent, achieved, yet inequality and violence go on.

Genders exercise power. This power is, however, distributed unequally. The juridico-political structure of many Western democracies was reformed in the last quarter of the twentieth century in ways that it has constrained the violent exercise of male power. For instance, committing violence against women is criminalized in these states, and courts are guided to take special notice of the ways in which patriarchal power shapes the administration of justice.[8] However, beyond the domain of law, the exercise of male power remains unchecked. While citizens in some sixty countries have been able to deny the state the

---

[8] The Urban Institute, *The Violence Against Women Act of 1994*. <http://www.ncjrs.org/vaw-hglt.htm>. (Accessed 22 November, 2003.)

right to capital punishment, they have failed to deny individual men the power to kill women. Very simply, law alone cannot disrupt the production and reproduction of patriarchal power.

While legalism's reduction of the complexity of gender violence to the question of 'the rule of law' is not productive, we should struggle to reform the juridico-political system in ways that it constrains, as much as possible, the perpetration of gender crimes. Part of this reform is to democratize or civilize the state itself by, in part, denying it the right to capital punishment, as it has been done in the EU, Canada, and about fifty other states. Equally significant is to democratize the administration of justice. As it is emphasized in the European Parliament's *Draft Report on Turkey's Appointment for Membership of the EU* (March 2003), the 'quality of the court system and the quality of judges' should be improved and 'a new legal culture at the service of the citizen' should be created.[9] The training of law enforcement agencies is also crucial.

Creating 'a new legal culture' demands great efforts on the local, national and international levels. A most urgent initiative is to promote the 'right to life' as a value in education, arts, media, literature, and popular culture. Individuals should realize that no one has the right to take anyone's life. Citizenship education should be given priority, especially the idea that citizens are denied the right to take the administration of justice into their own hands. In both the East and the West, but especially in the former, there is an urgent need for legal education.

Culture, Culturalization, and Cultural Relativism
The struggle against honour killing has suffered from current academic theorizations about the place of culture in contemporary life. These

---

9   European Parliament. Committee on Foreign Affairs, Human Rights, Common Security and Defence Policy, Rapporteur: Arie M. Oostlander, *Draft Report on Turkey's Application for Membership of the EU* (COM[2002] 700)–C5-0613/2000–2002/2014 [COS]). Provisional 2000/2014 (COS), PR\484772EN.doc, PE 320.271,12 March 2003/ <http://www.europarl.eu.int/meetdocs/committees/afet/20030324/484772en.pdf>.

academic debates have negatively shaped public policy in a number of Western states. Some of the questions that were raised in the wake of the murder of Fadime Şahindal in Sweden point to the significance of culture: Is honour killing part of Kurdish culture? Is honour killing an Islamic tradition? Was the killing a question of the conflict between two cultures, Kurdish and Swedish, Eastern and Western, urban and rural? What is the role of the Swedish government? What is the role of race and racism? There are at least two major ways in which the conceptualization of culture constrains or promotes our understanding of honour killing, and as a result our struggles against it.

Cultural Relativism and Post-Structuralism. Cultural relativism argues that values or truths are culture-specific and there are no universal measures or criteria to evaluate them. There are no universally accepted measures for understanding, for instance, 'good' and 'bad' or 'beautiful' and 'ugly'. The values of one culture should not be judged by the values of another culture; for example, the veiling of women or even honour killing as practised in Middle Eastern cultures should not be rejected as wrong based on the values of contemporary Western cultures.

Cultural relativism emerged in the early twentieth century, and played an important role in the theoretical and political struggle against modernist racism and its projects of racial purification, that is, eugenics. It emphasized the diversity of cultures, promoted tolerance and respect for other cultures, and rejected racist totalitarianism.

Since the late 1980s, the idea of respect for diversity has been re-theorized in terms of *difference*. In post-structuralist thinking, now dominant in academe and fashionable in media and popular culture, *difference* is the main constituent of the social world. Human beings, in this construction of the world, are all different, with their diverse and particular 'identities'. There is little, if any, common bond between human beings. The politics and everyday life of human beings are shaped by identities which separate them from all other human beings. In this world of particularized individuals, cultures, peoples, or nations, patriarchy is not universal, and gender oppression is too particular to be the target of struggle of women and men even within a single country.

Like cultural relativism, theorists of difference emphasize respect for cultural diversity, and tolerance. They oppose 'othering'. Thus, the politics of the two theoretical perspectives converge in their emphasis on diversity and tolerance. However, this tolerance sometimes translates into acceptance or even legitimation of oppression in 'other' cultures or societies.

Post-structuralist thinking turns into an obstacle to serious intervention in the status quo. It works as a conformist theoretical-political enterprise when it theorizes or rather eradicates the concept of *domination* and replaces it with the concept of *difference*. The world is not, in this view, divided into powerless and powerful blocs. Every individual, every woman, wields power. Power is not hierarchically organized; there may be a 'centre' and a 'margin' of power but there are no relationships of domination and subordination.

Although post-structuralists oppose violence, they prefer to remain silent about it, especially when it is perpetrated by 'others' whom they cannot judge due to cultural differences. There is, thus, an attempt to isolate honour killing from the patriarchal culture of the society that generates it. This is done by, among other things, reducing honour killing to a 'practice', that is, an individual behaviour not rooted in patriarchy as a regime or system (see below). Labelling the crime as a 'practice' relieves the academic specialist from the burden of criticizing culture and religion. As I have argued elsewhere, these 'strategies' are not helpful. In fact they do not allow a serious departure from neo-colonialism. A radical departure requires the abandoning of the epistemological and theoretical dictates of cultural relativism which has already ended in philosophical agnosticism (Mojab 2002). For instance, many academics are concerned that if they even discuss let alone critique oppressive traditions in other (for example, Middle Eastern) cultures, they would be accused of racism, neo-colonialism, or Orientalism. In her review of two documentaries on honour killing ('Crimes of Honour' and 'Our Honour and His Glory'), feminist anthropologist Mary Elaine Hegland wrote:

> The topic of honor killing, like clitoridectomy, spousal abuse, infanticide, elder neglect, rape, war, capital punishment, and premarital sex among other practices condoned by some groups but condemned by others, presents *dilemmas* to anthropologists, feminist scholars and others. Should anthropologists be apologists or advocates for their research group or social analysts? Should one's role be researcher or activist? (2001: 15, italics added)

This problematization of the dilemma of academic researchers is, at the same time, a positivistic statement of neutrality and objectivity. This position does not start from the interests of the several thousand women who are slaughtered every year in the name of male honour. To put it very explicitly, it does not have respect for the victims of this crime, their desire to live, their right to live, and their resistance to the murderers. In doing so, this 'respect' for other cultures is disrespect towards women who are subjected to harsh punishment for failing to abide by man-made rules of honour.

Anthropologists are equipped with conceptual tools for exempting culture and religion in the '*practice*' of honour killing. In her review of the two documentaries on honour killing, Hegland writes:

> The two videos clearly differ in level of professionalism, cultural knowledge, and analytical sophistication. *Crimes of Honour* promotes a more balanced, contextualized, analytical treatment of honor killing and the film team and activists portrayed take a more moderate, accommodating stance. Since the action is blamed on specific conditions rather than the society, culture, or tradition as a whole, the film provides hope that better conditions will serve to combat the practice.
> *Crimes of Honour* is less strident in tone. Activists are angry abut honor killing and the lack of effective means to protect threatened women, but they do not condemn culture, tradition, and religion as responsible.... (2001: 16)

But why should any one who opposes honour killing 'take a more moderate, accommodating stance' toward this crime and those who perpetrate it? What are 'better conditions'? What 'better conditions' can deter criminals from perpetrating the crime? Why should one hesitate to condemn the culture, tradition and religion that sanctions violence against women? An extensive and rich literature in all Middle Eastern languages since the late nineteenth century critiques the oppression of women, and unreservedly condemns violence against women. This literature includes journalistic essays, poetry, novels, short stories, cartoons, letters to the editor, satire, and academic research. Much like Enlightenment thinkers, reformers in the 'Muslim world' critiqued the culture, tradition, and religion of oppression including the clergy and their versions of Islam. Today's feminists of a cultural relativist tendency move in the opposite direction by denying that Islam and culture play any role in honour killing, stoning adulterers to death, or executing gays and lesbians; not only do they deny such responsibilities, they do their best to protect Islam and Middle Eastern cultures from any critique.

Anthropologists interested in absolving religion and culture treat honour killing as *practice*. 'Practice theory' claims that individual behaviour (e.g., Rahmi Şahindal's decision to kill his daughter Fadime, Uppsala, Sweden, 2002) does not derive from rules, norms, culture, rule-bound traditions, systems, or structures. Even when the existence of structures is not denied, these are not seen as constraining the mind or behaviour of the individual (Barnard 2000: 142–3). While practice theory has not made a major breakthrough in the debate on structure and agency, its application to the case of honour killing undermines feminist struggles against this crime.

Cultural relativism has shaped aspects of public policy in Sweden, Canada and a number of other Western liberal democracies (see, e.g., Bannerji 2000). Under the banner of respect for difference and diversity, Sweden allowed Muslim parents to deny their daughters the right to participate in co-educational activities such as school trips or swimming. Paved with good intentions, this policy contributes to the formation of a gender apartheid regime in a civic nation which promotes gender equality.

Racism and Anti-Feminism

In Western countries, the extreme right and racists explain honour killing as a part of what they call the 'barbaric culture' of immigrants from the non-Western world. This is an ideological position that smacks of the politics of eugenics and the Holocaust. It is the policy of racial purification, blood and soil, pogroms and concentration camps.

Racist culturalization of honour killing ignores the fact that killing women is a universal phenomenon in patriarchal cultures in both the East and the West. Males, white and non-white, continue to kill women. In the U.S., an average of ten women are killed every day.

Much like war and like violence against women, racism is not the error of the intellect, although it is very easy to demonstrate that racists are, intellectually and politically, on the wrong side. Racism is rather a means of exercising power in a world in which race is a source of power and this power is divided unequally. Individuals, groups, institutions, and states appeal to racial loyalty in order to exercise power.

It is racist to tie honour crimes to the Kurds as an ethnic people or to Kurdish culture. This racism has been experienced extensively in Europe and in Turkey. This ideological construction of the Kurds as perpetrators of honour killing constrains the struggle against the crime in many ways. For one thing, it overlooks similar gender crimes committed by non-Kurds, and as such legitimizes the racists' own regime of male violence. At the same time it generates racist attitudes in the target community, which has, in self-defence against racism, denied the indigenous nature of honour crimes and anchors them instead in Arab and Islamic cultures and traditions.

This conflict between racism and nationalism allows patriarchal violence to continue. It encourages women and men on each side to enhance racial and national attachment. It prevents the crucial cross-racial solidarity against cross-racial gender violence. It pits Western women, themselves victims of male violence, against non-Western women who are also victims of male violence. It is a misogynist project that ends in the perpetuation of patriarchy.

Kurdish culture is, like most contemporary cultures, very diverse. Until the beginning of the twentieth century, it was a predominantly feudal-tribal patriarchal culture. However, there is, in this culture, a century of ideas of gender equality and the struggle to achieve it. In the beginning of the twentieth century, Kurdish nationalists were inspired by the achievements of women in Nordic countries. The first Kurdish women's organization was established in İstanbul in 1919. By the mid-twentieth century, the greatest Kurdish poet of the modern period, Abdullah Goran (1904–1962), strongly condemned honour killing in one of his poems, *Berde-nûsêk*, 'A Tomb-Stone' (see Kurdish text and translation in Mojab 2004). In 1982, the Kurdish film-maker Yılmaz Güney strongly condemned patriarchal brutality in his movie *Yol* (Road).[10] Since the 1990s, there has been a considerable struggle against honour killing in Iraqi Kurdistan, where the 1988 genocide known as *Anfal* and the two Gulf Wars had destroyed the social fabric of society and unleashed waves of patriarchal violence. Kurdish feminists in Kurdistan and elsewhere

---

10 A central story in the film is the chaining of a woman by her in-laws in their village barn on suspicion of infidelity. She is delivered to her husband when he returns to the village after taking a leave from prison. Many Turkish nationalists did not hesitate to condemn the film for offering a negative image of Turkey, and the film was banned by the government until 1993. In his review of the film, Roger Scruton celebrated the film for portraying 'the Turkish army as a peace-keeping force imposing its rough justice upon a country torn by faction'. However, the reviewer did not extend his defence of the Turkish army to women, whose right to life is denied in the movie and in Kurdish/Turkish society. Scruton resented Güney's condemnation of violence against women by claiming that 'he is unable to contain his outrage at the resulting sufferings of women, and unable to share Yasar Kemal's countervailing sense of the support which women receive, in the form of unbreakable domestic affection' (Scruton 1983). Honour killers have usually made no secret that they love their victims, and their decision to kill is, in large part, imposed on them by tradition, religion, and culture, as well as the approval and expectations of family, kin, tribe, neighbourhood, and village.

have created women's organizations, media, shelters, literature, and have organized conferences. They have revolted against 'their own', indigenous, Kurdish, regime of patriarchy.

Nationalism
Kurdish nationalists have promoted the myth of the uniqueness of Kurdish women: Like some Western observers of Kurdish society, they claim that Kurdish women enjoy more freedom compared with their Arab, Persian and Turkish sisters. Whatever the status of women in Kurdish society, Kurdish nationalism, like other nationalist movements, has been patriarchal, although it also has paid lip service to the idea of gender equality. For Kurdish nationalisms, nation-building requires the unity of genders, classes, regions, dialects, and alphabets. They consistently relegate the emancipation of women to the future, that is, to after the emancipation of the nation. And since Kurdish nationalism achieved state power in Iraq following the 1991 Gulf War, its record in matters of gender equality has been bleak. Let's briefly look at this experience.

The Kurdish people have lived since the late 1870s in what Mark Levene has characterized as a 'zone of genocide' (Levene 1998: 393–433). This zone of genocide has also been an active zone of war. Numerous wars, since 1961, have destroyed the social, economic, and cultural fabric of Kurdish society; these have unleashed waves of male violence against women. This explains, at least in part, why there are more incidents of honour killing among the Kurds of Iraq and Turkey compared with the Kurds of Iran, whose experience of war has been less devastating.

In the aftermath of the U.S.-led Gulf War of 1991, when the Iraqi army attacked Kurdistan, millions of Iraqi Kurds escaped into the mountains. The U.S., U.K., and France created a no-fly zone, a 'safe haven', in order to return the refugees. Two major parties, the Kurdistan Democratic Party of Iraq (KDP) and the Patriotic Union of Kurdistan, which had been fighting the Iraqi government for decades, created the Regional Government of Kurdistan in 1992. This was a de facto Kurdish state with a parliament and administrative structure. However, in the course of parliamentary elections, male and female voters were segregated at the voting centres. Six of the 105 members of the parliament were women (5.7%). The two parties engaged in an internal war in 1994, which continued intermittently until 1996. Failing to resolve their conflict, they formed, by 1999, their own separate administrations. In the context of an unprecedented increase in honour killing and women's suicides, they adopted Iraqi law, which did not criminalize honour killing, and were lenient on the punishment of killers. Faced with opposition from women, the two parties, especially the KDP, have tried to justify honour killing as a Kurdish and Islamic tradition. In 2000, the Patriotic Union of Kurdistan issued two resolutions aimed at revoking Iraqi law, and criminalizing honour killing. The resolutions, which have the status of law in the absence of a legislative organ, have remained on paper in so far as the government has neither the will nor the power to enforce them. Later, the KDP, too, criminalized honour killing under much pressure from diverse sources.

The nationalist position in Europe is in part a reaction to the racism found in some of the mainstream media and in civil society. If racists call Kurdish culture barbaric, nationalists respond by claiming that honour killing is foreign to Kurdish culture, imposed on the Kurds by Arabs and Muslims. Hardly a defence at all, this is an equally racist position.

Honour killing, much like genocide, is a crime that few would want to be associated with. It tarnishes the image of a people, nation, country, religion and culture which allows it to happen. When its occurrence cannot be denied, the damage is controlled by reducing it to an isolated event, or the problem of the individual killer. For nationalists, Kurdish and non-Kurdish, the defence of the honour of the nation has priority over the rights of women.

Swedish Kurds condemned the killing of Fadime, and many used the occasion to protest all forms of violence against women.

However, there was a tendency to clean the image of the Kurdish nation. If White racists claim that honour killing is an essential part of Kurdish (or non-Western) immigrant culture, Kurdish nationalists and Swedish government authorities deny its cultural import.

The debate centred on the killer's motivations. A Kurdish website, KurdishMedia, raised a question, and asked visitors to 'vote' on three stated answers (accessed on 15 February, 2002):

I think Fadime's murder was mainly motivated by		
Religion	135	30.75%
Culture	96	21.87%
Lost father in Western Culture	183	41.69%
Other	25	5.69%
Total Vote	439	

There is no information on the ethnic or religious background of the voters. The poll does, however, show a strong inclination to reduce the crime to the problems of a father who has failed to integrate into 'Western culture'. A considerable number of voters also locate the killing in religion, in this case Islam. Although about 22% relate the killing to culture, the dominant tendency is to absolve culture of such responsibility. Concerned about racist and media 'demonization of Kurdish men and the stigmatization of Kurdish culture', a Kurdish male student tried to find 'a way out of this dilemma':

> I believe that many Kurds find themselves in a dilemma and a state of ambivalence in the wake of the murder of Fadime. This is a result of the fact that many Kurds want to admit that the murder of Fadime originated from a de facto existing notion of honour; but at the same time emphasizing that Kurdish culture *as such* does not sanction and legitimize honour killings.
> There is a way out of this dilemma in my view. At the same time as one admits that the murder of Fadime was a result of this notion of honour, one can also underlie the fact that an overpowering majority of Kurds cannot relate to this notion of honour, since

Kurdish culture is not homogenous. And like all other cultures it is in a process of constant change. Only on the basis of an essentialist view of culture is it possible to claim that honour killing is an essential attribute of Kurdish culture—which many in the Swedish media tend to do, implicitly or explicitly.[11]

A non-essentialist view of culture, however, does not offer a 'way out of this dilemma'. That cultures do not consist of immutable essences is rather obvious, and such a claim does not offer insight into the intricacies of violence against women; it also fails to account for the competing claims of nationalists and racists, and does not provide a feminist alternative to androcentric interpretations.

OVERCOMING PATRIARCHAL VIOLENCE

It took the murder of Fadime Şahindal to alert the Swedish government that it had to overcome its reservations about treating Swedes of Muslim or Middle Eastern origin as citizens of the civic nation who are equal before the law regardless of gender. It is difficult to guess how many more murders it will take for academic theorists to overcome their fear of treating patriarchy as a universal regime of domination that has no respect for women, their dignity, humanity, security and safety.

Relativists, culturalists or post-structuralists have to overcome the fear of recognizing the universality of patriarchal violence and the universality of the struggle against it. Taking this step, however, demands an appreciation of the dialectics of universals and particulars: Each regime of patriarchy is particular (Kurdish patriarchy is different from Italian patriarchy), however, patriarchies form a universal regime in so far as they perpetrate, without exception, physical and symbolic violence against women (Mojab 1998: 19–30).

In the (neo-) colonialist or Orientalist world view, the women of the Middle East constitute an anomaly, an exception, or abnormal-

---

11   Idris Ahmedi, 'Honour Killing Seen from a Feminist Perspective and from a Non-Essentialist View of Culture.' KurdishMedia. <http://www.kurdmedia.com/>. (Accessed on 5 February, 2002.)

ity: Unlike Western women, they are seen as blind followers of Islamic patriarchy. They are, according to neo-colonialist thought, without their own history since they do not struggle for equality or liberation.

Academic feminists of the cultural relativist persuasion, too, are constrained by their own ethnocentrist constructions of women in the Middle East. From their perspective, these women are an anomaly, too. Relativists fail to appreciate a century of Middle Eastern women's struggle against patriarchy. Women's struggle against patriarchy is, for them, another 'sensitive topic'. They may know about a century of women's press; a century of advocacy of women's rights; a century of writing; a century of poetry; a century of organizing; and a century of repression of women's movements by both secular and Islamic regimes. Talking about this history is 'sensitive' because cultural relativists, like Islamic fundamentalists, believe that Middle Eastern women's movements are inspired by Western women's struggles. Appreciating this history is difficult for these academic feminists because, in their opposition to neo-colonialist 'discourses', they often side with nationalists, Islamists, and nativists. They privilege the nativist position, which rejects feminism as a 'derivative discourse'. They treat feminism as a 'Western discourse' that is not compatible with the desires, wishes, and ideals of Middle Eastern women. They do not want to contaminate Middle Eastern women's movements with the struggles of the women of the West, with modernity, with the Enlightenment. In fact, some secular academic 'feminists' of Middle Eastern background have actively contributed to the construction of a 'Muslim woman identity'.

Patriarchy as the Exercise of Gender Power. In order to achieve the goal of *eliminating* honour killing, we need to move out of the prevalent range of debate, which reduces violence against women to questions of culture, religion, psychology, ignorance, practice, and law breaking. One alternative is to see patriarchy as a *system* of gender relations, which, much like the state, exercises political power. This system, much like capitalism or feudalism, has to survive through unceasing reproduction. It produces male domination, and uses culture, language, religion, education, the economy, and every other social formation in order to reproduce itself. Violence is one means of reproducing male rule.[12]

Feminist Education. Eliminating honour killing means denying patriarchy one of the means of its reproduction, that is, killing women. However, none of the contemporary societies has yet been able to eliminate gender-motivated killing of women. This means that we should continue to struggle for such a goal, especially eliminating killing for reasons of honour. We have to mobilize in all domains of human life, from language to law to arts to science to knowledge. Of all of these sites of struggle, I emphasize the spread of feminist consciousness, feminist knowledge, and feminist organizing.

While Heshu and Fadime should never be blamed for falling victim to their killers, it is obvious that they were not alerted to the dangers of patriarchal violence. Feminist knowledge about the nature and scope of male violence might have made a difference. Heshu's letter shows that she had sensed the danger and intended to leave. Had there been intervention, her life may have been spared.

In a long-term effort, which must begin now and never stop, we need a major confrontation with patriarchy in the realm of education. We need to promote feminist knowledge, especially about male violence, in schools, universities, religious establishments, government, mass media, and popular culture. This requires prioritization; this project requires the allocation of enormous economic and financial resources, although it will succeed only if it turns into a social movement; it should be an intellectual, cultural, and political movement. We should be able to set up institutions that are alternatives to age-old

---

12 The post-structuralist theorization of power seriously constrains the struggle against patriarchal violence. This perspective treats patriarchy as a non-hierarchical organization of gender relations, in which women, like the male gender, also exercise power, if not at the centre, at least in the margins. Even if this exercise of gender power is of a centre/margin order rather than hierarchical, the question becomes how the margin could move to the centre, and in fact how to eliminate the 'space'-based division of power between the two genders.

patriarchal centres of power, from women's studies courses and departments to the feminist-oriented print and broadcast media.

In each country, we should raise demands such as:

1. The promotion of the idea of the right to life for women, and its actualization through law and law enforcement;

2. feminist education in all levels of schooling;

3. the adoption of CEDAW, the UN Declaration on the Elimination of Violence Against Women, and Working Towards the Elimination of Crimes Against Women Committed in the Name of Honour as the laws of the country *without reservation*;

4. the creation of publicly supported feminist media, print and broadcast; and

5. financing the establishment and running of women's advocacy groups, especially shelters.

Kinship, Politics and Love: Honour in Post-Colonial Contexts – The Case of Turkey

NÜKHET SİRMAN

INTRODUCTION

The aim of this chapter is to provide an analysis of the social conditions that produce honour-related crimes. These crimes are defined in different ways in post-colonial societies in which they are prevalent. Those who live according to the code of honour see such violence as necessary for the protection of virginity and of gendered values, while those who try to struggle against them define these crimes and the value system they are related to as ways of controlling women and their bodies. The politically hegemonic groups in these societies, in their turn, see these crimes as remnants of a traditional order that will be eradicated through education and modernization. This paper is written from the second perspective, one that sees crimes of honour as punishment meted out to those women who will not (or somehow cannot) live according to the dictates of the code of honour. These punishments can today be categorized as an infringement of women's human rights, including their right to work, to travel, their rights to their own bodies, and finally their rights to life.

Following Stuart Hall, I use the term 'post-colonial' to refer to a social and political context in which social relationships and the cultural concepts through which they are understood and interpreted are saturated with comparisons to societies and cultures deemed to be more developed (Hall 1996). Defining the colonial both as 'a system of rule and power and exploitation, and... as a system of knowledge and representation', Hall refuses to locate the post-colonial in a particular space, that is, in societies that have been colonized (1996: 254). Instead, he proposes that the term should be used to cover global relations after a particular time, the time of colonization. In the temporality produced after the global experience of colonization, which Hall calls the 'Euro-imperial adventure', all localities start to produce their own identity in relation to others and according to the measure of civilization/development. The identity of both colonizer and colonized is thus constructed in a painful relation of identity/difference. Thus, in spite of the fact that Turkey has never been formally colonized, it can be argued that social practices, especially those related to the position of women in society, are assessed and rendered meaningful only in relation to those in the developed West. Nuclear families, and women active in the public sphere and dressed in the European fashion, therefore become signs of Turkey's modernity, and the concept of honour becomes laden with fears of backwardness.

The confusion regarding the concept of honour crimes is ubiquitous in Turkey as elsewhere, and this even among feminists who adopt the second point of view. This is mainly the effect of the dominance of the developmentalist perspective that sees both the honour code and the social relations it regulates as an anachronism in the modern society they hope to be living in. In spite of the fact that the term 'honour crimes' should be seen as covering the infringements of all the rights named above, today the term is often reserved only for honour *killings*. This definition then allows the speaker to use the term with reference only to a particular part of the world (or of Turkey) with the consequence that the term is seen to be irrelevant to the control of women in other (more developed) parts of the world (or

Turkey). In the context of Turkey, the relegation of honour crimes to the regions of the country where tribal structures have not been dislodged is signalled through the use of the term *töre cinayeti* (customary crimes) to refer to these crimes. Even feminists have engaged in a discussion about the correct terms to use, some arguing that the term honour crimes is not gendered enough to describe that what is at issue is men deciding to kill women.

The use of terms is important in the delineation of the course of action to take. Relegating the control of women to tradition and therefore to a particular region (defined in terms of its culture, that is, tribalism) gives rise to the dubious strategy on the part of some feminists of resorting to the law, that is, co-operating with the state in order to eradicate honour killings. Feminists in Turkey have long tried to change the clauses of the Penal Code that regulate honour-related killings. At the moment, such murderers receive a reduced sentence on the legal basis of 'grievous unjust provocation'; in other words, the law sees the woman who is suspected of bringing dishonour to her family as having provoked her murderers unjustly. This is in line with many other clauses of both the Penal Code and the 1926 Civil Code, abrogated only in 2002, which curtail women's rights in the name of family solidarity.[1]

The Turkish Penal Code is, at the moment, under review in an effort to bring it in line with EU prescriptions. Feminist demands to prevent perpetrators of honour and passion crimes from receiving reduced sentences under the terms of unjust provocation have met untold resistance. In fact, the Parliamentary Justice Commission, work-

---

1   Thus, for example, adultery was deemed a public offence until 1996, homicides received a two-thirds reduction until 1990 if the victim was proved to be a prostitute, a woman could not undertake paid work without the permission of her husband until 2002, and a man who abducts or rapes an underage woman is still set free if he agrees to marry his victim. I will have more to say on the Civil Code below. The concept of 'unjust grievous provocation' is also interpreted from a gendered perspective, such that a woman who murders her husband after suffering years of violent treatment is judged to have been under 'mild' unjust provocation, while affronts to the honour of the man and his family is considered to be a form of grievous unjust provocation.

ing on a draft proposal of the Turkish Penal Code, agreed to reject a reduced sentence in relation to 'customary' crimes, showing the extent to which a developmentalist imaginary dominates the law makers' imaginary.[2] The demand of feminists that crimes 'related to honour, custom or jealousy' not receive reduced sentences was not met in spite of considerable advances with regard to the rights of the individual, the most important of which was the classification of sexual crimes under the rubric of 'crimes against the individual' rather than 'crimes against public morality and the familial order'.[3] All of these show the extent to which state institutions not only share extant social norms regarding the concept of honour, but also are crucial agents that reproduce them under the modern patriarchal gender regime in Turkey.

The final aim of this chapter is to provide an explanation as to why modern state institutions endorse the concept of honour to such an extent. I will use anthropological models in order to show the various strategies through which bodies and personal behaviour are regulated in different types of social organization with different gender regimes. I will then show how these gender regimes articulate and adapt to each other in present-day Turkey in order to render visible the

---

2   I use the term 'imaginary' to refer to a domain of signification that is necessary for the production of all meaning within a particular society, a central signification that provides the meaning of the world, of life, and the basic orientation for that society (see Castoriadis 1987). During the months of discussion leading to the preparation of the draft of the new Penal Code, some jurists categorically refused to accept rape within marriage as a punishable act, while others even suggested that in cases where the rapist married his victim, his sentence should be commuted, thereby showing the extent to which the imaginary of kinship overrides their interpretation of women's human rights.

3   This was the formulation under which sexual crimes were penalized under the still-extant Penal Code that had been promulgated in 1926, three years after the foundation of the Republic of Turkey as an explicitly modern nation-state. The new Turkish Penal Code is still under review as this chapter is being written. Apart from the issue of honour crimes, feminist advocacy groups have found that: The new version does not offer enough protection to women who cohabit with men under a religious marriage; is prohibitive with regard to consensual sex between young persons aged 15 to 18; is prohibitive with regard to non-heterosexual relationships, does not protect young women from having to undergo virginity tests at the request of their family, school teacher, or other superior; and that the anti-pornography clauses clash with the freedom of speech and expression.

gender regime on which modern power rests. My hope is to be able to provide an analysis that will contribute to the efforts to devise modes of feminist intervention in a context where modernism as represented by the Republic is seen as having ensured gender equality.

KINSHIP AND THE 'HOUSE'

The anthropological literature is known for its efforts to build models of the structuring of kinship-based societies. The term 'kinship-based society' is used in anthropology to denote the use of relations of filiation or affinity as a model for forging forms of identity and constructing social relations. In other words, what is described is a society where the community is imagined as being composed of persons related to each other as kin. In this type of society, relations of production and distribution, of domination and subordination, and relations with the supernatural are structured according to kinship. Kinship serves to position persons vis-à-vis one another and provide them with a basic identity and guide to behaviour.

Turkish kinship terms provide us with a good sense of the way in which kinship serves in this context to regulate the identity and behaviour of persons. Persons of the same generation and the same parents who are older than ego are referred to as *ağabey* (eB) or *abla* (eZ),[4] depending on the gender of the persons referred to. These terms also serve as terms of address. Persons in exactly the same position but younger than ego are referred to through a genderless term (*kardeş*) and are either addressed by their names or by sounds to attract their attention. It is not important for ego to know the particulars of younger persons or persons from a lower generation and discern unnecessary details such as gender or even name. What this shows is the extent to which persons older than ego are deferred to, while persons younger than ego are either to be disregarded or else are treated 'too intimately' by calling them by their personal names. These forms

---

4   The symbol eB in anthropological writing denotes the term elder brother, while eZ refers to elder sister. The letter S is reserved to refer to the term son.

of behaviour denote hierarchy and show how kinship defines in a minute fashion how such hierarchy is to be expressed in all face-to-face relationships and thus provide a guide to everyday behaviour according to the accepted notions of hierarchy and subordination.[5] Kinship terms are widely used in Turkey today, not only with regard to persons one has filial and affinal ties to, but also with complete strangers. These terms provide a means of regulating relations between non-kin, thus extending the language of hierarchy and respect, age, and gender to cover a whole of range of relationships within the society in general.

In kin-based societies, persons with real or imagined kinship bonds form communities of different sizes and shapes that anthropologists have variously called lineage, tribe, or clan. In these types of communities the reproduction of the group depends completely on the sexual behaviour of the members and therefore personal sexuality is placed under the control and regulation of the community as a whole. It is in these types of societies that honour emerges as both the identity of the person vis-à-vis others and the sense of worth that a person has of himself or herself; it is the internalized form of a person's social standing. Thus, although it is a concept that is linked with sexuality and sexual behaviour, it extends to cover the total sense of self of the person. In present-day Turkey, the term 'honour' (*namus*) makes sense both for men and for women. The term connotes the ability of the person to live up to the standards of masculinity and femininity as set by the society. The difference in what honour entails for men and for women is the difference in gender. Thus in Turkey, a dishonourable man is one who is not trustworthy, and therefore unable to undertake his social responsibilities nor to control his own sexuality and that of the women he is responsible for. A woman's honour, by contrast, is

---

5   The same distinction can be seen at all levels of the kinship terminology. For example, an older brother's wife is referred to and addressed with a term of respect (*yenge*), while a younger brother's wife is both referred to and addressed as *gelin*, a term that is used to mean 'bride' but literally means 'the one who comes'.

linked only to her sexuality. Honour, in kin-based societies, is deemed to be a moral issue regardless of gender. Thus, dishonourable men or women are seen as posing a threat primarily to the moral rather than the social fabric of society.[6]

In this type of society sexuality is lived primarily as a relation of antagonism between groups, within groups, and at the level of the subject.[7] Relations between communities are basically antagonistic involving power struggles over land, pasture, and labour power (people). These antagonisms mean that other communities are cast as immoral and weak and that relations between them (including marriage alliances) are fraught with danger and deep-seated hostility. The communities that are thus turned into the Other may include neighbouring villages, lineages, or even families. A good description of these relations of antagonism is provided by Abu-Lughod regarding the relations between the Awlad 'Ali Bedouins of the north-western desert of Egypt and Egyptian peasants. While the Bedouins see themselves as honourable and moral, they regard Egyptians as lowly people unable to contain their sexuality. Any practice can become a sign of this immorality: men sleeping in the same room as their wives while on a visit with the Bedouins or husband and wife holding hands in public.[8] Honour thus becomes an important axis along which relations of competition between and within groups are carried out. Thus, under the regime of kinship, sexuality becomes a bundle of emotions and behaviours charged with untold tensions and conflicting loyalties.

And yet, neither the Turkey of today, nor the Ottoman Empire two to three hundred years ago, can be described by any stretch of the

---

[6] See Abu-Lughod (1986) for an excellent description and analysis of the way the morality of honour is naturalized in a patriarchal, patrilineal kin-based context.

[7] This is especially the case in patrilineal societies where a woman's virginity is part of the bundles of rights and obligations that are exchanged in the course of marriage transactions. Some matrilineal societies do not link virginity to morality.

[8] I saw a similar approach to urban sexuality among peasants of Western Turkey while doing fieldwork in the 1980s. Women would poke fun at couples holding hands, asking whether the wife would run away if her husband did not hold on to her.

imagination as a kin-based society. Turkish society, which today is organized as a nation-state, had indeed been ordered for long years under the Ottoman rule as a kinship-like system, but one in which a conquering dynasty rather than an imagined community of kinsmen provided the imaginary of rule. This form of rule was organized through the house rather than the lineage, clan, or tribe. Those who pledged and demonstrated loyalty to the dynasty were admitted within the household as members without necessarily being adopted as kin, but with the possibility of being made into kin through sexual relations, whether in the form of marriage or concubinage. In house societies,[9] it is this personal loyalty that organized both everyday life and the political order. In order to obtain status and power, persons had to attach themselves to the houses of powerful (and usually older) men who themselves had acceded to this position by virtue of their ties to another (more) powerful patron.

Identity and status as well as rights and obligations accrued according to the position a person occupied within the hierarchal organization of this house. This hierarchy was structured around the head of the household whose personal ties of dependency had secured him the position in the first place. Those men and women who belonged to the house were ranked according to their relationship either to the head of the house and/or the heads of the houses they belonged to previously. Unmarried and unattached persons were kept outside the boundaries of the community and were made to live in bachelor's houses. Men could only begin to compete for power and prestige once they were married.[10] In spite of the fact that kinship con-

---

9   I use the term 'house' societies in the sense proposed by Lévi-Strauss as 'a type of social structure' that indicates 'a corporate body [*personne morale*] holding an estate made up of both material and immaterial wealth, which perpetuates itself through the transmission of its name, its goods, and its titles down a real or imaginary line, considered legitimate as long as this continuity can express itself in the language of kinship or of affinity and, most often, both' (Lévi-Strauss 1982: 174.; the quotation here is taken from Joyce and Gillespie 2000).

10 See Lindisfarne 1994 for an analysis of the constitutive relation between marriage and true manhood.

tinued to provide the main code according to which hierarchy and identity was imagined, new positions derived from the political relation to the sovereign were also articulated to this basic code. Persons who attached themselves to large houses began to be known according to the role they played in the normal functioning of the household: Thus, for example, those who controlled the stables had their own special name (*seyis*), as did those in charge of the kitchens, the education of the children, the personal secretary of the household head, and so on. These were statuses proper to the organization of the big house and provided its incumbent with status and power.

The biggest house of the empire was, of course, the palace, Topkapı. The status and the rights and obligations these statuses entailed were set out in minute detail in the palace and most of these statuses were also important political positions. Governing the house and governing the domain was one and the same thing and the head of the Ottoman house, the sultan, sat at the apex of the personal ties of dependency that linked all big houses of the domain to one another in relations of dependency. Sexuality also played a key role in this personalized form of governing. Contracting marriages between households were used to strengthen relations of dependency between households and young men tried to shore up their position within a big house by becoming the household head's son-in-law. As shown by Leslie Peirce's brilliant study of gender relations in the palace, power struggles within the house were regulated through a norm-bound competition between contenders carried out through the medium of sexuality and reproduction.[11] In this model kinship still provided the code through which personal relations and hierarchies were imagined but it was regulated by the political imperatives of empire. This produced a

---

[11] Peirce, in her *The Imperial Harem: Women and Sovereignty in the Ottoman Empire* (1993), shows that sexual relations between a concubine and the sultan were geared to the production of an heir, after which all such relations would end. The mother-child dyad would then form the core of one of the contenders to power, with the different parties in the palace supporting one or the other dyad.

homology between the organization of politics and kinship, but one in which heads of household lost their autonomy and had to accept the ultimate sovereignty of the head of the ruling house. In everyday life, these now-dependent heads of households emulated the trappings and rituals of power of the palace, including generous giving and regulating their dependents' sexuality and identity, that is, their honour.

LOVE AND THE NATION-STATE

It was the nation-state that sought to regulate sexuality on the basis of another emotion: love. This emotion was constructed in such as a way that instead of tension and antagonism, attachments between persons were to be based on amity. Love, as the bond that would bind both the spouses to one another and the person to the nation, was invented in the course of nationalistic politics within the empire, and it was used to refer to love as in *amour passion*—but tempered through reason.[12] Through love, the relation between the nation and the individual was construed as a relation of submission the individual chooses to enter into out of his or her own will, rather than being the result of a type of coercion as under the empire. In this type of social order, the conjugal family, rather than the house, becomes the unit that sustains both the political and the gender regime. This conjugal family was produced by shedding all the now unnecessary dependencies and bonds linking it to other units in the polity. The Turkish Republic institutionalized this arrangement by promulgating its Civil Code in 1926 whereby the (conjugal) family was proclaimed as the constituent unit of the polity and no other bonds that linked persons to one another were recognized legally. The individual owed his or her allegiance only to the nation-state, with the family as the only recognized mediating structure. Individuals within this family were to be bound to one

---

12 For my account of the production of love in nationalist politics in the Ottoman Empire, see Sirman, 'Gender Construction and Nationalist Discourse: Dethroning the Father in the Early Turkish Novel' (2000a) and 'Writing the Usual Love Story: The Fashioning of Conjugal and National Subjects in Turkey' (2000b).

another by no other tie but love, a relationship they would enter into out of their own volition. Through love, the individual turns into a self-monitoring subject. The 1926 Civil Code, amended as late as 2002, designated the husband as the head of the household and charged him with the task of providing for his family.[13] The inequality in this arrangement was rendered invisible through various ideological discourses that declared love and sacrifice the duty of all citizens vis-à-vis the nation. But this duty was inherently defined in a gendered way, and women, as mothers of the nation, had to make just that many more sacrifices and had to love just that much more.

Within the regime of the family, the control of sexuality becomes the duty of the individual, rather than the group as a whole. It is assumed that spouses will control their sexuality out of love and through reason. Thus, in societies based on the conjugal family, it is assumed that the concept of honour will lose its salience and that individual identity would depend on love, tempered by reason[14] and the value received in the labour market by exercising this faculty. Thus, identity, in this model, would be regulated through the concept of human rights rather than honour. It is imagined that those individuals who have the ability to exercise this faculty well will finally enjoy equal status within the family and enter into only contractual relations based on reason in society at large. In such societies honour thus becomes in theory an archaic concept that infringes on individual human rights, and through the concept of human rights, human bodies and their sexuality are rendered genderless.

Women's human rights advocates today accept this latter model and try to ensure that social life and the legal institutions that regulate it are organized accordingly. Unfortunately, their strategies are rarely

---

13   The new Civil Code does away with the terms husband and wife, using the gender-neutral term 'spouse,' and designates both spouses as responsible for material sustenance and decision-making. However, this code is only applied to those couples married after the law was passed.
14   The concept of reasonable love is rendered in Turkish by a different word (*sevgi*) than the word '*aşk*' which is reserved to denote passionate love.

successful, especially in post-colonial conditions, because they ignore the manner in which the gender and political orders of the kinship, household, and family are articulated to one another in the present.[15] Social science practice that compartmentalizes social life into neat little boxes composed of the economic, the political, and the familial makes it impossible for feminist advocates to see the extent to which power and sovereignty are implicated in this articulation. The belief that the distinction between the public and the private is an adequate model of social life further occludes the extent to which everyday life, the body, and the emotions are constituted by power, and this in spite of the critical feminist insight of the 1970s that the personal is political. Human rights activists and feminists castigate what they call traditional societies for the exploitation and subordination of women that kinship and household systems entail, but they fail to link the operation of these systems to the power order of the societies in question. Similarly, casting love as a genderless relation occludes its role in constituting power relations in so-called modern societies. Academic research has repeatedly shown that romantic love in most parts of the world (including Latin America, Japan, Turkey, and Europe) serves to create feminine subjects desiring to willingly subordinate themselves to men, and indeed women have been the target population of romantic films and cheap romances for a long time.[16] This construction of femininity is often linked to capitalism but rarely to the operations of political systems in Western liberal democracies. And yet, as feminists have long claimed, neither love nor reason has been able to put a stop to domestic violence and male domination.

---

15 The changes in the Civil Code and the Penal Code in Turkey are a case in point. They not only were changed as a result of the government's strategic decision to get a date for the EU–Turkey negotiations by the end of 2004, but the demands put forward by feminists regarding honour crimes were not met.
16 Nevertheless, women's subjectivity has generally been studied through sexuality rather than love, mainly as a result of Foucault's influence.

HONOUR AND THE NATION-STATE

Just as kinship became an important code for the operation of house societies, modern societies too have adapted the structures of kinship and of the house to fit the requirements of the nation-state and of modern forms of power. The articulation between a kinship order and the conjugal family is apparent in many aspects of life. Critiques of the concept of honour were not part of discussions regarding the place of women in modern society in the period of transition from empire to nation-state. In the 1880s, for example, Şemseddin Sami, a modernist thinker, writer, and critic argued that modern education for women would mean that they would cover themselves not with a piece of cloth but by using reason. Thus, rather than striving to eradicate notions of honour in the control of women's bodies and actions, modernists have merely sought to devise new and more effective means of sustaining it. There are many other examples that show the effectivity of kinship and the house in ordering everyday life, especially in a country such as Turkey that bases its claims to modernity on the new forms of familial arrangements and of the new status of its women.[17] Arranged marriages are still the most common form through which individuals find a spouse, marriages between kin are very widespread despite campaigns by the Ministry of Health that aim to show that such marriages are genetically very risky, men are undisputedly dominant both in the family and in public, and people depend extensively on kin in everyday life for purposes of mutual aid and socialization. As I tried to show above, the legal institution recognizes the key role played by kinship and the family in the political order and organizes the clauses of the Civil and Penal Codes so as to protect the social and familial order rather than the rights of the individual.

---

17 In spite of the fact that Turkey seeks to differentiate itself from other nations of the Middle East on the basis of women's position in Turkish society, and in spite of the constitutional claim that all Turkish citizens are equal regardless of gender, none of the modernizers at the turn of the century argued that men and women should be equal in society. Even feminists of the period did not openly articulate such a demand, denigrating some feminists in the West and embracing their identity as mothers and wives. See Muhittin (1931).

Nationalisms themselves reproduce these power relations by turning them into those sacred traditions and mores that are taken to define national identity. Most post-colonial nationalisms that build their claims to nationhood on arguments of cultural difference in the end only end up by reproducing these power relations that characterize kin-based and house societies. But the nation-state cannot allow kinship groups or houses to exercise real political power. Many of the reforms that Turkey undertook to modernize its society also served to cut off the sources of power that houses could draw upon. From the discouraging of arranged or kin marriages to the promulgation of the Surname Law in the space of three months in 1934, these reforms had the effect of preventing the emergence of any other locus of power that would pose a threat to the monopoly of power of the nation-state. Thus, under the name of modernization, the Turkish Republic was able to implement those changes that would articulate the forms of power and sovereignty of kinship and house societies to the organization of power of sovereignty under the order of the nation-state. In this order, state sovereignty was delegated to the heads of families who would enjoy this privilege as long as they remained loyal to the state.

It can thus be argued that the power regime of the modern nation-state in Turkey depends on a pact between the state and men—especially married men—that links gender to the way sovereignty is exercised in the polity as a whole. The ease with which the 1926 Civil Code was passed through parliament is testimony to the acquiescence by men to this new order, an order, which, moreover, legitimized itself by promising to bring about equality among men.[18] The speeches made in parliament at the time indicated that the code was introduced as recognition of the countless sacrifices 'the Turkish Mother had made for centuries' and was deemed to be an example of the 'generosity' of the Turkish man.[19]

---

18 See Zihnioğlu 2003 for an account of the circumstances under which the Civil Code was passed in 1926.
19 The quotation is taken from Zihnioğlu 2003: 181. The capitalization is in the original.

What the code in fact accomplished was to make all men, whether rich or poor, educated or ignorant, legally equal as husbands and heads of families. This was in line with reforms regarding marriage that had begun to be undertaken since the last decades of the nineteenth century. The main impetus then had been to make marriage accessible to all classes by limiting the amount of the Islamic dowry (*mehr*) a woman could ask by legally reducing the costs of marriage celebrations which, it was thought, led to the creation of a large segment of unmarried men in the population.[20] This measure could serve to limit the degree of inequality that existed among men and was largely reproduced through marriage only in a house society. The Republic, which had specifically made equality one of its founding tenets differentiating it from the imperial order, thus went a step further and declared all men equal by making them all legally heads of families once married. Thus the new order underwrote what appears to be a principle of modern democracy by accepting wholeheartedly the meaning attached to true masculinity in house societies. That the modern order should seek to uphold the power relationships defining traditional masculinity should come as no surprise if one remembers that (Turkish) nationalism, which legitimized these transformations, was mainly a male discourse that began in the 1870s. Furthermore, it is from this perspective that it becomes possible to see the role of gender as a power relation in the constitution, exercise, representation, and reproduction of all kinds of power relations in society.

CONCLUSION: HONOUR AND THE POST-COLONIAL NATION-STATE

The concept of honour is crucial for this modern order to work. To see honour as a traditional concept is to render invisible the modes through which it still regulates the identity and the life of all women, and to imagine that it will disappear with development and education.

---

20 See Ortaylı 1985: 93–104 for an account of the legal changes in Ottoman marriage practices in the late nineteenth century.

What is more important is to try to locate the mechanisms through which women's bodies and emotions are controlled under present post-colonial conditions. The gendered understanding of love produced through nationalist discourses in Turkey shows that notions of honour are still operative in the regulation of feminine identity. Under modern conditions, a woman will not feel honourable if her love does not include sacrifice, while a man will demonstrate his love by providing for his family. A woman will show her love for family and country by controlling her own sexuality while a man will do so by being prepared to die for family, country, and honour. Thus love, rather than displacing honour by producing the presumably free subject who chooses to act according to his or her own personal emotional attachments, serves to replace the kin group or the house with nation and family, the two imaginaries constitutive of the nation-state, in the operation of honour.

What this analysis has shown is that the concept of honour is internal to the operation of power within the post-colonial nation-state and that in these polities the violence of the sovereign becomes visible in the crimes and violations of rights perpetrated through claims to honour. Thus, honour is not simply a cultural relation; it is for the most part a political one that has as much to do with public regulation as with personal relations. Honour as a gendered relation of power is operative in post-colonial nation-states where political order is imagined as depending on the family as a modern institution. This imaginary is rather different than one in which inter-personal relations are imagined to be based on a contract willingly entered into by free and rational individuals. It is this latter imaginary which produces the notion of human rights. Feminists have long shown that in this kind of social order, women's subordination is perpetuated through recourse to notions of women's nature. Whether the notion of human rights will prove to be effective in a context where discourses and practices based on honour rather than nature serves to control and subordinate women is highly doubtful.

Many women's organizations have indeed been trying to provide training on women's human rights to poor women in shantytowns as well as to members of the state bureaucracy such as the police and members of the judiciary. These training programmes take the individual as their starting point and pay no heed to the numerous social and familial networks in which women of different social classes are presently embedded. As a result, women learn about rights *theoretically* without being provided with the means to exercise them, or given an understanding of the social context in which they have to struggle. Without the means with which they can juggle these abstract human rights with the moral obligations and emotional attachments in which they are entangled in everyday life, women often do not see any relevance between their lives and what they learn in the training sessions. The same also applies to the bureaucracy.

The attachments that constitute the unspoken aspects of everyday life often involve a wide range of kinsmen and women and not just husbands, fathers, and children, and define a feminine subjectivity that is constituted in relation to what I would like to call 'the law of kinship'. The Turkish state, on its part, attempted to provide women with another set of principles according to which they could forge a modern feminine subjectivity. It is these principles that were enshrined in the Civil Code of 1926, constituting what I would like to call 'the law of the state'. The law of the state attached the morality and rights defined by the law of kinship to family and nation (defined as a family writ large), thus putting the former to the service of the latter. In its haste to rewrite social relations in accordance with its imaginary of modernity, Turkish law chose to disregard the multitude of ties that bind persons to kin outside the immediate family, instead defining it simply as being composed of the father, the mother, and the children. The Turkish Civil Code gives secondary importance to all non-contractual relations between persons outside of the family, relations which are binding according to what I have called the law of kinship. In the absence of any mechanisms that would bridge the gap between the law of kinship and the law of the state, feminine subjectivity in Turkey became dichotomous between the modern and the traditional. This dichotomy can only be entertained if context is completely ignored and the effects of kinship in the regulation of relations between kin as well as non-kin in the modern Turkish order are disregarded.

Feminist interventions simply compound the problem. They proceed from 'the law of abstract human rights', disregarding both the law of kinship and the law of the nation. Context is thereby doubly edited out of their imaginary of a properly modern social order. They thus compound the problem of dissociating the exigencies of everyday life from their imaginary society composed of relations between equal individuals in the hope that the law will, in the end, institute these egalitarian relations. Thus, in the absence of adequate social institutions and networks needed to provide women with the ability to exercise individual human rights, they end up by proceeding in exactly the same fashion as did the Turkish state in trying to bring about the desired social transformation: They ignore what exists in order to supersede it, making it impossible for the women they target to implement the proposed strategies. Thus, when faced with pressures and threats based on concepts of honour, many women are left to their own devices, which, in the absence of any institutions devised to cope with the problem, inevitably turn out to be the larger kin group and familial alliances. Hence, the passing of the new Penal Code based on the notion of individual human rights will not, unfortunately, bring women any protection in a context where honour and the family set the frame for all social, cultural, and political relations at the level of the everyday.

Honour Killing, Patriarchy, and the State: Women in Israel

NAHLA ABDO

INTRODUCTION

The so-called 'honour killing' is one, albeit extreme, form of sexual violence against woman's being. This is a global phenomenon and an integral part of the culture of private property, patriarchy, and the colonial order which characterizes many states all over the world (East and West, North and South). Sexual violence against women, including torture and murder, is not uniquely Arab nor is it rooted in Islam as a religion or culture. Historically, the phenomenon of sexual torture and murder of women existed in various forms and many cultures, such as the Western/European tradition of burning witches during the Middle Ages, the practice of using the 'chastity belt' later in the seventeenth and eighteenth centuries, or more currently, the phenomenon of 'crimes of passion' within the Brazilian context or 'dowry deaths' in Indian culture.

The so-called phenomenon of 'honour killing' is just another one of these multiple forms and practices of extreme sexual violence (including murder) against women. Like sexual violence in general, 'honour killing' is not confined to the poor, uneducated, and illiterates as is sometimes claimed. While its frequency under such conditions could be higher than in other places, the phenomenon itself criss-crosses all cultural boundaries, classes, races, and nationalities. It is an exclusively gender/sexual phenomenon, often legitimated by legal structures, state policies, and the national character of the concerned states, and moulded by masculine decisions and patriarchal norms and customs. The historical roots of sexual violence against women could be as old as patriarchy and private property, and as such, there is nothing uniquely Arab or Islamic about this phenomenon.

What is worthy of analysis and comprehension here is the historically specific conditions which not only give rise to such phenomena, but also colour the perpetrator and the victim with the colour of 'otherness', or of the 'other culture'! In other words, an analysis of this phenomenon would explain who are the 'we/us' and who are the 'they/them' in the discourse.

This paper argues that the cultural-as-religious plays a very small role, compared to the cultural-as-political, in analysing the phenomenon of 'honour killing'. The forces responsible for the perpetuation of the phenomenon of violence against women, including their murder, it is argued here, must be sought/located within the state and its institutions such as the juridical (e.g., courts and police), the legislative (e.g., laws, policies, and national agenda), and the structural, including the social, the educational, the economic, and the political. In addition to these forces one should add the ideological structures of the state and society, such as nationalism and religious movements, including fundamentalisms which also affect the phenomenon. As a form—albeit extreme—of sexual violence, 'honour killing' is also found in other structures which pre-date the state, for example, communal and community structures such as tribal, clan, or family organizations.

This paper does not absolve family, tribal, or clan structures from their responsibility in perpetuating the phenomenon of crimes against women on the basis of the so-called 'family honour'. After all, the overwhelming cases of 'crimes of honour' are perpetrated by family members, mainly brothers, cousins, uncles, fathers and husbands. Moreover, in communities with relative isolation, entrenched patriarchal structures, lack of education and engulfed with the culture of poverty, it is not rare to find female family members also involved in the criminal act. In such communities, women are more prone to the internalization of patriarchy, used by them as a coping mechanism to deal with both their survival and the survival of their families.

Finally, it is no surprise to find that the practice of 'honour killing' is more prevalent among communities, societies, and collectivities with strong adherence to customary laws and other forms of unwritten codes. Nonetheless, whilst it is true that customary laws and other forms of unwritten codes of conduct largely have been produced to regulate patriarchal constructs of the family, tribe, and clan, through control over women's bodies, movements, and actions, neither the family not the tribe nor even the corresponding laws and regulations are independent; nor are they floating systems of organization. This is particularly true since the emergence of the state (be it colonial, settler, liberal democratic, etc.) which has taken over many of the roles and functions of the family (or tribe or clan), and integrated them within its structures, policies, and projects. We can see this, for example, in the case of education, wherein the state has replaced the family in educating and socializing children, and also in the case of the economy, where the capitalist state with its commodity-driven market has transformed the land and its direct producers into 'objects' and sheer commodities, transforming the family from a self-contained institution into a state-dependent organization.

No matter how much the concept of 'honour killing' is attached to 'family-honour', the reality is that the family as we see it and experience it is not the ahistoric, unchanging, and 'ideal/pure type' family that is often depicted in the literature and discourse on 'honour killing'. By removing its economic power and independency, the state has also managed to re-mould and re-shape the power structure and ability of the family to make decisions, using it in the process as a means to serve the state's own interests. Simultaneously and on the other hand, the development of the modern state and the commodity/capitalist market have opened up a wider public space for citizens, nationals, or residents, allowing more room to move some 'private' and 'domestic' issues outside of their confined borders to the public realm, allowing for the negotiation of social and political concerns, including the phenomenon of 'honour killing', through state laws, policies, and programmes.

However, in a world of uneven development, where the Third World makes up about two-thirds of the world population yet amasses most of the world's poverty, unemployment, oppression, and subjugation, the extent to which the public space is open and capable of negotiating phenomena otherwise considered private is an issue which requires further investigation. For the very poor conditions under which the majority of the world population lives creates its own dynamics and cultural norms and laws. Herein lies the concept/context of historical specificity which requires scholars to go beyond generalization and into particularization.

Between the 'modern' state in the form of Western liberal democracy with a relatively highly developed public space, and the underdeveloped and dependent state in the Third World with a much narrower public space, there also lie other forms of states where the public and the private take a more complicated and complex form. One example which concerns us in this paper is a form of state which tends to combine features of the developed 'liberal democracy' and under-developed 'Third World', yet simultaneously differs from both of them—this is the state of Israel, which will be used as a case study. Israel, as will be argued in this paper, is 'liberal' yet exclusivist and exclusionary; it is also 'democratic', but simultaneously settler-colonial. Its specificity lies in the way in which it has been able to combine these oppositions and contradictions and reflect them differentially among its citizens, through different sets of policies and practices.

The approach used in this paper is critical feminist and uses an anti-racist methodology.[1] This paper will deal with the case of Israel as a historically specific case—but definitely not a unique case, as some would want us to believe. Thus, the methodology used here questions not only the religious justification for Israeli/Zionist racism and its exclusionary nature, but also the frequent usage of 'religion', particularly Islam, as an explanatory means for the phenomenon of 'honour killing'.

Islam as a political ideology/religion, as organized movements (e.g., Hamas, Jihad, Muslim Brothers, and so on), while exercising more influence on the private/family sphere than on other state political structures, remains a political structure, shaped and re-shaped by local, national, and international political economic changes. This type of Islam, as most ordinary women and men would say, is not God-given, but rather 'man'-made. Responding to my question on how she views Hamas (the Islamic movement in the Occupied Palestinian Territories), Abeer articulated her answer as follows:

> Islam the religion is about my relationship to God. No one has the right to invade my person and decide how I should respect, love and connect with my God. Hamas is not Islam, nor is it the representative of God in Gaza.... I do not want to talk about the women in the organization.... I feel sorry for most of them, because they cannot think for themselves, nor do they seem to know how they have been dragged to this position! It is the males and leaders in the movement that scare me. These people are only concerned with their own political career and how they can control us, women, if and when they take control over the state and turn Palestine into an Islamic state. (Interview, 21 May, 2004, Gaza/Palestine)

The above example is not intended to serve as the final word on the phenomenon of Hamas nor on any other political religious organization, nor is there any inclination to simplify a complex phenomenon such as political Islam in any and all of the different forms it

---

1 For more on this approach see Abdo and Lentin (eds.) 2002: 1–30.

takes. The power which such phenomenon have and exert on the social, political, and economic structures of countries as well as on people's daily lives is well understood. Also recognized is the role played by globalization and the hegemonic Western culture, not only in terms of the horizontal and vertical strengthening of such phenomena, but also in terms of the process of 'otherization' forced upon these phenomena, resulting, consequently, in the production of a relatively new culture of 'humiliation', 'hate', 'rage', and oppositional stances currently characteristic of the relationship between most forms/organizations of political Islam and the West.

This paper will argue that both Israel as a state and the phenomenon of 'honour' crimes within this specific case have ramifications beyond their national and geo-political boundaries. Discussion around these can be used as material and examples for comparisons as well as experiences to learn from. The female groups that are affected by sexual violence, including 'murder', in this case do not exclusively belong to the 'indigenous people', or Israeli's citizen Palestinians only. This phenomenon is equally present, and perhaps in a larger proportion, among the state's 'proper' citizens, the Jews of different backgrounds.

By choosing Israel as the case study, this paper intends to highlight several important issues. These include:

1. The role played by colonialism in sustaining and perpetuating the phenomenon of 'honour killing' as a mechanism for the colonial tempo of 'divide and rule';

2. The role played by racism and militarization in intensifying violence in general, and sexually-based murder in particular;

3. Demystifying the notion that 'honour killing' is a product of Islamic culture and religion; and,

4. The divide between the 'us/them'/'we/they'!

'HONOUR KILLING': WHOSE FAMILY IS IT ANYWAY?

Most literature (East and West) has tended to explain away the phenomenon of 'honour killing' within the limited context of Islam by using a culturalist approach in which religion becomes the main if not only ingredient of people's culture, or in which culture becomes limited to the religious ideological form. Islam, more than any other worldly and spiritual religion, has been used as the major and sometimes only explanatory ground for the phenomenon of killing women under the pretext of preserving 'family honour'. This has been the case for much of the local male/masculine discourses on 'honour killing', and an increasing number of Western academic scholars' writing (national and international) on the issue. The discourse on 'honour killing' has lately received ample air-time on major national TVs in most Western countries. It has also received plenty of international attention through a myriad of conferences, panel discussions, and workshops with the presence of local, national, and international feminist/activists and the scholarly community.

This paper does not intend to belittle the role played mainly, albeit not solely, by direct members of the family (fathers, brothers, cousins, uncles, and husbands) in killing female members. After all, these are the direct agents, or perhaps tools, responsible for the crime; they perform the act, legitimate it, and defend it if and when caught. These are the subjects whose words and 'logic' are often heard, reproduced, and taken as evidence to the 'familial/tribal' character of the phenomenon. Whether the concepts of 'family honour', 'religious norms', 'traditional behaviour', or the preservation of the status quo are evoked in explaining/justifying the act or not, these same concepts are often reproduced as the raison d'être for the phenomenon of 'honour-crimes'. One might only recall the relatively recent documentaries produced about 'honour killing' among Palestinians and Jordanians by the BBC Director, Shelly Seawell (1999), with wide coverage in North America, as well as that by ABC's Dianne Sawyer.

Patriarchal ideologies around which families, tribes, clans, and in most cases institutionalized religions are structured are no doubt contributing factors to the perpetration of honour killing. In fact, patriarchal ideology in this limited and narrowly defined concept of subjective culture has more reason to survive and even outlive ideologies that are objectively structured, including the state. This is particularly true if families, clans, and ethnic/religious communities find themselves isolated, marginalized, or placed in a hostile, foreign, racist, or colonial state or setting. Thus, in addition to the fact that the violence of militarization can easily find its way into subjugating women citizens to different forms of violence, including killing, most women victims of the phenomenon of 'honour killing' in a colonial settler state appear to be indigenous peoples as well as immigrants and refugees, especially those fleeing political persecution in their own countries. Before responding to the question of whose family and whose 'honour' is being protected and saved by killing one's own female members, a brief discussion of sexual violence and the murder of women in Israel will be provided.

Israel's militarized and settler-colonial nature has placed it among the most violent states worldwide. While the political violence against the Palestinian population is the most pronounced and manifest form of this, other forms of violence—including sexual violence against women, both Israeli Jews and Palestinian (Arab) citizens—is equally rampant.

Historically, the gendered/sexed Israeli state has turned a deaf ear to violence perpetrated against women and especially to crimes committed on the so-called basis of 'family honour'. The state's general disinterest and inaction towards sex-crimes were not exclusively oriented towards 'its' Palestinian citizens only; they also included its own female Jewish nationals/citizens as well. The only difference, as will be elaborated on later, is the ideological underpinning which motivated Israel's action, or lack thereof.

Elsewhere (Abdo 2005, forthcoming), I have referred to the official treatment of the phenomenon of 'honour killing' by Arab governments and leadership in general, and Palestinians in particular, as *tabtabeh* (literally, 'a pat on the back'), which means paying lip service to the crimes perpetrated against women; however, this 'policy' is not simply an Arab one. Until quite recently, and largely as a result of the awakening of the Israeli feminist movement and the Palestinian national and feminist movement in Israel, the state has used a similar strategy/policy, albeit for different reasons and under a different pretext.

In addition to the crimes inflicted on women and caused by Israel's mammoth (one billion USD a year) sex industry centred around the trafficking of women, violence in the form of 'honour killing' against Israeli Jewish women has been an equally serious problem. Israeli official and highly conservative statistics put the percentage of 'domestic violence against married women' at ten per year, of which 7 per cent are said to be exposed to ongoing abuse. Available data, based on police and hospital reports (an equally gross-underestimation of the true extent of this phenomenon) suggest that only one out of every six battered women actually reports to the police, raising the percentage of battered women in Israel to about 20–25 per cent of the total Israeli population, or approximately 50 per cent of the female population. In addition, rape and incest is also widespread among the Jews in Israel. Based on information gathered from police and other centres in 1994, for example, the Help Centres (Israeli feminist centres) reported 848 cases of 'rape'; 133 of 'attempted rape'; 104 of 'gang rape'; 162 'paternal incest' cases; 83 'fraternal incest' cases; 186 'incest by other' individuals; and hundreds of cases of sexual harassment and sexual abuse.[2]

---

2   For more, see my forthcoming book, *Sexuality, Citizenship and the Nation State: Experiences of Palestinian Women* (forthcoming, 2005, Chapter 5); see also <www.no2violence.co.il/Statistics/Statistics010.htm>.

TABLE 1
Murdered Women in Israel by spouse, former spouse or family members 1992–2001
(Reproduced from Abdo, 2005: Ch. 5 [forthcoming])

		Veteran Israelis		New Immigrants		
Year	No. of Victims	Jewish	Arabs & Druze	C.I.S.	Ethiopa	Foreigners
1992	18	5	2	9	2	-
1993	19	9	1	8	1	-
1994	19	10	4	4	1	-
1995	17	6	5	4	2	-
1996	21	10	4	6	1	-
1997	21	9	5	6	1	-
1998	18	8	4	5	1	-
1999	13	7	2	2	2	-
2000	23	10	9	4	-	-
2001	28	8	8	8	3	1
Total	197	82	44	56	14	1
%	100	41.62	22.34	28.43	7.11	0.50

Sexual crimes perpetrated against women on account of the so-called 'family honour' have been on the rise since 1992, mostly among Jews (and 'new immigrants'), but also among Palestinian citizens. Table 1 documents some of these statistics. As it reveals, the overwhelming majority of women murdered on an 'honour' basis in Israel are Jewish ('veteran' and 'non-veteran' Jews as they are officially called). New immigrants, particularly under the category of 'C.I.S.', which refers to Russian immigrants and others from the Eastern Block, come second, at 28.43 per cent. As for Ethiopians, the rate of 7.11 per cent is extremely high compared to their representation in the Israeli demographic in general. In terms of overall representation, female murder among Palestinians in Israel, albeit high in terms of their overall representation in the Israeli population (19 per cent within the Green Line—that is, the population before the 1967 occupation, and 25 per cent with Jerusalemites included), appears to be, by Israeli standards, a lesser a problem. This, however, did not absolve Israeli state officials, academics, cultural/ideological producers/disseminators, including feminists, from flagging the phenomenon as Arab (Palestinian) only, insisting on its Islamic religious and Arab cultural bases. This culturalist (academic, feminist, and official) discourse, incidentally, is not very different from other official (including feminist and academic) Western European and North American discourses which continue to see the phenomenon as Islamic.

To take the Israeli example one logical step further, the questions that present themselves are: What family? Which family? And who is being 'honoured' or 'protected' here?

As already mentioned, Israeli official numbers for both Jewish and Arab women murdered under the pretext of 'family-honour' constitute a gross underestimation of the actual number. The Israeli-based Arab Association for Human Rights (HRA), for example, estimated the number of Palestinian women murdered between the years 1992–1998 at about sixty-six. The numbers of battered, raped, and murdered women have grown steadily in the past four years or so, especially due to the further militarization of the state and the consequent increased violence within Israeli society. Still, this has not motivated the state to take up measures adequate to limit the occurrence of the phenomenon or redress such injustices. This is true for the cases of all women involved, including women in the 'favourite' Jewish category (i.e., Ashkenazi Jewish women). Except for a handful of women's shelters built in the Jewish cities, and one shelter only to serve the Arab 'sector' (whose inhabitants make up about 22 per cent of the Israeli population), no serious discussions, let alone any practical measures, have been taken by the Israeli official establishment to redress women's victimization since then.

Unlike other Palestinian immigrants and refugees, say in the European or North American context where they are considered as ethnic groups and treated as such, Palestinians in Israel are markedly different. In Israel, and despite Israeli official academic insistence on categorizing them as an 'ethnic' group, the state places them in a specific category as an 'undesired' group, as a 'hostile' collectivity and, therefore, as the 'enemy', rather than as citizens. Yet, when it comes to issues concerning sexuality, sexual violence, and political rights, Palestinians become 'Arabs' and 'Muslims' par excellence! Thus, when the issue of 'honour killing' is raised, it is never raised as crimes against women, but rather as an exclusively 'Arab/Muslim' phenomenon. It is brought out as a product of the Arab and Islamic 'mentality', an indication of their 'backwardness', compared to the 'modernity' and European-ness of the Israeli Jews. An emphasis on the individual cultural heritage of Arabs is designed, as will be seen below, to differentiate Arab-ness from Jewish-ness and create an us vis-à-vis them divide, justifying in the process the policy of non-action.

For Israel, the issue is to ensure the perpetuation and expansion of the Zionist project of settler colonialism through deciding on who is or can be a Jew and who isn't and cannot be a Jew. This, regardless of the fact that the 'Jew' in the Zionist ideology and Law of Return is any person with Jewish blood who immigrates/settles in Israel and thereby immediately becomes a full citizen! It is fascinating to note here that the 'Jewish' immigrant/settler does not have to be or might not have been a Jew prior to his/her immigration/settlement. The recently revealed fact that the majority of Russian Jews (more than one half of them) were/are not Jews is an indication of the Israeli use of religion (Jewishness) as a political tool for its settler-colonial interest rather than an indication of its declared 'representation' of world Jewry.

For Israel, the question of 'Jewish-ness' does not denote more than those who can serve the political ideology of the Zionist/racist state. One needs only remember the well-known 'Ethiopian Blood Scandal' (the blood gathered over a period of time from Ethiopian Jews in Israel, only to be considered as contaminated and disposed of!). What this suggests is that the Jewish-ness of the Ethiopians (many of whom were re-Judaiized upon arrival in Israel) is not the type of

Jews or potential Israeli nationals that the state is looking for as citizens. After all, Ethiopians are Africans and Blacks and not White or European. On the other hand, one is struck with another example for defining Jewish-ness, as in the case of Russian Jews. In this case, over one-and-a-half million Russians were brought to Israel over the past two decades as 'proper Jews' and made into full citizens upon arrival. This group of people is considered White and (Eastern) European and appears to fit the Zionist ideology of a proper Israeli citizen (White and European) and, in tandem with their Ashkenazi origin and long-time rulers, are leaders and the face of the state. Russians are considered 'proper Jews', despite the incredible irony recently uncovered about their past and current 'religious' affiliation: A recent study by Israeli academics has pointed out that the majority of Russian immigrants to Israel remain mostly non-Jews (namely, either Christians or unbelievers/communists).[3] Notwithstanding this, Israel continues to treat this fact with total oblivion.

INDIGENOUSNESS, ETHNICITY, AND THE SETTLER-COLONIAL STATE

The debate over whether Palestinian citizens of Israel are a national group, and hence an 'indigenous population', or whether they are an 'ethnic' collective as Israeli official policy (academic and otherwise) refers to them, has been discussed elsewhere (e.g., Abdo 2005, forthcoming). As will be asserted here as well, the major force which has been lost throughout the Israeli discourse is one concerning the history and character of the state at stake, namely, whether the group has immigrated or sought asylum as refugees, or migrated to the existing state; hence the reference to an 'ethnic' or 'cultural' collective becomes a closed definition. Or, on the other hand, whether the state itself has 'migrated into' an already existing 'nation' or collectivity, or 'found itself' settling on a land already populated by another group of people

---

3 For more on Russian Jewish immigrants to Israel, see Majid Al-Haj 2004.

(living on and off it); in this case, the reference is to an indigenous people or national group.

These definitional issues are not introduced here with the intention to set up a new divide, nor are they meant to value-judge or prioritize one marginalized group over another. Putting it differently, the concept of 'history of origin' is not important in itself. Its significance, rather, is in the political/ideological context, often used by the state, particularly the settler-colonial state, in promoting certain identities and minimizing/marginalizing or suppressing others. Calling attention to the historical context, I argue, is particularly significant to the advancement of critical and analytical thinking and writing. Historicity in this context helps in comprehending not only state policies towards sexual violence (including murder) against women, but also helps us understand the intersectionality between gender, sexuality, ethnicity/nationalism, and racism. It also helps identifying the nature of the state as expressed in its legal, juridical, and socio-economic policies towards marginalized and ethnicized or racialized women.

This paper does not intend to take up the concepts of 'femicide' or 'ethnocide', both of which have been used in connection with the murder of 'indigenous' women. The former concept has been primarily concerned with women (within and outside of the dominant nation/ethnicity), while the latter focuses on the killing of women from the 'other', non-dominant ethnicity (or ethnicities) as a means to fully subjugate, if not wipe out, the entire undesirable ethnicity.[4] Avoiding such concepts here by no means belittles the role of the Israeli colonial state in perpetuating and even encouraging the phenomenon of 'honour killing', nor should it be taken to mean that Israel has not been engaged in a process of *genocide* against the Palestinians.[5] The primary reason for not using these concepts is to demonstrate the complexity of the relationship between the colonizer and the colonized as

---

4   For more on this issue, see Shalhoub-Kevorkian 2002.
5   See Ilan Pappe's *The Making of the Arab-Israeli Conflict 1947–51* (1994).

expressed in the historically specific conditions under which the Israeli state has been operating in regards to its Palestinian citizens.

In contradistinction to the situation in most Arab countries, including those in the Palestinian Occupied Territories where the phenomenon of 'honour-crimes' is largely hushed up and considered a 'social or cultural taboo', in Israel sexuality in general is not considered a social taboo. Sex education has entered into most government schools, sexual relations (as in love, dating, and so forth) are public events, and sex magazines are publicly displayed in the market. Despite all this, issues pertaining to personal status laws or family law remain overwhelmingly in the hands of religious authority, the Rabbinical courts, and not the civil courts. This suggests that, for issues pertaining to women's bodies and sexuality (particularly within the family context), in terms of the legal context these issues are still outside of the civil jurisdiction. In the past five years or so an improvement in the status of Israeli women was achieved as the Knesset (Israeli Parliament) approved the changing the law regarding women's rights for custody and alimony, allowing women to take their cases into civil courts and thus outside of the religious courts. As marriage and divorce remain parts of the religious Israeli laws for all citizens, sexual violence within the family (including Jewish families) continues to be under the grip of the male religious authorities.

It is worth noting here that the achievement in legal changes mentioned above, which was largely due to the activism of the Israeli Jewish feminist movement, also occurred through the women's/feminist Palestinian (Arab) movement and activities which are not less important. For over a decade and a half now, an increasing number of organized Palestinian feminist groups, such as 'al-Fanar' (The Light House), 'Assiwar', and 'Badeel' have been working hard to expose the phenomenon of sexual violence, especially in the form of women murder (honour killing), to the media and public through public discussions, workshops and conferences, and through activities with the youth—especially at schools for raising students' awareness on violence against women. Citizen Palestinian women have been and continue to network individually and collectively with other Jewish feminist groups in lobbying government for changing various sections of the family law. In the past four years or so, and largely due to a strong campaign initiated by Jewish feminists first and taken up later by citizen Palestinian feminist groups, an important change to the Israeli Family Law has taken place. The Palestinian feminist campaign to change sections within family law did not proceed without major objections, resentment, and ridicule by Arab media, and Arab national and political leadership—and most importantly religious leadership—, all of whom accused these women of being 'loose', 'Westernized', and even 'Israelized'!

Despite all of the difficulties, they succeeded in pushing for a law which gives women the right to take their cases of custody and alimony outside of the religious courts and into the civil courts. In their strong lobbying, and their use of the changes just achieved by Jewish feminists in regards to the Jewish Family Law as a precedent, Palestinian feminists were able to have this law passed and implemented.

It is interesting to note here how even at this level of activism, the colonial motto of 'divide and rule' tries its best to define the national/cultural identity of women. The Druze in Israel, who are a part of the Arab Palestinian people with a developed variation of Islam, have been a concern for the state since its establishment. Israel from the outset tried to absorb the Druze by isolating them from their Arab environment. This was done through a power play between Israeli leadership and the Sheiks of the Druze, whereby the latter would provide males for Israeli conscription and Israel promises to give them a special status. The law which passed regarding alimony and custody was lobbied for and presented by Jewish feminists and activists. The surprise was that despite the absence of a Druze feminist group working with Jewish women, the law was passed for both Jewish and Druze women. Who spoke on behalf the Druze? Who decided that the Druze are not Arabs? What is the role of the Jewish feminist movement in this? None of these questions were ever answered. The only indication here is that the state can create, change, and re-create identities through its legal, economic, and political power. In this case it can decide to give a preferential treatment to the Druze in the false hope of isolating them from their national/cultural and linguistic collective, the Arabs.

Israel's concern with the concept and institution of the family and the family as a reproductive organization is limited to the colour/type of nationality of the family. The Jewish family, and within that the Ashkenazi type, is what is important for the state. It is the 'white' Jewish offspring that Israel is most interested in, not Arab Jews, Mizrahi Jews, or Ethiopian Jews and *definitely not Arab Palestinians* (Abdo and Yuval-Davis 1995).

Here is what is rather unique in the case of citizen Palestinians when it comes to issues of family and 'family honour' and 'honour killing'. Because of its realization that the Arab (Palestinian) family is the basis for Palestinian national identity, national reproduction, and expansion, Israel perceives of it as a "national" (read: Jewish) threat to the Jewish "race" in Israel. Most Israeli policies towards citizen Palestinians have been directly oriented towards the Arab family. These include the policies used to curb Palestinian growth through various racist and exclusionary practices and actions (house demolitions, preventing Arabs from obtaining building permits, high unemployment, poor services in Arab cities and villages, and so on). Israel also realizes that much of the sanctity placed on Palestinian nationalism and culture originates from the sanctity placed on the Arab family. It is the latter that Israel exploits, plays with, and ensures the status quo of, in order to keep using it against Palestinians as a national resistance group.

Herein also lies Israel's interest, or perhaps obsession in the issue of honour killing among Palestinians. Israeli policies and action—or rather inaction—towards the so-called 'honour killing' among the Palestinians has always demonstrated a particular interest in these crimes, verging on an obsession on the part of Israeli academic and official representatives. Historically, Israel has been active in adopting and implementing polices and programmes aimed at keeping the Arab family and culture around the family under its total control. This was not done in a manner whereby the state would take over issues concerning 'family-honour' under its *direct* control. Rather, it kept all things believed to be related to Arab 'culture', 'tradition', and 'family' within the community and used them as a cultural marker of the 'other' family, as a rod for differentiating 'us' from 'them'.

'Honour killing' among citizen Palestinians in Israel has been dealt with by the state through the policy (practice) identified earlier as *tabtabeh*. To date, killing in the case of 'honour killing' in Israel is not considered a crime (it is not criminalized), perpetrators are not considered criminals, and if and when caught are not punished accordingly.[6] If anything, throughout the history of the state, Israel has responded to such actions by largely ignoring them. The official discourse has run as follows: 'This activity is part of Arab culture and traditions, religion and customs, and we do not want to interfere in their private business....' This intentional policy of hushing/silencing means not only that Israeli police, for example, would not show interest in registering the case, follow it up, finding the murderer, and using existing legislative or executive procedures to prosecute. Israeli official policies and practices used to silence this phenomenon have resulted, in most cases, in the police actually co-operating with the murderers, or the Sheikh of the village, or the Head of Palestinian extended family (*Hamula*) in 'resolving' the issue through traditional patriarchal and often 'tribal' means.

---

6   Partly due to advances in information technology, and partly due to the struggle of Arab women, the issue of violence against women in the Arab world has been receiving more publicity. Several sites and web sites pages are currently available on and around such issues. See, for example <www.wclac.org/defaultold.htm>; The National Jordanian Campaign to Eliminate 'Honor Crimes' in Jordan: <www.amanjordan.org>; and Rana Husseini's various contributions to the *Jordan Times*.

Traditional means often used in 'solving' family or *Hamula* disputes (e.g., divorce, battering, violence including sexual violence against women, rape, incest, and etc.) have largely been conducted through the so-called *Sulha* (a traditional system used for reconciliation of differences). The *Sulha* system involves an arranged gathering of male heads of both the victim's and the victimizer's families at a neutral or third-party location, where the two families with the facilitation of a third party are expected to work out a form of resolution to the 'dispute'. The 'solution' often involves a form of material compensation (a certain payment) made to the victim's family, and the two families would be expected to go back to living in peace!

In cases of pre-marital rape, attempted rape, battering, or any other form of sexual violence, a tradition has developed whereby the families decide to marry off the rape victim to the rapist or to return the battered wife to her batterer's house. No matter how cruel and anti-human such practices are, the state, through its deafening silence, becomes an equal accomplice in doubly or even triply victimizing Arab/Palestinian female citizens.

The state's so-called policy of staying outside of the 'Arab'/'their' (the state's own) citizens' traditional cultural norms is a calculated policy/mechanism aimed at keeping Palestinian citizens socially and culturally under the grip of their traditional leadership, thereby enabling Israel to maintain its control over its Palestinian citizens.

But what Israel, Israelis, Westerners, and others concerned with these issues fail to understand is that the Palestinian Arab family, proclaimed to be the cradle of traditionality, backwardness, and the so-called 'Arab mind', is not the primordial type of family that became stuck in its form and structure sometime back in desert times! The family is not an ahistoric phenomenon at all. In fact, the Arab/Palestinian family has changed tremendously since the establishment of the state of Israel. Israeli colonial rule, which stripped the 'indigenous' Palestinian family from its land, its major means of survival, production, and reproduction, has very much led to the nuclearization of the *Hamula* extended family. This rule has sent many family members into the city as wage labourers and increased economic and social differentiation between families, with probably a trickle down positive feature: increased education among the new generations and a change in some patterns of life and marriage among others. However, these historical objective changes were not the only force of change undergone by the Palestinian family. Direct intervention by the Israeli colonial state in the order and functioning of the Palestinian *Hamula* has in fact had a long-lasting effect in terms of strengthening or even re-inventing patriarchy and women's suppression within the Palestinian (Arab) family.

Losing the overwhelming majority of the land to a small minority after the expulsion of about 80 per cent of the Palestinian community in 1948, and finding themselves in a hostile and foreign state and culture, citizen Palestinians used family structures as a familiar and safe refuge. However, in many senses, Israel has reinvented a strong patriarchal culture within the Palestinian family by (re-) creating the position of the *Mukhtar*.[7] The *Mukhtar*, which in Arabic means 'the chosen one,' has historically represented a pre-capitalist, peasant way of life whereby the village, extended family, or the community chooses an elder to manage the social, economic, and political life in the said community. The coming of the Israeli state, assuming control over Arab/Palestinian economic and political life, has led the state to seek new ways to reinvent an Arab social structure which the state can depend on politically (i.e., to ensure loyalty to the state) and socially (i.e., to keep traditional control over its members and in particular to manage the lives of its female members). The *Mukhtar* who was entrusted in these tasks was often rewarded by the state, either finan-

---

7   The phenomenon of the *Mukhtar* within citizen Palestinians in Israel has received special attention among anthropologists. See, for example, Khalil Nakhleh 1977; Abdo 1987. On the politics of the *Mukhtar* and the counter public politics which emerged among Palestinians who began to refer to the *Mukhtar* as *Ameel* (Israeli collaborator), see Zeidan 1995.

cially or through other incentives (including access to state security or even weapons). The powers delegated to the *Mukhtar* has given the latter a very strong hand in controlling family members, and most importantly females, as he had power over decisions on marriages, divorce, and all other social issues.

Although second and third generation Palestinians (women and men) have fought and continue to fight against such archaic forms of social/family organizations, the colonial legacy of intervention in the lives and culture of the colonized continues to take its toll on citizen Palestinian women, particularly concerning sexual violence, including murder of women.

Israeli colonial policies and practices did not only attempt (and succeed) to create a new and tighter mode of cultural intervention in the Palestinian family, it also played out and reinforced what it considered to be 'Arab cultural markers', such as the phenomenon of 'honour killing', to serve its own colonial purposes. For example, the phenomenon of 'family-honour' was (and still is) used as a means to de-nationalize and de-politicize citizen Palestinians by using it as a tactic to force out confessions from Palestinian political prisoners and break down their national and anti-racist resistance. Israeli prison authorities have often forced confessions out of male political prisoners by, among other things, threatening to sexually harass, rape, or torture their female kin (be they a mother, wife, sister or daughter). In several documented cases, female kin of prisoners were brought to the prison and were threatened with sexual acts.

With female political prisoners, rape and other forms of sexual violence has been used as a form to de-politicize the whole family. Sexual harassment and rape of Palestinian women political prisoners is amply recorded and documented.[8] In other words, Israeli officials use issues such as 'virginity' and the consequences of loosing it prior

---

8 For an update on Palestinian women political prisoners, see 'The Palestinian Initiative for the Promotion of Global Dialogue and Democracy' (MIFTAH), an organization initiated and headed by Hanan Ashrawi: <www.miftah.org>. See also Langer's *In My Own Eyes* (1978).

to marriage and 'family honour' within the Arab context as a political mechanism of control. In keeping with the state's colonial racist policies towards its Arab citizens, Israel as a state undoubtedly has ensured the perpetuation of traditional patriarchal norms (those it found in place and others it has created) and used them as means to control the colonized.

SEXUAL CRIMES, RACIST POLICIES, AND THE ISRAELI STATE

At the outset and since its establishment, Israel has announced itself as a democratic state/country, as part of Europe, and as antithetical to Arab or Muslim cultures; it has thereby tended to dissociate and differentiate itself from its geopolitical environment. Compared to other Middle Eastern countries, Israel has indeed developed a 'democratic' form of rule based on public formal and regular elections, the separation between state bodies (the legislative, judicial, and executive bodies), and a legal system largely based around individual rights. However, a critical examination of the state's 'democratic' structure reveals its limitations and its rather exclusive and exclusionary policies and state ideology.

There is a partial truth in the Arabic proverbial saying—uttered partly by citizen Palestinians—that 'Israeli democracy is good only for Jews'! This proverbial saying holds true only if one sees Israel as having two 'harmonious' yet oppositional communities, say, Palestinian/Arab and Israeli Jews. The reality, however, is that there is no one 'unified' or harmonious Jewish community (let alone ethnicity or nationality) within the state. Since its establishment, the state of Israel has considered itself 'White', 'Western', and 'European', with the select among European male Jews being in control of the country's economy, politics, and military structure. On the other hand and within the Jewish context, Mizrahi Jews who for over 40 years in the life of the state have made up the majority of the population have been largely excluded from policy-making and decision-taking positions, have been kept marginalized economically, politically, and socially, and have been discriminated against at all levels. In other words, Mizrahi Jews in Israel were never seen as the 'preferred' Jews nor were they treated as equal Jewish citizens.

The marginalization of Mizrahi Jews, or Arab–Jews, as some refer to themselves, has caught the attention of a large number of progressive Jews, both Ashkenazi(s) and Mizrahi(s), particularly feminists who in the past two decades have been very vocal against Israel's hypocritical policies towards Jewish-ness. The works of feminist scholars such as Amy Gottlieb (1993), Simona Sharoni (1993, 1994), Nira Yuval-Davis (1980), Abdo and Yuval-Davis (1995), and Ronit Lentin (2002) present ample analysis around Israeli racist policies towards its 'own' Jewish nationals. Especially in the past decade and a half, criticism of the state of Israel in this area has developed among an increasing number of Mizrahi feminist scholars. Scholarship by these feminists has produced evidence about the oppression, exploitation, and discriminatory policies applied by the state against its non-European Jewish citizens (Shiran 1991; Shohat 1988, 1996; Shohat and Stam 1994, 2002; Lavie 2002; Motzafi-Haller 1997; Dahan-Kalev 2003). All of these scholars attribute Israel's racist policies, giving the upper hand to Ashkenazi Jews while socially and economically marginalizing other Jews, to a discrimination against 'non-' or 'less' White/European Jews predicated partly on cultural grounds and partly on economic grounds. The situation insofar as Palestinians are concerned is somewhat different. In the case of citizen Palestinians, Israeli Zionist racism is integral to the state's structural, institutional, legal, and judicial systems. It is a systematic and built-in form of racism which is characteristic of Israel as a settler-colonial state and society.

Without going into any details here, suffice it to mention a couple of examples to demonstrate the legal, institutional, and structural forms of racism practiced against citizen Palestinians. David Kretzmer, an Israeli Jewish legal Professor at the Hebrew University, classifies

Israel's racism and exclusionary principles into three categories in his *The Legal Status of the Arabs in Israel* (1990):

1. 'open Discrimination', which refers to forms of discrimination fixed in law;
2. 'hidden Discrimination'; and
3. 'institutional Discrimination'.

'Open Discrimination' refers to the 'Law of Return' and Israel's 'Land Laws'; whereas the former law considers the land of Palestine as 'Jewish', opening it up for Jews all over the world to immigrate ('return') and make it their country upon arrival, the 'Land Laws' considers Palestinian land as 'the sole property of the Jewish people and not the citizens'.

Included in the 'hidden Discrimination' is the preferential treatment and benefits made by government to Jews over citizen Palestinians. 'Hidden Discrimination' as Kretzmer maintains refers to all policies, rules, and regulations which favour Jews under the guise of 'military services', thereby excluding almost all indigenous Palestinians. As the vast majority (90 per cent) of citizen Palestinians are not required to serve in the Israeli army, they do not receive the wide range of benefits such as larger mortgages, partial exemptions from course fees, and preferences for public employment and housing.

The most serious form of racism is the 'institutional' form which gives government institutions the power and ability to allocate budgets (for municipalities, social, health and education services, as well as for housing) as they feel fit. 'Institutional racism' also includes 'Emergency Regulations' (inherited from the British) which are applied to Arab citizens only. In concluding his remarks, Kretzmer suggests that 'on a decidedly fundamental level there is no real equality between Arab and Jew in Israel. The state is the state of the Jews, both those presently resident in the country as well as those residents abroad... even if the Arabs have equal rights on all other levels the signal is there: Israel is not their state' (Kretzmer 1990: 42–3).

Structural, institutional, and systematic racism against citizen

Palestinians undoubtedly marginalize women further, enhance their dependency on the traditional family and obstruct any major change or improvement in Arab/Palestinian traditional social-cultural norms, particularly around gender/sex relations and issues. Although marginalization, socio-economic dependency, and exclusion are the lot of all citizen Palestinians, males and females alike, the latter are still doubly or triply affected. Palestinian women share a similar lot with Mizrahi Jewish women when it comes to marginalization and an inferior status, for example, in terms of their exclusion from equal educational, economic, legal, and political participation given otherwise to the 'preferred breed', the Ashkenazi Jewish women; yet on the other hand, as Palestinians they are not equal to any Jewish citizen in Israel. Hence, the racial/national hierarchy of oppression and marginalization is created within the same sex/gender.

On the other hand, and in addition to their oppression and subjugation on racial/national grounds, a feature they also share with their male counterparts, Palestinian women citizens of Israel are also discriminated against and marginalized within their own family/community and 'society' at large on strictly a gender–sex basis. To reiterate, Israel, as a settler-colonial state, expands onto territories, water, and other natural and human resources which belong to the Palestinians, not only those living in the territories occupied after 1967, but lands that continue to belong to Palestinians who became state citizens. Stripping Palestinians from their land, their sources of survival and reproduction, means impoverishing them and turning them into state dependants. Yet, when racism is used to inform almost all state policies, structures, and institutions, the burden of 'indigenous' citizens becomes double if not triple. These conditions unquestionably turn the whole community or collectivity inward and strengthen its familial, tribal, and national character, with dire consequences on the female members.

CONCLUSION: SEXUAL VIOLENCE AND FEMINIST(S) CHALLENGES

As much as this paper has tried to outline the theoretical context within which sexual violence against women and particularly 'honour-crimes' occur, it also is concerned with delineating some conceptual and practical tools which would help ameliorate the marginal status of women and reduce, or perhaps eliminate, the phenomenon of 'honour killing'. The following discussion recognizes the fact that sexual violence and crimes against women are a global phenomenon, and as such, it emphasizes the role played by global forces in the perpetuation and sometimes even expansion of all forms of violence, including sexual violence. Such forces, which among other things include colonialism, racism, patriarchy, Western cultural hegemony, and the recent emergence of the U.S. as the unipolar economic, military, and political force in the world, all these, it is argued, make up the wider context within which violence must be understood and theorized.

'Thinking globally' constitutes the threshold for critical, anti-racist feminist methodology. Thinking globally helps expand feminist horizons and articulate the phenomenon outside all forms of parochial borders, limitations, and boundaries, including the religious, the national, and the cultural. It also has the potential for creating feminist solidarity among women of different cultures and national and religious backgrounds. However, because of the uneven development and the differential ways in which global forces impact on different countries and states, particularly in the Third World, such differences and specificities of each country/state become equally important and demand special attention. The state's or country's or society's historical specificity, in other words, ought to become the starting point for feminist analysis of social-cultural phenomena, including 'honour killing'. The local/national context (even in its colonial or dictatorial form) should serve as a frame of reference for the necessary legal, juridical, socio-economic, and political changes required to fight all forms of violence against women.

Highlighting the importance of the state, be it colonial or 'democratic' or a special combination of both—as in the case of Israel—, the built-in racist policies within the structures, institutions, and bodies of the state and the racism experienced in the daily lives of residents, immigrants, or indigenous women, it is argued, constitutes the first challenge for critical anti-racist feminists concerned with eliminating violence against women. Operating within this context, the question becomes how feminists can contribute and work locally to contain or eliminate this phenomenon.

It is true that there is no one fit-for-all prescription here, especially at the practical/empirical level of operation. Feminist movements throughout the Arab/Muslim world have worked long and hard trying to move, shake, and change situations and conditions in their own countries. One particular area in which major efforts have been invested is the area of Family Law or the Personal Status Code. In Egypt, for example, the feminist movement has succeeded in affirming the *Khulo'* law, that is, the law which allows women to ask for divorce by returning to their husbands all they as wives have received in the marriage contract. The reference here is to the part of the marriage 'dowry/bride-price' known as *Muakhar*. In Jordan, the women's movement has also succeeded in placing their demand to raise the current age of marriage to 18 (from 16) as well as place the *Khulo'* law on the agenda of the Upper House. Although the Lower House (Parliament) has just rejected the law (as of June, 2004), enlightened higher officials in Jordan are determined to keep the law alive until the Lower House (Parliament) approves it.

In Palestine, both laws, along with a number of other legal changes in favour of women and against discrimination against them, are currently placed on the agenda of the Palestinian Legislative Council for voting and ratification. In fact, during the month of July, 2004 an agreement was reached between the higher religious authorities in Palestine and the Minister of Women's Affairs whereby the age of 18 was acknowledged and ratified as the official age for marriage in both the West Bank and Gaza. In Israel, where the age of marriage is already at 18, the Arab (Palestinian) feminist movement fought for and succeeded in giving women the choice between the religious and civil courts in matters of alimony and custody, as mentioned earlier. Such efforts and consequent changes, it should be emphasized, are no minor achievements, as they have implications for male and female education, increasing the age of marriage, a greater ability for self development, and hence more awareness about violence against women.

Women throughout the Arab/Muslim world have also been heavily active in providing safe places for battered women by renting 'secure homes', building 'shelters for battered women', training and sensitizing their own 'national' police force around gender issues, and so on. Palestinian women, for example, are also working on raising awareness and sensitizing judges and lawyers concerning gender issues and particularly making them aware of the debates around victimology as a gendered concept.

Speaking from a personal experience, I can say that the women's/feminist movement in many of the Arab/Muslim contexts is alive and committed to working towards the improvement of women's status. During the months of April–August, 2004 I was entrusted with writing the strategy and putting an action plan into place for the newly established Ministry of Women's Affairs in Palestine. As I was observing and following up the development of the staff in the Ministry (most of whom are women), I could see the enthusiasm and commitment of the individual women in advancing themselves and their sisters' lot. Despite the tremendous difficulties and challenges these women face daily at all levels, the energy and devotion they demonstrate while at work has been remarkable. This they exhibit in spite of the patriarchal familial context within which they live. It is worth noting that these women in general have little or no support from husbands or other male family members. In some cases they are the only bread winners for relatively large families; they face daily humiliation and obstructions, including physical and sexual harassment by the

Israeli colonial check-points and the special burden of the Apartheid Wall. These military check-points rose in number from one hundred prior to the second Intifada of 2002 to around 700 at present; they have been erected between Palestinian communities and also within villages and cities. All of this notwithstanding, hard work and commitment to changing and improving women's conditions in Palestine is clearly on the make.

I also made a similar observation during another mission in Jordan, as I was working to incorporate a gender strategy in the structure and institutions of the Ministry of Education. Jordanian women/feminists, I would add, demonstrated no less enthusiasm and commitment to improving women's status through ensuring better quality education and participation in the labour force. In this case, and with support and what seems to be a serious push from men in upper leadership positions, I am confident women can make important strides in improving their situation at large. There are various other practical moves and actions taken up by women all over the Arab/Muslim countries towards achieving gender equality and improving the status of women which this paper cannot address.

Still, no matter how effective these incremental practical changes are, without changes at the structural, institutional, and legal levels, the efforts remain disorganized and can be short-lived. The role of agency, in other words, constitutes only one part in the overall complex of efforts required for challenging existing situations and improving women's lot.

Both agency and structural/institutional changes, I argue, are in themselves in need of a context or a conceptual framework to guide their policies, programmes, and actions. During my long-time research and activist years in the Arab world, especially among Palestinian women in Israel and Palestine, I learned that good will on the part of women's NGOs and centres working on gender issues, and particularly on sexuality, as well as commitment on the part of one leader here and one decision-taker or policy-maker there, are important but insufficient. What is lacking, rather, in terms of dealing with sexuality in general and sexual violence against women in particular is what I refer to as a 'theory of the sexual'.

One primary challenge facing Arab feminists, particularly academics, in dealing with and changing the phenomenon of violence against women (especially in its sexual form) is that of writing or theorizing the sexual. Theorizing the sexual or providing an analytical framework for contextualizing sexual violence is needed throughout the Arab/Islamic world in order for a real move on violence against women to take shape.

Not unlike in other parts of the world, the gap between academic feminism and committed and activist feminism remains wide. Throughout the last two decades or so, much of the academic feminist scholarship within the Arab world has been more reactive than proactive. Academic feminism has largely been concerned with engaging in global feminist debates about Western presentation of Arab and especially Muslim women rather than contributing to a theory of sexual position within the Arab context.

It is understandable that writing the sexual is not an easy task. It is a major challenge that involves a clear critical stance against one's own 'national' state or government. It involves a critical reassessment of the existing legal, juridical, socio-economic, and political structures as well as the cultural/traditional forces which impede the women's movement and progress within it. Theorizing the sexual also involves providing an alternative vision for changing sexual violence and 'honour killing'. While an outline of a comprehensive theory is beyond the scope of this paper, some of the characteristic ingredients of such a proposal will be suggested here.

In a context where issues pertaining to sex, sexuality, or women's bodies are considered private—the 'business of the family'—and hence need not be exposed to the public, yet alone negotiated outside of the private realm, the primary feminist academic role must be ensuring the removal of the sexual from the private realm and into the public sphere. In other words, a contextualized theory of the sexual would first and foremost begin with challenging the social cultural 'taboo' built around the concepts of sex, sexuality, and sexual violence. This involves challenging society's 'hushing' attitudes towards the phenomenon, challenging the state/government policy of silencing referred to earlier as *tabtabeh*, and challenging the reluctance and hesitation in taking bold steps towards providing practical solutions for potential victims of 'honour killing'.

Such a challenge, it is proposed, could benefit greatly from politicizing the sexual and removing the sacrilegious connotations often attached to women's bodies and sexuality, particularly around women's 'virginity'.

This theoretical exercise, admittedly, requires strong commitment and bold determination to delve, objectively, into existing hegemonic fundamentalist movements; to reveal their political nature and motto; and to treat them as a part of the existing patriarchal structure of political order. Politicizing the sexual could as such lead to promoting a discourse and encouraging public and media debates around issues such as the virtues of sex education at schools, open discussions around safe sex, raising issues of birth control, contraception, and family planning as issues pertaining to women's bodies, and affirming women's rights to ownership and full control over their bodies.

Moreover, theorizing the sexual requires concerted efforts by academic feminists to work together in a participatory approach with activists and feminist NGOs in order to build on already existing successes and achievements at the community level. It simultaneously requires trying to find alternative methods for dealing with failures, set-backs, or obstacles faced.

Theorizing the sexual, it must be emphasized, is a process and not an act of the moment. It is not an activity, but a long term visionary and strategic project that requires constant and consistent efforts at re-locating the sexual from its domestic confinement into its proper public space as a political issue.

Moreover, writing the sexual involves turning the sexual into the cultural, by changing the concept of the cultural from its existing male hegemonic order of the traditional-as-static into a dynamic culture which incorporates women as half of society's members into it. In other words, the strategy for theorizing the sexual should be able to bring out the historic and contemporary contributions of Arab women in making their society, history, and culture. For, like their female counterparts throughout the Arab and/or Muslim world, Arab Palestinian women have and continue to leave their imprint on all fields of life, be it through their productive and reproductive roles or through their tremendous political contributions to the national struggle.

Theorizing the sexual as the cultural by simultaneously re-writing the cultural is all the more important in the Arab world, and perhaps in other contexts as well. For even within the context of feminist activism and women's/gender NGOs, there is a tendency to work within the framework of 'cultural relativism'. Cultural relativism, one needs to remember, in the past two decades or so has been given a strong impetus and a major push largely due to the onslaught of globalization and the U.S. cultural hegemonic practices in the region. This has produced a clear tension among local women's activist groups, particularly as they try to balance foreign imperial and cultural intervention with local fundamental and conservative forces which find a virtue in the status quo and view change as imposed from outside. This situation has led, in a number of women's NGOs, to the adoption of an approach towards sexuality that is far below the desired level of action. Despite the presence of well-intentioned feminist activists in a number of NGOs, a number of the solutions attempted in dealing with sexuality and sexual violence have in fact resulted in causing more disservice to potential victims of sexual violence than otherwise would have been the case.

For example, in various countries including Palestine, Jordan, Egypt, and Lebanon, women/feminist activists and NGOs, including those that have been working hard to establish shelters and hotlines for women victims of sexual violence and to provide other related services, are often ambivalent about dealing directly and publicly with cases of honour killing. Their line of argument is that they do not want to be seen as working against Arab 'norms', 'culture', and 'customs' and fall into the hands of the 'imperialists' or 'Western culture'. 'Cultural relativist' approaches adopted by women's/feminist groups—or rather pseudo-feminists—sometimes means co-operating with the authorities, including the police, or the 'working out' of an agreement between the battered and her batter, resulting in various cases in the woman returning to the violent house only to be more severely battered or even killed. This situation might also mean the refusal on the part of feminist-activist help providers to speak out publicly—albeit anonymously—on the volume and enormity of the problem regardless of what the national political leadership position is.

A theory of the sexual, therefore, must provide not only the contextual and conceptual framework for articulating, discussing, and debating sex, sexuality, sexual violence, and 'honour killing'. It must also provide an outline and a guide to inform better decisions for feminist/women service-providing centres. Such a theory, in fact, could be of great value and incentive for policy-making and decision-taking leadership (the overwhelming majority of whom are male) who might be interested in gender equality but who require education and consciousness-raising. The absence of such a theory, on the other hand, simply helps to maintain the existing status quo via its absence or even worsen the current context in regards to women's situation. This challenge, I believe, is currently at a high historical moment as we witness the increasing strength and resilience of fundamentalist movements throughout the region. More and more people appear to be absorbed within existing political religious movements, especially in rural areas and areas containing the marginalized in the cities and towns.

Like all theories, the sexual as political and cultural will not start from scratch. The beginnings of the theory of the sexual in the Arab world, albeit in a highly descriptive manner, are available not necessarily in academic writings per se, but in literary and cultural products. Examples here include the works of Nawal Saa'dawi (1980, 1997), Muhammad Shukri (1996, 1998), Bu Ali Yassin (1996), and Fatima Mernissi (1985, 1991), particularly the book in which she used the pseudonym Fatina A. Sabbah (1984).

Life-and-Death Honour: Young Women's Violent Stories About Reputation, Virginity, and Honour in a Swedish Context
ÅSA ELDÉN

Just a few years ago, the concept of 'honour killing' was practically non-existent in the scientific, political, and media vocabularies in Sweden. Whenever it occasionally appeared, it awoke associations of distant and foreign places. Today, we have seen extensive and heated discussions in the Swedish public discourse about cases of (mortal) honour-related violence. Honour killing has become a common concept open to everyone's opinion and definition. Honour killing is today a Swedish reality.

The Swedish debate on honour killing began in the second half of the 1990s, dramatically growing after the murder of Fadime Şahindal in January 2002. The debate has mainly focused on one question: Is violence in the name of honour 'similar' to, or 'different' from, violence against Swedish women? In official documents, another question has been given importance: Can there be said to exist 'ordinary' (Swedish/worldwide) and 'special' (honour-related) violence against women? In my opinion, both these questions redirect the focus from the main issue: men's use of violence against women in different situations and different cultural contexts.

The aim of this chapter is to argue in favour of a feminist comprehensive perspective in analyses of honour-related violence. My analytical tools are collected from feminist research on men's violence against women, and I hope that this may prove to be a fruitful strategy to analyse and combat honour-related violence. When using a comprehensive perspective, I argue that violence must be understood in its context, for example in a gender-cultural context. I also argue that different forms of violence must be kept grouped together, as well as violence used by different men directed towards different women. Throughout the paper, I will use empirical examples from my dissertation: young women's violent stories from legal cases concerning violence in the name of honour and interviews with Arab and Kurdish women, both from the Swedish context (Eldén 2003; Eldén and Westerstrand 2004).

During the process in which the empirical material of my dissertation was collected, the topics of *reputation, virginity, and honour* gradually emerged as the essential and interconnected centre of my study. In the analyses of the interviews and legal cases a main focus was the insistence that a woman has to be a virgin at the time of her marriage, and that she must protect her reputation, so as to not bring dishonour on her family. The three central topics mentioned above came into focus through descriptions of severe violence against women from male relatives, but also in experiences characterized by the women as 'dad's concern'. I saw that reputation, virginity, and honour were interrelated in a manner more complex than the simple connection between a woman's loss of virginity through sexual intercourse reflecting unfavourably on her family's honour. It was the woman's *reputation*, and not what 'really' happened, that brought dishonour to her family.

In the analysis of my interview material, I show how good or bad reputation is given crucial meaning by the women in the stories of their lives. I interpret this focus on reputation in the light of cultural conceptions of divided femininity, in which 'virgin' and 'whore' appear as essential and mutually exclusive categories of women (cf. Svalastog 1998; Lundgren 2001a). I also interpret it in the light of honour, meaning that a man's honour is related to what female relatives (by blood or marriage) show to others. A woman who has been defined as a 'whore' must be socially or physically extinguished to restore the honour of the family. Connecting the conceptions of reputation, virginity, and honour may create tools to understand how cultural conceptions of 'virgin' and 'whore'—which on a conceptual level appear to be static categories—become physical and concrete in women's stories about their lives. For a woman who is branded as a stained 'whore', who can never again become a 'virgin', these categories may become static not only on a conceptual level, but also in actual life. A woman that once has got a bad reputation will leave one category for the other. Only when a woman branded as a 'whore' no longer exists will the honour of the collective—the male family members—be restored. For a woman who is forced to live with highly normative demands, no matter if she follows or violates them, her reputation may become a matter of life and death.

In my analysis I call this 'a cultural context of honour'; a frame of interpretation in which the behaviour of the individual (woman) cannot be separated from the honour of the collective (of men), and where men's honour is connected to women's sexual behaviour (cf. Bourdieu 2001; Delaney 1987). I do not see this frame as determining people's lives, but rather as more or less normative. When creating gender, men and women make use of normative cultural conceptions; presumptions that tell us how men and women 'are' and 'should be' (Lundgren 2001a). It is possible both to break and to confirm these conceptions in different contexts and situations (Lundgren 2001a).

When interpreting their own lives, the women I have interviewed use the concepts of 'Swedish', 'Arab', and 'Kurdish' as conceptions of community, separated from and contrasted with other communities. 'Swedish' is purported to signify values of the individual's precedence over the collective, and with ideas of gender equality and women's independence. Comparatively, in the concepts of 'Arab'/'Kurdish', the collective takes precedence over the individual and is perceived as constraining and oppressive against women. When one mutually exclusive contrast (Swedish vs. Kurdish/Arab) is connected with another (gender equality vs. oppression against women), and one side is loaded positively and the other negatively, a hierarchical relation is created between the two sides.

This creation of contrasts makes sense as an emancipation project: Through these contrasts the women create a distance between that which is desired (liberty) and what is desired to be left behind (constraint). I interpret the contrast between Swedish and Arabic/Kurdish as a way of making the emancipation project intelligible in a Swedish cultural context, in which the concepts of Swedish vs. Arab/Kurdish are loaded in a way similar to this contrast of gender equality vs. constraint. The creation of a contrast between 'gender equal Sweden' and 'oppressive immigrant cultures' can be understood as a way to create a contrast between 'us' and 'them', and to uphold the image of Sweden as a world champion of gender equality (Molina and de los Reyes 2002; Lundgren and Westerstrand 2003).

However, this loading of culture as contrast is not unambiguous. The women oscillate in their stories: The substance of the contrast remains constant, while its loading changes. By way of example, 'Arab'/'Kurdish' may be filled with a content where the collective takes precedence over the individual, while at the same time its loading may alternate between positive (safety, community, love) and negative (limitations, constraint, subjection).

A similar oscillation can be found in a speech given by Fadime Şahindal in the Swedish Parliament, shortly before she was murdered by her father in January 2002. Fadime portrays herself as affected by Swedish values, while her family is portrayed as unchanged Kurdish even though they have lived many years in Sweden. In the story told in her speech, the Kurdish collective is loaded positively (with 'community') during her childhood, and later loaded negatively (with 'constraint') after the family's move to Sweden. Through this change, 'Kurdish' becomes contrasted with 'Swedish', which is loaded positively (with 'independence' and 'liberty of the individual'). Also in her family's understanding, as presented by Fadime, 'Swedish' and 'Kurdish' are contrasted, but they carry a reverse loading as 'Swedish' is loaded negatively (lack of morality, free sexual habits). Fadime interprets her own conduct as 'frightening' to the rest of the family.

The oscillation of loading found in Fadime's story is comprehensible if connected to conceptions of gender and to her story about experiences of violence. Within the chronology of her story, the control, threats and violence used by Fadime's male relatives began with her desire to 'live a Swedish life'. In the eyes of these men, as portrayed by Fadime, 'Swedish' is equated with 'whore'. A woman who is considered Swedish by male relatives is a woman with a bad reputation—a whore. I analyse this in the light of what I earlier mentioned as cultural conceptions of divided femininity in a cultural context of honour. In her story, Fadime's family perceives her as a Swedish whore, who will never again be a Kurdish virgin. To restore the honour of the family, she must be socially excluded or die. This shows a highly normative situation where cultural conceptions of 'virgin' and 'whore' are seen as exclusive categories not only on a conceptual level, but also in the actual life of Fadime. Fadime 'is' a whore that brings dishonour to her family; she runs away from her family and is murdered by her father.

In her story, Fadime makes control, threats, and physical violence 'intelligible' by connecting them with an understanding of culture as contrast, and to cultural conceptions of divided femininity within a cultural context of honour. Since she, in the eyes of her family, 'was' a Swedish whore and could never again be a Kurdish virgin, her male relatives 'had to' threaten and use violence against her. Such a connection makes the oscillation of loading in the contrast between Swedish and Kurdish comprehensible. As mentioned, the loading of 'Swedish' alternates between positive and negative—depending on whether Fadime or her family load the concept—may excuse male relatives' use of violence against and control of women close to them.

On an analytical level, I see culture as created through human acts and interpretations, carried out in contexts where the individual relates to more or less normative frames of interpretation (Geertz 1973; Lundgren 2001a). Individuals can choose to interpret their experiences and actions as determined by a cultural frame, like Fadime does when she sees herself through the eyes of her family; her male relatives 'have to' threaten and use violence against her to restore the honour of the family.

In the stories of Fadime and the women I have interviewed, culture, gender, and violence are given meaning through being interconnected. Culture is created as a contrast ('Swedish' vs. 'Arab'/'Kurdish'), and is related to conceptions of gender (divided femininity as 'virgin' vs. 'whore') and experiences of violence (control, threats, and physical violence). The 'Arab'/'Kurdish virgin' is contrasted with the 'Swedish whore' who figuratively or literally must be extinguished—threatened, battered, murdered.

The basic supposition and common characteristic of feminist research is that gender and power are connected in so far as men are structurally superior to women. In a feminist interpretation, an act of violence must be understood as given meaning in its context (Lundgren et al. 2001; Mellberg 2001). In my project, this can consist of culturally accepted forms of control and normative conceptions of gender in a cultural context of honour. This requires a comprehensive analytical perspective, which connects culture, violence, and gender.

Men (and women) may refer to conceptions of reputation, virginity, and honour to make control, threats, and violence against women 'intelligible' and accepted. A comprehensive feminist perspective highlights the connections between a murderer's argument that the killing was necessary to restore his honour, and the women I have interviewed constantly referring to—and being aware of—their reputation. In their stories, a bad reputation is fatal for a woman. In a woman's actual life, the connections between culture as contrast, cultural conceptions of gender, and experiences of violence may be a matter of crucial importance. If she, in the eyes of male relatives, lives a Swedish life—'is' a 'whore'—this may become a matter of life and death.

I will further argue for a feminist comprehensive perspective when interpreting honour-related violence by taking an example from the second part of the material that forms the basis of my dissertation: legal cases. The example is taken from an article written together with doctoral candidate in law Jenny Westerstrand: *Defender of Honour: The Judicial Handling of an Honour Killing* (Eldén and Westerstrand 2004). In the article we analyse the Swedish judicial judgement of the murder of Sara in December 1996. Our focus is to concretely understand connections in women's reporting of violence, between different forms of violence (like threats and physical violence) as well as different perpetrators and different victims. We also show how men's violence against women, in order to be comprehensive, must be understood in a (gender) cultural context; in this case what I have previously referred to as a cultural context of honour.

In December 1996, sixteen-year-old Sara, originally from Iraq, was murdered by her brother and cousin. Sara's murderers were convicted of murder and also of uttering severe illegal threats during the weeks preceding the murder. However, in our interpretation of the legal material, a picture is drawn of an everyday exposure to violence, in which the violence and threats used by the young men form parts of a whole.

Sara was controlled, threatened, and battered for years before she was finally murdered. According to the legal material, the persons involved in the control and violence were several of Sara's relatives. Among them we find the two young men who were convicted, but also—maybe to a higher degree—her father and uncles. The male relatives seem to have acted collectively; they gathered to discuss Sara's behaviour, they made a decision to kill her, and threatened and used violence against other female relatives.

I argue that Sara's male relatives used cultural conceptions of divided femininity in a cultural context of honour in controlling her. In their eyes, Sara was branded a 'whore', and the control, threats, and violence were connected with normative demands of not being a 'whore'. To restore their honour she could no longer exist, and was condemned to death.

When using a comprehensive perspective to understand this case, several *connections* become visible in Sara's life. Violence and control were always present—in different forms, used by different men, against different women. The acts of violence were carried out by a male collective in a cultural context of honour.

Nevertheless, the prosecutor chose to prosecute only the two young offenders. When handling the case, the Swedish court failed to visualize the violence Sara was exposed to, and failed to punish most of the men responsible for this violence. I will take one example to show this failure: the gap between the legal understanding of threats and the threats in Sara's everyday life.

The legal understanding of threats is limited to a concern with a momentary offence, an act 'of the moment'. The regulation condemns threats for causing serious fear for a person's safety, but does not include threats as part of a process in a gender cultural context; threats that aim at controlling women's space of life. Men's control of women is passed over in silence. How can this understanding—threats as an act of the moment—grasp the threats Sara was exposed to?

If we understand the threats from the male relatives to be threats expressed in a cultural context of honour, they may be interpreted as part of controlling a woman branded as a 'whore'. The threats do not disappear in the moment after they have been expressed. If we further understand these threats in the light of the difficulty—or impossibility—of getting rid of a bad reputation, and that the woman lives with and daily confronts the men who see her as a whore, her life situation will appear extremely dangerous. From this point of view, to understand threats as a momentary offence appears as a poor instrument to catch the meaning of what Sara was exposed to. In the Swedish judicial handling, men's use of threats as a way of controlling women is passed over in silence.

In the preliminary investigation of the case, there are statements that Sara's mother lived with constant threats, but also that she was threatened after the murder. It is stated that a male relative called her and told her: 'Now it is your turn.' The violence—control, threats, battery and finally the murder—does not end because Sara is dead. There is a reality of violence both before and after the murder. When the violent acts are defined as the woman's own fault—Sara was branded as a 'whore' who had to be extinguished to restore the honour of the men—an honour killing may be understood as a direct threat against female relatives. If they also come to be seen as 'whores', they may meet the same fate as Sara. A feminist comprehensive perspective shows connections between different forms of violence (here threats and murder), and between violence used by different male relatives. This perspective also makes visible connections between different female victims.

In order to understand men's violence—which is a condition to be able to combat it—we must see how culture, gender, and violence are interconnected. Wherever it appears, men's violence against women must be analysed in its context and related to culturally accepted forms of control and cultural conceptions of gender; how men and women are and should be. This interpretation makes the question of whether or not violence against Swedish women and honour-related violence should be understood as 'different' or 'similar' meaningless. To combat men's violence by comparing and contrasting it with what is perceived as different is hardly a constructive way to go. If violence is interpreted in its gendered cultural context, there is no such thing as ordinary or special forms of violence. There are simply men using different cultural conceptions of gender to control women's life and death.

Honour Killings:
Instruments of Patriarchal Control
NICOLE POPE

Honour killings tend to be perceived in the West as an exotic and gruesome form of murder, far removed from the reality of Western society. Western media usually describe honour killings, somewhat misleadingly, as an Islamic custom. The underlying message is usually that these murders are committed by backward people coming from distant cultures, and bear little in common with forms of violence prevalent in the West. A line is therefore drawn between 'us' and 'them', which creates an apparently unbridgeable gap.

But any type of violence, whether it happens in the developed or in the developing world, is always framed in a particular cultural context. While violence against women in Western societies is rarely perceived as a problem of 'culture', but rather as a social issue, murders committed in minority communities in the West or in developing countries, particularly if they are Muslim, are broadly attributed to 'culture' rather than to the patriarchal element within the culture, and therefore perceived to be unavoidable. This perception reinforces prejudices and racism, and leads to the rejection of the entire culture.

In her book *Is Multiculturalism Bad for Women?*, Susan Moller

Okin (1999) states that: 'In the case of a more patriarchal minority culture, no argument can be made on the basis of self-respect or freedom that the female members of the culture have a clear interest in its preservation.' She goes as far as suggesting that women could benefit if some cultures were allowed to disappear. 'Indeed, they *might* be much better off if the culture into which they were born were either to become extinct (so that its members would become integrated into the less sexist surrounding culture) or preferably, to be encouraged to alter itself so as to reinforce the equality of women—at least to the degree to which this value is upheld in the majority culture.'

But how does one define culture? It is composed of many elements—music, literature, art, language are all part of culture. Social practices and traditions which discriminate against women can also be the product of culture, but Western observers often fuse all these elements together when looking at minority cultures, and conclude that these societies are monolithic and unable to change, and therefore backward and unworthy of respect.

Honour killings, in my view, are an extreme—*the* most extreme—form of patriarchal control. But patriarchy takes many shapes and forms, and it certainly still exists in Western liberal societies, even if we sometimes too confidently believe women have reached equality. Honour killings are culture-specific in the way they are carried out, and therefore need culture-specific solutions, but the concepts of pride and shame that underlie these tragedies exist in various forms everywhere.

At the level of the community, crimes committed in the name of honour cannot be viewed separately from other forms of discrimination against women. Forced marriages, exchange of brides, underage marriages, and routine domestic violence all contribute to creating the conditions that can lead to murder. They are part of the same problem—the concept that a woman is just a commodity, and her 'owners', her male relatives, have the right to make decisions on her behalf without consulting her. The job of ensuring that this commodity is not spoiled, which would decrease her value and that of other members of the clan, is entrusted to the male members of the community. Their pride is hurt, and their masculinity challenged, when they are seen to have failed at this task.

The level of control seems motivated by an underlying fear of female sexuality, often perceived to be so potent that girls, if left unsupervised by their male relatives, will immediately stray off the straight path of social convention. Women are not believed to be capable of making adequate choices on their own or of defending their own virtue. Nafisa Shah, a well-known women's rights activist from Pakistan who is a member of a large feudal family, recounts in her thesis how her female cousins, women in their forties, would only be allowed to watch harmless documentaries on television, while the men congregated in the garden around a TV set showing Baywatch (Shah 1998).

Tribal codes of honour have been around for millennia, along with the murders they have inspired. But deciding what television show a woman can honourably watch on television is obviously a contemporary issue. Culture cannot stand still, and although there is a direct line that links old cultural traditions and murders committed in the name of honour today, each murder case has its own, modern, dynamic, and it is usually the result of a complex mix of traditional, socio-economic, political or even religious factors.

Culture and traditions may have a strong influence on people's behaviour and their understanding of the world around them, but they do not put people on automatic pilot. There is a temptation to think that it is perfectly natural for a Kurdish father to kill his daughter if he believes she had illicit relations with a man she wasn't married to, but each murder is still the result of a decision, taken by one or several individuals. Families grapple with these issues, and the disputes don't always result in killings: Women who had to seek help in shelters to save their lives sometimes manage to negotiate a return to the fold of the family.

In spite of the pressure of tradition, and above all the pressure of the community, some families manage to stand firm and resist the call to do 'the right thing' and cleanse their honour. Others will kill without hesitation, believing it is the easiest way out of a scandal that has had a disastrous impact on their lives. More often than not, the murder only compounds the problem: The parents have lost a daughter, and despite a tendency by courts to be lenient in such cases, one or several members of the family may end up in prison.

Prosperity and education make it easier for a family to seek alternatives to killing, for instance by sending away a 'disgraced' girl. But, as the murder in April 1999 of Samia Sarwar, daughter of the chairman of the chamber of commerce of Peshawar in Pakistan, showed, money and education do not always guarantee a more liberal approach. The young woman was shot to death in the office of her lawyer Hina Jilani in Lahore for seeking a divorce from her abusive husband. The gunman was brought into the lawyer's office by Samia's own mother, a doctor. The culprits were never sentenced, and the Upper House of the Pakistani parliament rejected a motion condemning honour killings brought in response to this tragedy.

From a broader perspective, honour killings may not be as far removed as we, Westerners, liked to think from other forms of violence against women that are still prevalent in liberal Western societies, such as domestic violence, rape, and crimes of passion. Is there a connection between the jealous and possessive man in Europe, who kills his lover because she wants to leave him, and the father who kills his daughter in Kurdistan or in Pakistan? I believe there is. In both cases, the murders are triggered by wounded pride, a wish to exercise power and the notion that women can, and should be, controlled.

The line is often very thin, for instance, between crimes of passion and honour killings. As Westerners, we can 'understand' (though obviously not condone) a crime of passion, but we find it more difficult to comprehend the emotions involved in honour killings. The fact that a girl's own parents or siblings—the very people who should be protecting her—can cold-bloodedly make a decision to kill her and become her executioners astonishes us, as does the lack of determination of the law enforcement agencies to crack down on such violent acts.

The main difference lies in the structure of the family, and the response of the local community. In strict patriarchal societies where honour killings are still common, the sense of ownership is not limited to the immediate partner, but extends to the entire clan. Also, the society at large, from judges to legislators, tends to take a tolerant view of murders committed for honour.

The legal framework in the West makes it easier to punish the perpetrators of violence against women, although the surprisingly low rate of conviction for rape in developed countries such as Britain (7.5 per cent) or Ireland (under 2 per cent) suggests women still have trouble convincing judges and juries that a sexual assault was unprovoked.

We don't need to go far back in history to find evidence that women's sexual behaviour was a matter of community interest in our societies as well. 'The Magdalene Sisters', a powerful film by Peter Mullan set in Ireland in the 1950s, follows the story of 'fallen girls', locked up in church-run institutions and condemned to a life of servitude and indignity, in some cases for life, for the same kind of 'crime' that warrants execution by relatives in other countries. The last of these institutions closed down in 1996.

We sometimes forget how recent progress in women's rights is in Western societies, and how fragile the gains remain. Despite the enormous progress accomplished thanks to the feminist movement in the past few decades, violence against women is still rife: Over 100 women are still killed by partners or ex-partners every year in countries like England and Wales, and figures in other developed, liberal societies are just as alarming. Furthermore, the wave of right-wing conservatism that is creating wider political divisions between East and West, North and South, is also threatening these social improvements. The language used in the debate against abortion rights, particularly in the United

States where the religious right is intent on banning terminations, often ignores a woman's rights and suggests her body is nothing more than a vessel carrying the unborn child. The leap from that standpoint to the notion that the purity of women has to be preserved so their body won't pollute the family bloodline is not that great.

Control of a woman's reproductive ability lies at the core of traditional practices against women. It is largely because a man can only be certain of the paternity of his child if his wife is kept away from other males that women's sexual behaviour is under such tight scrutiny the world over, and virginity is a prized commodity.

Until quite recently, on the rare occasions when the issue of culture was invoked in court in Western countries, it was usually to grant extenuating circumstances to men from minority communities who had committed violent acts, usually against their women-folk. Luckily this is changing. Landmark cases in Sweden, and more recently in Britain where for the first time a Kurdish man was sentenced to life imprisonment in September 2003 for the murder of his daughter, show that our understanding is evolving and cultural relativism is on the decline. Increasingly, our knowledge of the dynamics within a community is used to extend protection to all its members, and particularly women. Patriarchal community leaders are no longer the only intermediary between the authorities of a host country and its immigrant members.

Discriminatory practices against women often evolve to take into account modern factors. Urbanization and migration, which often leads migrant populations to feel uprooted and uncomfortable in their new surroundings, can reinforce the attachment to customs and traditions, and they can widen the gap between generations. Social, political, and economic conditions prevailing in a country are also crucial elements influencing the way women are treated. Almost everywhere, women are still the lightening rod of social change, and bear the brunt of social upheaval, whether it is a nationalist struggle, a war, economic depression, or religious awakening.

There are also differences in the way honour killings are carried out from one country to the next, sometimes from one tribe or one village to the next. In Turkey, for instance, perpetrators of honour crimes seldom invoke religion, but usually mention tribal traditions to justify the killings, and it is still relatively rare for men to be killed. In Pakistan, where religious fundamentalism is on the rise, religion is used as a tool to strengthen patriarchal control and men are more likely to be murdered as well if they are involved in illicit relations. In India, it is often marriages or affairs between members of different castes that trigger social rejection and violence.

In many cases of crimes of honour, money is also a crucial motivating factor: Women have a financial value in strongly patriarchal communities. In Pakistan's Upper Sindh, where poverty and feudal abuses are fuelling a climate of violence and lawlessness, murders, allegedly in the name of honour, have become a business with the complicity of corrupt feudal chiefs. Men can kill a female relative, then choose a prosperous member of the community and accuse him of having had illicit relations with the dead woman. Unless the man pays hefty compensation, as ordered by tribal courts whose members often get a share of the deal, he risks being killed, even if he was not involved.

As this case demonstrates, culture does evolve, but not always in the direction of greater rights for women. The patriarchal order is quite selective in the way it adapts to modern conditions and sadly, women's rights come last.

When we talk of patriarchy, we usually think mainly in terms of gender—of man versus woman. There is however another dimension that also needs to be taken into account. The pyramidal, hierarchical structure of the extended family is an obstacle to change. In liberal Western societies, the breakdown of the extended community and the focus on the nuclear family empowers younger people—sometimes with unfortunate side effects, as older people are sidelined and abandoned in homes for the elderly. In the course of my interviews in regions where honour killings are still practised, I was struck by the fact that young men as well as young women living in these strongly patriarchal societies complain bitterly about the tyranny of their elders. Boys have greater freedom than girls, and they don't risk their lives carrying the heavy weight of honour, but they, too, are at the mercy of a patriarchal decision on whom to marry, what job to choose, and how to conduct their private affairs. Marrying the groom her parents have chosen without her consent may be unappealing to a young girl, but her prospective husband may also resent his family's choice.

As members of the clan get older, they gradually climb the echelons of the family hierarchy and gain more power. Women, as well as men, can wield strong influence within the group, even if their power of decision rarely extends much beyond the walls of the family home.

By the time frustrated young people reach middle age, the incentive to force change has often diminished. They are finally enjoying the rewards of power, as it becomes their turn to lord it over younger members of the family. All too often, the oppressed turn into the oppressors. One hears countless stories of young brides tortured mentally, and sometimes physically, by a mother-in-law who, most probably, was maltreated or exploited when she was young.

Because honour killings involve the entire society—from government officials who turn a blind eye to the issue, to judges who implicitly condone the practice by passing lenient sentences and nosy neighbours who spread lethal gossip—a multi-pronged approach is needed to combat the scourge of honour killings. Empowering women, making them aware of their rights, and providing them with access to education and protection if they are threatened are obviously important elements of this struggle, but I believe it is important to co-opt men—young men, but also judges and legislators—into the battle for greater women's rights.

Secluded women can contribute little to the welfare and prosperity of the community. An educated mother can bring up her children more efficiently, and supplement the family's income.

Emotionally, too, men have a lot to gain from establishing more equal relations with women: They may control their womenfolk through fear, but receive little emotional comfort as a result. It is therefore important to convince men that relaxing their control over the women would not just in fact improve their life and that of their children, rather than just take away ancient privileges.

Westerners can best contribute by keeping an open mind and listening, as well as offering advice, to all members of the communities where women still suffer routine violence and discrimination. Dialogue must not be one way only. Reforms have greatly improved the lot of women in Western society, but individualism taken to its extreme can also lead to loneliness and isolation. While individuals, especially women, are often oppressed by the extended family, a community respectful of all its members can offer warmth and succour.

Supporting efforts to develop local solutions to ensure that women are given the individual rights they are entitled to within their community, rather than imposing ready-made Western solutions, would allow brutal practices such as honour killings to be phased out while preserving the better elements of various cultures.

SECTION 2

Community Struggle Against Honour Killing

The Cultural Basis of Violence in the Name of Honour

NEBAHAT AKKOÇ

I want to start the first presentation of the symposium by commemorating Anna Lindh, the late Swedish Minister of Foreign Affairs. I hesitate to do this, as you might perceive it to be a simple gesture like people do after the death of someone—but it is not.

Anna Lindh reserved the most important part of her visit to Turkey for Diyarbakır and especially for KA-MER (Kadın Merkezi, 'Women's Centre').

When she visited KA-MER, a large delegation and about twenty-five journalists accompanied her. We gave her information about our work and she announced that she was going to support the work of KA-MER. This support is very significant and must be recalled.

Then, we all went to visit the 'Women's Street Market', which was launched under our 'Women Entrepreneurship' programme. All those women working in stands of the market were illiterate, immigrant women who did not speak Turkish. She talked with them in such a friendly way....

They understood each other, sometimes with the mediation of a translator and sometimes without—as if they were speaking the same language. I was watching her from a certain distance. Then someone from the delegation came and told me that Anna Lindh was calling me. I went near her. She asked me to walk with her for a while. I realized that she wanted to be alone with me for a little while. We walked quickly side by side. The crowd followed us. She turned her face to mine, looked into my eyes and asked, 'How are you? Are you really o.k.? Can you work and live comfortably?'

At that moment we were two mothers, two feminist women against violence who were aware of the difficulties of women. She was neither a politician nor a diplomat at that moment. She was a friend.

For me, her question addressed a number of issues. And I answered with all my sincerity. 'Yes, I am o.k., I am not faced with any challenge I cannot cope with.'

We agreed that we should cook a dinner together if I would be able to go to Sweden one day. She explained that she had friends from Diyarbakır and she knew about our cuisine.

Thus, while I am commemorating Anna Lindh, I also have this short, private and meaningful meeting in mind, in addition to all her other identities. When I commemorate her, what I have in mind is the friendly communication she established through a female language, both with me and with the women in the market.

One morning I woke up and saw that the marketplace Anna Lindh had walked around in was destroyed. Women selling vegetables in a street market had become intolerable for some people. And they destroyed the marketplace. This ate my heart out. I recalled our short, friendly conversation.

One morning I woke up and learned that Anna Lindh was killed. She must have become intolerable for somebody.

Violence, reinforced by the same source, never ceased. A few weeks ago, two terrorist attacks following upon each other occurred in İstanbul.

For a while I thought that our seminar in İstanbul would be cancelled. Then I started to receive reconfirmation of the seminar from the Consulate-General. As you see, this was the best answer to give to the violence.

They want us to remove ourselves from the world, to leave the whole space to them. But we will continue working. Perhaps we will be fearful, but still we continue working with no rest.

KA-MER, which states as one of its most important principles that it is 'against violence', was established in 1997. Since its establishment, we have tried to provide support for women who are faced with violence. However, the first particular project for women killed in the name of honour started by the end of 2002. And we received our first support at the beginning of 2003 from Anna Lindh after we had applied to the Swedish Consulate.

Our project to prevent honour killings had two particular objectives: First, to open channels for possible victims to reach KA-MER and to provide them with life security; second, to determine and try to transform cultural practices that cause killings that are committed in the name of honour. The latter would be possible only through finding ways to meet with potential victim's close friends and families.

Almost a year has passed from the beginning of the project. In order to show the progress we have made, it will be meaningful to discuss the first and the last killings that occurred during this time; however, in both cases victims were not in able to apply to us, but we will assume here that they did.

The first case involved Şemse Allak, who was killed by *recm*—by stoning. The killers had left her because they thought that she had died. But she was found by police forces while in a coma and was taken to the Medical Faculty of Dicle University. Şemse Allak was five months pregnant when she was *recm*ed.

The last one was Kadriye Demirel. She was also thought to be dead and was taken to the Medical Faculty of Dicle University by police forces. Her head was smashed by a stone and her body was full of slashes made by cleavers. She was six and a half months pregnant.

In the first case, KA-MER was all alone. All our members

worked for months in order to help Şemse Allak survive. We left no stone unturned. We did all we could. But Şemse died six months after the *recm*.

We could not litigate, of course, because Şemse did not have the physical power to sign papers giving the right of representation to a lawyer and we could not find any of her relatives to file a lawsuit. We were about twenty women who buried her in a pauper's grave. Someone brought the two families together and reconciled them, while Şemse was still alive. The two families had a peace dinner. The men of the two families reconciled. During the dinner, nobody even recalled Şemse's name.

Kadriye Demirel was also hit on the head and was left because her killers thought that she was dead. She was put in the bed Şemse had used in the Brain Surgery Department of the Medical Faculty of Dicle University.

When KA-MER heard about the case and went to the hospital, we saw that all the non-governmental organizations were there to take care of Kadriye. Kadriye did not need KA-MER. Everyone was there.

Kadriye lived for two days. She was never left alone in these two days. A great number of people were there to take care of her when she died. The funeral was quite crowded. Associations, trade unions, and human rights defenders were there to attend the funeral. Women's rights had started to be perceived as human rights. Moreover, some women had visited Kadriye's mother and persuaded her to attend the funeral. Her mother was at the grave of Kadriye, the death of whom she could not prevent. She was keening for Kadriye.

We were also there as KA-MER. Our distress upon the death of Kadriye was mixed with the happiness of observing the large number of people who took care of her.

Well, this was the progress that had been made in just one year. We are glad to see that there have been significant improvements in terms of the creation of social sensitivity.

Two more women's bodies were found on the day Kadriye was

killed. One was found on the highway between Diyarbakır and Elazığ, close to the security point nearby the district of Maden; and the other was in Siverek district of Diyarbakır.

Security forces in Maden were trying to find relatives of the woman by showing her photograph to the cars they stopped. A man in one of the buses they stopped informed us about the situation. We learned about the body in Siverek from the newspaper.

People had not taken care of them as they had Kadriye. But, someone had reached KA-MER to give us information about the two bodies.

While those who killed Şemse and the brother of Kadriye who hit her were pridefully wandering about, having 'cleaned' their honour, other killers prefer to stay hidden. In fact, those who kill women to clean their honours get public attention as heroes, because it is the society that gives this duty to them. So they show everyone that they completed their duty.

Things are changing gradually, because laws are changing in Turkey. Social sensitivity is changing. Those who have killed in the name of honour cannot always show themselves in public with pride anymore. Some are trying to hide themselves, as in the last two cases.

Of course these killings are not peculiar to Diyarbakır. Our projects are not limited to Diyarbakır as well. We are working in twelve different cities of eastern and south-eastern Anatolia; and we will continue working. Our burden is lighter now. We are not needed in hospitals and at funerals any longer as our representatives replace us there, and so have more time to deal with the creation of social sensitivity around the issue.

We never forget that all existing institutions and organizations are products of the system and that for a final solution, all institutions and organizations should discover and consider factors that cause and feed sex discrimination or that conserve the patriarchal system. They may even need to restructure themselves.

I used the examples of Şemse and Kadriye to compare the

progress we made after a year-long project. KA-MER had twenty-one cases during this project. Şemse and Kadriye died but the others are still alive. In order to explain the cultural fundamentals of killings committed in the name of 'honour', we investigated the reason for the 'judgement' for a 'death sentence' in all of the cases we received in the past year. Each time the reason for the judgement was to clean someone's honour.

The reason for the killing of Şemse was her secret love for a man and having a religious wedding ceremony while she was pregnant.

The reason in the case of Kadriye was that she had been raped—not the offender but the victim of the rape was punished. Thus, being raped was a cultural basis for judgement and as such was a crime that 'deserved' death in turn.

We mentioned Şemse and Kadriye by name because they are not alive anymore. The other women are still alive. So I will mention them with their report numbers. The reason was the same in the first, seventh, and the thirteenth cases. If there is gossip about a woman, this is accepted as a valid basis for punishing her. Moreover, we know that the gossip in one of the cases was created purposefully and maliciously after the woman had rejected the advances of a man.

If a woman acting more comfortably, laughing, decking herself out, or talking more than others, is enough for the gossip to arise. Following upon this gossip, she is considered guilty and is punished.

Only two of the twenty-one cases were sentenced because of sexual intercourse with a man. If a young woman has sexual intercourse before marriage, this is certainly a reason for her to be killed.

This is not, however, the only reason for being killed.

Our fourth applicant is also a single young woman. It was decided that she should be killed because she had rejected the candidates her family offered as husband and had told them that she wanted to marry someone else.

According to the family, she was potentially guilty because of this behaviour. She was a troublemaker that would cause shame for the family, if not today, then tomorrow. So they thought of getting rid of this troublemaker and making the family peaceful.

Fortunately, the woman managed to get away from her family, marry the man of her choice, and established a life according to her will.

Our fifth case is a married woman. A death sentence was imposed on her because she did not obey her husband. In other words, her guilt is disobedience. We could not learn which instructions she did not obey. Whether justifiable or not, right or wrong, obeying the husband is a supposedly unquestionable task in society; doing otherwise is cause enough for punishment. Basically, the major reason receiving judgement in the name of 'honour' is disobedience. Men slap women during the first night of their wedding, or even use violence in such a way as to cause injuries. These practices are used mainly for ensuring the obedience of women.

The guilt of our sixth applicant was her statement that she wanted a divorce from her husband who used violence against her, who was much older than her, and to whom she was married by force. In our culture, one of the men at home says into the ear of the girl leaving home with her wedding dress: 'You are leaving here with your wedding dress; you can only come back with your white shroud.' This tradition is used to explain at the beginning that women do not have the right to divorce.

Kadriye Demirel was killed because she was raped by a male relative who could easily get into her home.

Our eighth applicant was judged because of her disobedience caused by the issue of her being harassed by her husband's drunkard friends. The woman faced harassment on many occasions, so she asked her husband not to bring his friends to their home. For this reason, her husband accused her of paving the way to *taciz* ('harassment'). Fortunately, her family understood her. Now, she is living with her family. As we can see from these two cases, women must always protect themselves from harassment and rape. This is their responsibility. Being unable to carry out this responsibility for any reason is accepted as an offence that deserves punishment.

The ninth, eleventh, fifteenth, sixteenth, seventeenth, nineteenth, and twentieth cases—two of whom were single and the rest married—were also judged on the basis of disobedience.

The sixteenth and twenty-first applicants were judged because they left their homes where they faced constant violence. Women do not have the right to leave their home without permission, even when they are faced with violence. They did not obey. It is a fundamental rule that women should obey all men at home. Otherwise, they have to be punished. Responding to the words of men, not doing what they say and resisting their wishes requires punishment. These situations may occur for reasons that may seem insignificant to us—like getting out of the home, talking with someone the man does not like, going to the father's home without permission, going shopping, and so on. The basic thing is to discourage women from telling or living their personal choices in any issue. It is supposed that disobedience starting from ordinary reasons in daily life today may reach huge proportions in the future, so men try to prevent this from happening. It is well known that in our region there are some practices whereby women are not killed after their first disobedience, but rather are punished through the infliction of some bodily harm.

The crime of the tenth applicant was 'falling in love' and not hiding her feelings from her family. She had showed an unusual courage with this behaviour and proved to be a potential danger for the future, and she was judged for this reason.

The fourteenth applicant got married without the permission of her family. Then she was left alone by the man she married. She sought shelter when she was left alone with her child. She applied to KAMER with mediation of a relative when she realized that her family would kill her.

We can show thousands of reasons considered to be valid to punish women. What is common in all cases is that the women do not behave in accordance with their social roles. The things I have told you up to now are the results we drew out of cases that were investigated by KA-MER.

The cultural reason used for punishment of the woman, whose body was found in Urfa–Siverek as I mentioned at the beginning of this chapter, was that she was going to her family's home in Adana without the permission of her husband. This was such a crime that both the husband and the father found her guilty.

Were not two women killed in Urfa two years ago, one for going to the cinema, the other for requesting a love song from the radio?

Fadime in Sweden was also killed because she was together with a man from a different culture.

In each culture there is a different set of rules valid only for women. These rules decide the norms of 'honour' in that culture and thus the mode of punishment. For instance, after migration from rural to urban areas in our region, people try to maintain village rules in the city as well. However, women in rural areas who can go to the field to work without restraint; if however, they go out in the city, they are punished.

In conclusion, we can sum up the cultural reasons for the punishment of women in one sentence; it is possible to collect hundreds of practices of different cultures under a single heading:

> To maintain the secondary status of women.

In the meeting of AKADER (the 'Academic Research and Solidarity Organization', an interdisciplinary co-operation at Diyarbakır University), Dr Aytekin Sır described the rationale for these practices as follows: 'to preserve slavery status as valid for women'. We totally agree with this description.

'Honour' is the norm of culture for controlling women. Honour means *not* laughing, wandering, loving, requesting a song, wanting education or information, talking, enjoying sexuality, and a hundred more things as well. Honour does not only mean virginity as most people assume; issues around virginity are just one of the hundreds of reasons for violence. 'Honour' means to obey, to come to heel.

The source of all these norms across the world is the 'patriarchal system' that oppresses women with various cultural practices.

At KA-MER, we first started from the universal and turned our face to the local; now after analysing the local, we are looking at the universal again. For instance, while we were evaluating our results, the young divorced mother Amina Laval was sentenced to stoning in Nigeria, and we discovered the similarities in concepts of honour at the universal and local levels, as I mentioned above. The system operates with a heavy hand as a whole.

The system creates thousands of reasons in each culture to survive and to feed itself.

The problem is the patriarchal system—the system that oppresses women, that restrains them from being individuals and that makes them dependent on men.

We, the women organizations working in Turkey and throughout the world, are trying to alter a giant-like system by fighting against the practices of our cultures that make women suffer.

Nineteen women managed to survive thanks to our project this year. Their struggles paved the way for the creation of significant sensitivities.

Therefore, looking at the local, working at the local level, leading the creation of social sensitivities and cultural transformations, and providing support is crucial.

Supposing that theories that were developed in other parts of world are valid and satisfactory, and basing our work on these theories, is often inadequate and sometimes ends up with destructive results.

We believe that being aware of the universal dimension of the problem but still being interested in the local level—working with care with the positive values of the local, without ignoring local values—is the best thing to do.

The most important thing while doing this is to avoid language and behaviours that will cause total rejection. For instance:

• The Universal Declaration of Human Rights provides for the right of travel for each human being. What we frequently saw categorized as 'disobedience' is that women go out of the home, neighbourhood, or sometimes the city without permission. If a woman is judged for such a reason, we cannot go to the family and say, 'But she used her right emanating from the Universal Declaration of Human Rights.' It is a matter of process. Saying that would cut the relations. The necessary language can be best developed by those who know the local norms.

• We have to be careful about our dress and the language we use when we visit an injured woman or attend a family *divan* meeting. Otherwise, nobody would take us seriously.

When a woman has had sexual relations and loses her virginity outside of marriage, it may seem natural to say, 'but she has the right to have a voice over her body'. In local practices, however, these words would be useful, rather, they would result in the condemnation and exclusion of the speaker of the words. We will need to work for dozens of years before we will be able to say these words.

I can give a number of similar examples. It was for this reason that KA-MER started to work with twelve different organizations in twelve different cities in south-eastern Turkey. Because, although we have the same ethnic identity, we believe that it is not right to use the same methods in Diyarbakır as in Urfa, Bingöl, or Van. Only women who were raised in the cultural and traditional practices of the region, who are aware of their secondary status and decided to struggle against these practices, can develop the necessary language for that region.

As women who are part of the same culture and who are defenders of women's human rights, who are familiar with the cultural basis of killings committed in the name of honour, they will be able to co-operate with governmental and civil institutions. Meanwhile, we will have to solve some general challenges through co-operations on a national level.

We need to co-operate on the following issues:

1. There is a lack of women shelters in Turkey. Social Services and the Society for the Protection of Children have a limited number of guest-houses. If a woman is escaping death, she should immediately be taken to a shelter. But insufficient conditions results in serious danger for both the applicant and the non-governmental organization.

2. The non-governmental organization that sends a woman to a shelter cannot have any contact with her again. Thus, we cannot develop permanent solutions for the applicant, and when the woman has to leave the shelter she is sent back to the place from which she fled, and so we have to work on the same case once again.

3. The women who cannot get psychological support in the shelters come back with psychological problems.

4. Women organizations cannot open shelters because of financial difficulties and complicated conditions. When women's human rights are violated, this is perceived as a problem of the women organizations, not of the state.

5. KA-MER developed co-operation with governmental organizations in Diyarbakır. But the attitude of both male and female staff in governmental organizations of other cities causes trouble both for the applicant and the related non-governmental organization. These people either do not know or ignore the fact that that these women organizations are trying to carry out one of the major responsibilities of the state.

6. When a woman is taken to hospital by police forces, as with the two cases I told of at the beginning, hospitals may demand that the non-governmental organization that takes care of the woman also cover her medical expenses. Either the university or public hospitals should cover these treatments from their own resources.

7. A society that has established its relations with women based on violence can develop alternative non-violent behaviours and communication methods through a process that takes examples from other parts of the world.

The challenges I mentioned above, and others I have not mentioned, can only be solved through co-operations on a national level.

The local practices can be handled only by women of that culture who work with an appropriate language and a careful investigation. This investigation is dangerous as well. As you know, murderers are hiding or are claiming that their murders are actually suicides. The patriarchal system is resisting. The method of struggle should take all these things into consideration. We prepared the next step of the Project for Killings Committed in the Name of Honour with all these discoveries in mind.

Violence against women has not ceased anywhere. Our female guests from the European Parliament tell us about the challenges they are faced with.

We are ten years behind many countries. This struggle is such that it will continue until the patriarchal system ends.

But I believe that killings committed in the name of honour will end in a shorter period of time. With this belief, I would like to state my hope that we draw concrete ideas from each other and that we find ways to co-operate, and I present my respectful greetings to you.

The Story of Ayşe
KA-MER

The story told below was dealt within the framework of the 'Project about Killings Committed in the Name of Honour' of KA-MER (in Diyarbakır). The real name of the applicant has not been used. Our reason for telling this story is that we believe that the meeting on 4–6 December will be more productive if our discussions are based on real experiences.

A male relative of Ayşe as well as her husband Veli approached KA-MER on 12 December, 2002. Ahmet is a middle-aged man who has lived in a European country for many years. Both while he was abroad and after he returned, he reacted against various human rights violations experienced in our region. When we first met, he came with another man who had arrived from İzmir about this matter. He was the head of the family council that decided that Ayşe must be killed.

Ahmet explained why they came as follows:

> Ayşe has disappeared for the last two days. The family council came together on the assumption that she had run away with another man and decided to kill her. But I suggested that we should

contact a women's organization and listen to their views. They accepted when I insisted. I brought you together. Now let's talk.

I immediately realized from these words that Ahmet was trying to prevent the killing. But the head of the family council insisted that Ayşe had run away with a man. This caused back-biting in the village. She had to be punished by death. There was no way to make him give up this idea—he believed that he had to kill Ayşe if he wanted to live honourably in İzmir. Otherwise, it would be a bad example for other women, his business would fail, and his prestige in society would be shaken.

At the end of a one-hour-long negotiation, the two men accepted our demand to meet with Ayşe. We had managed to convince them with examples of many innocent women who had suffered because of unfounded rumours, and as such that the rumours about Ayşe might simply be untrue and that they may come to regret any action later.

The head of the family council had one condition before he accepted our wish to meet with Ayşe: We would help him to understand whether the rumours were true or not. He had some questions. He wanted us to ask these questions to Ayşe, and convey the answers to him. If the information supported the claim that Ayşe had run away with a man, she would be killed. This task was incompatible with our working principles. But there was no other way to see her.

During this negotiation, our colleagues at KA-MER were in a meeting. We were making a monthly evaluation meeting as we had done for the last five years. Jülide Aral was there as the group facilitator. We conveyed our talks with Ahmet and the head of the family council and their demands to the group. We discussed the issue and we all agreed that we should take Ayşe away from the family. But we would not ask those questions.

Ahmet gave us his mobile phone number and took our numbers. He said they will call us. And off they went.

After a short while, Ahmet called us. He said that he was happy because we had won some time. He did not want to witness the killing of one more woman. He had seen too many killings in the past. While abroad, he had realized that women there were given more value. But he could not relate his ideas in the family council, because he was afraid to be excluded. He offered to arrange a meeting with Ayşe for us. And he wanted us to prevent the killing of Ayşe.

Ahmet and three women from KA-MER rented a car and set out on the way to the village in the evening. It was very cold and snowy. When we arrived at the address they had given, we realized that Ayşe—to escape from death—had taken refuge in her aunt's (her mother's sister) home after a six kilometre-long barefoot walk in snowy weather. Ayşe stayed with her aunt that night. However she was moved to another place since she might be found there easily. They did not want to give the address of the new place to us. They gave us the address of a grocery and told us we should find the store, turn of the lights of the car, and wait. They said that a man would come and lead us to the place where Ayşe stayed.

We found the grocery and started to wait. I guess they gave the number plate of our car. A young man came and told us to follow him. Electricity was cut off. We could not see the face of the young man. We went up to the last floor of an apartment building in a ghetto. It was dark. There was an old man and a woman. Ahmet had informed them. After a while, Ayşe came to the room where we were waiting.

She was a slim, beautiful, and young woman. She was afraid. She examined us with her eyes. We introduced ourselves and explained why we were there. We tried to make her believe us.

The host, a *Hacı*, stated that he believed Ayşe was slandered and that he would help her. We gave information about KA-MER to the *Hacı*, too. We gave our address and phone numbers. He promised to protect Ayşe.

We had a chat with Ayşe. That night she told us the following: She was not sent to school. When she was 10 years old, her father forced her to marry a man who was their relative. She gave birth to five children but two of them died after birth. There had been some slandering of her, and she was living in continuous fear and realized that the family council came together. After a female relative told her that 'They will kill you', she ran away early in the morning and sought shelter in her aunt's home in another village.

They thought that she would not be safe there so she was taken to the place where she now stays. And the man who welcomed us was her brother. We did not ask Ayşe any questions. We convinced her brother to bring Ayşe to KA-MER, because she needed to meet with a lawyer. This offer was accepted.

The next day, Ayşe came to KA-MER with her brother and a cousin. She explained her experiences as follows:

> A cousin of her husband has started to disturb her recently. By phone, by words and by glances, everywhere he saw her. He told her that that he loves her and he wants to have a sexual relationship with her.

After hiding her situation for a long time, Ayşe explained it to her mother-in-law who had been suspicious about the telephone calls. However, the mother-in-law did not attempt to help Ayşe. They were both afraid, since another woman in the family had been killed under similar circumstances. First they tried to strangle her with cheesecloth in front of all, women and children of the family, but when she resisted, she was killed with a gun. The husband of the murdered woman was arrested and stayed in jail only for thirty-four months. Then he married again and had children. Ayşe takes care of two daughters of the murdered woman.

Meanwhile, the harasser was threatening Ayşe, saying, 'If you do not yield to me I will see to it that you will be killed like the other woman.' When Ayşe did not surrender, the harasser—who was now doing his military service—started to slander Ayşe.

Ayşe related that she ran away when she heard from her sister-in-law that she would be killed. She did not trust anyone and implored us not to leave her alone. She said, 'I want to struggle for my rights with your support.'

We wanted to engage a lawyer but she did not have an identity card or a civil marriage. So first we had to get an identity card. Then she could report the crime.

We knew from Ahment that Ayşe's husband, Veli, knew that his wife was innocent. But he did not know that she had been harassed by a relative. He was angry with her because he thought that she was behaving in a provocative manner.

We called Ahmet and the head of the family council and told them that Ayşe ran away alone and explained to them the reason for her escape. But we kept the harassment a secret since that otherwise might turn into a cause for a blood feud. They wanted us to give them a few days. We started to wait and we talked with Ayşe by phone every day.

We learned later that the family council had met again. They decided that the most senior three men would talk to Ayşe. Negotiations were held. At the end, they decided that Ayşe was innocent and that she should come back to the village and continue to live with her husband.

Ayşe was still staying at *Hacı* Mehmet's home. According to the decision of the family council, a brother would take her back to the village. They did not want us to know about these developments. There was a knock at *Hacı* Mehmet's door at midnight. They opened the door with fear. It was the brother of Ayşe. He told them that he would take her home and entered the room where she was sleeping. He woke Ayşe up. Ayşe thought that she was being taken to death and started to cry and to tremble. She could not stand up. And when she stood, she could not walk because her legs could not carry her. Her brother threw her over his shoulder. Ayşe was continuously crying and shouting, 'Inform KA-MER, call Nebahat!'

We learned all these things—afterwards—from *Hacı* Mehmet. *Hacı* Mehmet, who was illiterate, searched and found KA-MER with the help of a little child showing around the address card of KA-MER to people. He was crying while he was talking. He explained that he could not forget the screams and the fear of Ayşe and could not sleep all night. He wanted us to take care of her. He said that he would be with us when we needed him. He did not quite understand what KAMER was all about but stated that he trusted us.

We called Ahmet again and told him that we wanted to go to the village of Ayşe. Ahmet also felt disturbed when Ayşe was taken to the village. He talked with the husband of Ayşe and learned that he also needed support, because he had accepted his wife back, in spite of all the slander.

Life would never be the same for husband and wife again. The villagers would always judge and reject them. We went to the village to talk with Ayşe and her husband. Ayşe, her husband, children, mother-in-law, mother, father, and the two daughters of her murdered sister-in-law were at home. Ayşe could not talk much in front of her husband and the others. Her husband said that he knew his wife was innocent and trusted her. But he also knew that life is difficult for a man if he cannot get rid of his dishonour in the eyes of the family and society. But he accepted his wife back. He told us that he did not know how long he could stand against the pressures of villagers, brothers, and family.

When the family learned the facts, their anger turned against the harasser. Someone had to be killed. They wanted the man to die.

Our role had changed. A blood feud was about to start. We had to prevent this.

We visited the village many times. On every occasion we heard provoking words like 'honour, virtue, dignity, death' from honourable members of the family. They wanted the case to be concluded. They would kill Ayşe if she was guilty. If not, the harasser would be punished. Otherwise, they would not be able to look at the face of the other villagers. They would even reject their own son if he could not get rid of the 'dishonour'. They declared these things sometimes in anger, sometimes crying.

The harasser started to phone again. Ayşe told this to us and to her husband. Ayşe also recorded one of the phone calls thinking that it might constitute evidence for the family to understand things better. A copy of the cassette was given to the office of the public prosecutor and another copy to the family of the harasser. Meanwhile, Veli's family was also convinced.

A week after these developments, we had a meeting with Ayşe's husband and two moderate men of the other family. We came to a common decision in the meeting. A new family council meeting would be held with the participation of KA-MER and those who have a say in these matters. Following this decision, a family council meeting was carried out in the village with a group of party leaders, lawyers, and KA-MER.

The brother of the harasser also attended the meeting. Everyone had uniformly agreed that Ayşe was innocent. The main problem was about what to do with the man who dishonoured his family by harassment. The brother of the harasser explained his ideas as follows:

> I am desperate and confused. I do not know what to say. First I had thought that my brother was victim of a slander. We listened to the cassette you gave me. It was my brother's voice. I told him that I know that he is guilty. But he denies it. I know that the voice of the harasser belongs to my brother. But he insists in denying it. He wants to come to the village and make an oath. I know that he is guilty. But if he accepted to come and commit perjury, he may come and do so. And this case will end. There is my brother on the one side and 'honour' on the other.

This suggestion was quite positive, since we were in an impasse. The military service of the harasser would end after a short while. So we accepted the suggestion. We said: 'We all know that he harassed Ayşe, slandered her and was about to cause her death. But if he rejects this, we might think that he regretted. He may make an oath. And we can leave him alone with the shame of being a perjurer.'

Ayşe's family asked: 'And then?' It was said that the harasser could not live in the village and should be punished. After this demand, the case came to an impasse again. We decided to meet again and left the village.

In this meeting, where the honour of the woman was cleared, there was a difficulty about what punishment to give the harassing man.

The family council did not come together again. Events heated up once more, because Ayşe was innocent. It became apparent that the guilty party was a man. If the guilty party was a woman, she would be killed. But it was difficult to accept that a man was guilty. So at this point, everyone turned against Ayşe again. The easiest solution was for her to disappear. There was nothing we could do anymore....

In the meantime, both Ayşe, her husband Veli, and the family were isolated. In our visits to the village, Veli greeted us on the outskirts of the village and we walked to his home on the other side of the village together. He did so consciously. He wanted to show the villagers that he had friends and that he was not alone. Sometimes he tried to say hello to the villagers. But nobody responded to his hello. They turned their heads and did not look at him.

We learned that Ayşe's children were also excluded. One of the teachers of the village school told a friend from KA-MER that Ayşe's son became subject to rape and he was stoned. The girls were not sent to school anyway.

In KA-MER, we were about to organize a meeting about killings committed in the name of 'honour.' Many governmental and civil organizations would take part in the meeting. Ayşe said that she wanted to attend. We would solve the problem there. The day for meeting ultimately came. The Governorship, Diyarbakır University Psychiatry Department, the UNDP, the Health Office, the Bar Association, and friends from Diyarbakır, İstanbul, and Ankara were all there.

Ayşe attended the meeting. First she could not talk for many reasons. Then we made her feel comfortable. And Ayşe explained. She told about her experiences and her fears.

Suggestions for a solution came out of this meeting. The desperate Ayşe and her husband accepted all the decisions that were made. The Governorship provided Veli, who was working for the government, with a job in the city. A home was rented, paid for by the Governorship. They were given aid in kind for their home and aid in cash for the education of their daughters. Now, Ayşe and Veli live in the city.

But Veli cannot walk around honourably. He is ashamed, confused, and has some difficulties.

Ayşe is trying to get used to the city. Sometimes confused, sometimes cheerful, sometimes fearful. Because she is still disturbed.

The harasser came back from military service. Now he lives in the village.

But Ayşe and Veli had to migrate to the city. We are used to the expulsion of the guilty one. But this time the victim was a woman and the guilty party was a man. Thus, the practice changed. The guilty one is staying in the village and the victim is trying to continue her life in the city, with worry and depression.

In the Name of Honour*
Leylâ Pervizat

'You, women, stand side by side and finish this practice. This is not the first one. It will not be the last one. Allah will not forgive this; neither will the Prophet. Our hearts are aching with sadness.' These words were spoken to me by a graveyard keeper as I was leaving the Diyarbakır Cemetery for the Destitute and Without Family after visiting the burial site of Şemse Allak last June. Şemse was stoned by male family members in late November of 2002 in Mardin, Turkey. After spending seven months in a coma, she died in June 2003. Her body was buried by a large group of women activists in an unusual religious ceremony. According to the practices of Islam in Turkey, women are not allowed to conduct the religious burial prayer—they may only stand on the sidelines and watch. However, in this case, women performed the service for Şemse, a first in our memory.

Şemse was a victim of so-called honour killings. Honour killings—one of the most horrendous violations of women's human

---

(*) Reprinted with permission from *Human Rights Dialogue,* 2.10 (Fall 2003), Special Issue on 'Violence Against Women'. © 2003 Carnegie Council on Ethics and International Affairs <www.carnegiecouncil.org/viewMedia.php/prmID/1061>.

rights and a form of extrajudicial execution—target individuals who believe, or are perceived to believe, in values and standards that are at odds with the social norms of their society. Although they are a most severe form of violence, honour killings are not the only type of violence faced by women in Turkey. Women are also subject to abuses such as marital rape, female genital mutilation, nose cutting, bride price, forced marriages, polygamy, and forced virginity testing. To make matters worse, the state fails to recognize its duties and responsibilities in eradicating these forms of violence, and legitimizes them by deeming them 'family problems' or 'domestic situations'.

Soon after Şemse's burial, our project team of KA-MER, an independent women's organization in Diyarbakır, held its first open meeting, inviting representatives from the government, judiciary, media, police force, health groups, the community, and other NGOs to discuss ways of eradicating honour killings. As a women's rights activist and a feminist researcher, I am working with KA-MER to prevent honour killings in south-eastern and eastern Turkey. We take a broad approach by trying to address the problem before the execution occurs, in addition to dealing with killings after they happen. We work both on the community level and with government officials to create awareness and eventually to eradicate this practice.

Unfortunately, Şemse was stoned before KA-MER heard about the danger she was in and could intervene. Her case received worldwide public attention, partly because stoning—as opposed to shooting or stabbing—a woman or man in the name of honour is very rare in Turkey. Religious leaders' attitude toward honour killings is very clear: They denounce the practice. Similarly, activists working on the issue have never cited imams, the Qur'an, or Islam as sources of the problem in Turkey. This point was made clear to me when, during my visit in Urfa, one of the most religious and conservative cities in the country, I challenged the concept of honour killings by arguing that the Qur'an does not permit women to be treated like this. A very religious Muslim tribal leader responded, 'This is honour, what has that got to do with the Qur'an? Men's honour comes before the Book.' Our exchange made me realize that invoking the Qur'an is not a useful way to denounce this violence. Instead, the concepts of masculinity, culture, and tradition, which are rooted in the community, must be studied and utilized to end honour killings.

One of the obstacles that women's human rights activists face in their work is the fact that Turkey's judiciary often justifies honour killings on the grounds of tradition, culture, and assault on a family member's manhood. While the Turkish Penal Code does not have a specific clause relating to the concept of honour, courts often cite honour as a mitigating factor in their judgements, stating that a challenge to honour causes a heavy provocation to the perpetrators of honour killings.

Another obstacle is mainstream human rights activists in Turkey who downplay the significance of the crime. For instance, a well-known human rights activist working against capital punishment once complained to me and other activists that the recent media attention devoted to honour killings was 'exaggerating this women thing to the level of a human rights violation and therefore diminishing the power of human rights'. For many such human rights activists, honour killings do not belong on the same level as torture, lack of freedom of expression, or extrajudicial executions.

Violence against women is legitimized by the attitudes of state actors, many mainstream human rights activists, and Turkish society at large because ultimately gender imbalances are the status quo. Challenging the parameters of these power dynamics is complex since they are imbedded in interpersonal relations, family, community, and culture. In short, women lack autonomy—they suffer when they assert their rights as individuals and go against established societal norms. Often women are seen as the battlegrounds for men's struggles to assert and reclaim their masculinity. Honour killings are seen as the lesser of two evils since, in some instances, they are thought to prevent feuds that could destroy the stability of the whole society. Thus, people in Şemse's village claimed that her death was necessary to prevent endless violent feuding between her family and that of the man who supposedly dishonoured her through extramarital sexual relations.

In order to prevent honour killings, it is crucial to redefine the concept of honour within the community. From the moment a woman or girl transgresses a norm—which she could do by losing her virginity or by calling the radio station and asking for a favourite song—until the moment she is murdered in the name of honour, her family and the community she lives in go through a decision-making process in which they make judgments about her moral standing. When her name is out as a transgressor, her male relatives cannot walk in the village with heads high. To reclaim their manhood in the eyes of other men, they cleanse their honour by stabbing or sometimes stoning her.

Because such a concept of honour is so imbedded in Turkish culture, and cultural variables are what we try to understand, use, and hopefully transform when interfering in these cases, we do not use a human rights framework when we intervene preventively at the local level. When talking to families, a cultural discourse proves to be very effective. We believe that male family members are also victims of the concept of masculinity—they suffer throughout the decision-making process. We try to give men what I call cultural and psychological space where their masculinity is not challenged and they do not feel forced to kill in order to cleanse their honour. To do this, and in order to help create space for long-term change, we take advantage of some of the positive aspects of Turkish culture that offer individual men an excuse to avoid violence. These include special occasions and gatherings where non-violent negotiations are encouraged or where authority figures can act as intermediaries, in which we can make use of traditions of hospitality toward guests or respect for elderly people's recommendations as tools to prevent these crimes.

However, when we talk with government officials, we use a human rights framework because it is an effective tool for achieving official recognition that honour killings are a form of extrajudicial execution. One of our main goals is to use the UN General Assembly resolution 'Working Towards the Elimination of Crimes Committed in the Name of Honour', of which Turkey is a co-sponsor, within national courts to show that honour killings are not isolated incidents and should be recognized as human rights violations. We also refer to the UN Commission on Human Rights resolution on extrajudicial, arbitrary, and summary executions, which Turkey has also signed. We think that using these human rights instruments offers an opportunity for women's human rights defenders to achieve official, government recognition of this issue as a human rights violation and to put violence against women on the same plane as extrajudicial executions and torture.

Şemse's horrendous death brought people to their feet not only in Turkey but also around the world. In order to eradicate this atrocious crime in Turkey, activists must use all possible advocacy tools—changing society's discourse by using some of its own terms of reference, reforming the judiciary, and incorporating a gender perspective into the human rights advocacy being conducted in Turkey.

Gendering Multiculturalism
DILSA DEMIRBAG-STEN

INTRODUCTION

There are now over 150 different ethnic groups living in Sweden. The country is very much a multicultural society. Swedes are no longer only blue-eyed blondes. As a result, Sweden has aspired to a more diversified policy that takes the ethnic diversity of society into account. There is an integration minister whose task is to monitor the work of diversity and to prevent discrimination against non-'ethnic' Swedes.

Unfortunately, despite this, there is still racism and discrimination of immigrants in the country. Immigrants have a 60 per cent less chance than Swedes of finding a job. There are housing areas where over 80 per cent of the inhabitants are immigrants. These areas are characterized by a higher degree of criminality and unemployment than the 'ethnic' Swedish housing areas. The schools in Stockholm that show the worst results in the national tests are in the ethnically segregated areas. The statistics are easy to interpret. An immigrant has a higher probability of being unemployed and facing exposure to racism and discrimination if he/she is from a non-European country. There are great differences within the immigrant group. The immigrants coming from the 'Western' cultural sphere have better chances than immigrants from Asia and Africa, for example. The reasons for this and how to overcome them are a hot political issue.

HOW THE DISCUSSION STARTED

During the election to the Riksdag (Swedish parliament) in Sweden in 1991, the right-wing populist party Ny Demokrati received almost 7 per cent of the votes. The most important issues for the party concerned immigration. The political line was similar to that of Le Pen in the French election. This fact embarrassed and horrified the political and intellectual establishment in Sweden, who preferred to see Sweden as basically a tolerant and liberal country. The advance of Ny Demokrati created national shame and uncertainty. Integration issues became a minefield. The climate of discussion hardened and positions were locked.

A more positive effect of the election was that people now speak more openly about structural racism and discrimination against immigrants. Immigrants also participate to a greater extent in the public debate. Different ethnic and religious groups are now increasingly raising their voices and demanding their rights. They are demanding that employment should not based on ethnicity and mother-tongue, but rather should be in line with their qualifications and education, and the right to practice their culture and religion—a new situation that mainstream society does not seem to know how to relate to. In aiming to work in the spirit of multiculturalism, demands have been accepted from various ethnic groups that contravene human rights. One such example is a law allowing child marriages for immigrants but not for Swedes. The UN has criticized this law in Sweden on several occasions but without result.

In my opinion it is ignorance concerning the new Swedes' cultures that causes this clumsy and at times downright dangerous approach to the demands of the various ethnic minorities. The attitude to different cultures and religions is flat and static.

The murder of Fadime Şahindal is an example of how mainstream society fails to regard other cultures and ethnic groups with the same complexity and dimensions as its own.

Fadime Şahindal was a young Kurdish woman born in Turkey, who chose to defy her family's expectations of her and chose to live with a Swedish young man without being married to him. The family threatened her and demanded she return to the family. On one occasion she was assaulted in the street by her younger brother. He himself had a Swedish girlfriend. Fadime Şahindal's boyfriend died in a traffic accident. On 21 January, 2001 she was murdered by her father, witnessed by her mother and sisters, in Uppsala.

When her father was asked why he murdered his own child, he replied that he was forced to do it to clear his honour, *namus* in Turkish.

Killing a female relative to clear one's honour is no unusual phenomenon in some countries and cultures. Honour killing is a sign of women's oppression that exists in countries where a good woman is a virgin when she gets married.

Honour killings were something new to Swedes. Sweden was shaken by the event. The whole country mourned Fadime Şahindal and many people wondered how a human could kill his own child. Sweden was in shock.

That is how a public debate on honour killings started.

A DEBATE WITH TWO MAIN LINES OF REASONING
The debate can be roughly divided into two lines of reasoning. One explains honour killing as the deed of a mad person. Traditions and cultures provide no explanation. Making such a claim, according to them, is racist. Their mantra seems to be that no culture is more equal than others. In addition, they believe for example that calling the Kurdish culture a culture of honour detracts from the structural oppression that exists for Swedish women. One should speak of the general global patriarchal oppression of women. By speaking of one

specific culture or pointing out differences in degrees of women's oppression, one risks feeding racism, they continue. The mechanisms behind the murder of Fadime Şahindal are, according to them, the same as those behind a Swedish man's murder of his girlfriend. These people seem to be unaware of the fact that the collective praises a person who has killed his sister in order to clear his honour and that the law in many countries reduces the penalty for a person who has killed for the sake of honour. Supporters of these views seem to find it difficult to hold more than one thought at a time. Those who represent this attitude are mainly ethnic Swedish feminists and male immigrants. In order to avoid nurturing racist forces or in the worst case being themselves labelled as such, many intellectuals, politicians, journalists and others also rejected culture as part of the explanation of the murder of Fadime Şahindal. The motive for not wanting to single out a culture as less equal may be well meant, but from a feminist perspective is counter-productive as the denial prevents constructive development. The attitude in my opinion betrays a static view of foreign cultures. People seem to think that by criticizing certain phenomena in other cultures they are consigning them to eternal barbarism.

The second line of reasoning is mainly represented by women from the cultures being singled out as cultures of honour. I am one of them. I feel a great love for my culture but accept with sorrow that the ethics of honour are a degenerate variant in Kurdish culture. It is true that the culture of honour is not something only found among Kurds. Unfortunately, the problem extends over nations and religions. There are factors that influence and strengthen the degree of control of women. Some of these are social, political and economic conditions. In general it can be said that the more vulnerable the man is, the greater the need he seems to have to control his women. Failing to discuss the ethics of honour openly would in my opinion be a betrayal of the millions of women who live in that reality.

DON'T GENERALIZE THE OPPRESSION OF WOMEN!
We who live in cultures of honour can, by making a relevant analysis, work towards changing that part of our culture that oppresses women. Irregardless of whether it is in Sweden or in Turkey. I object to a generalization of women's oppression. Not speaking of different types and degrees of patriarchal oppression keeps the problem at a superficial level. It does not lead to a penetration of the oppression and its mechanisms, which makes it hard to lay a realistic foundation for preventive measures. I consider, therefore, that I am honouring my culture by criticizing it and working for change.

The first approach in my opinion repudiates the description given by the women concerned with their reality. In addition it belittles the perpetrator's explanation of his actions, which is not done for example in the case of abused Swedish women.

Another problem that was raised in connection with the debate on honour killing was how the white middle-class and well-educated Swedish women were given the preferential right of interpretation. The fact that they in turn rejected the description given by the girls concerned did not improve matters. There were plenty of immigrant men who gave support to these feminists. In that way, in trying to avoid being racist, they were both racist and sexist. People seem to be unaware that women in Iran, Iraq, India, Pakistan, and, like Nebahat Akkoç, in Turkey, are working daily with women exposed to honour-related crimes. I assume that no-one would dare to call these women tools of racism.

This constant fear of being singled out as post-colonial, racist, and the creation of the Orient as the opposite of the Occident is an obstacle to many vulnerable women. At the same time there are many of us who feel that we can now start discussing a problem that existed before in secret in Sweden. The predominant message still seems to be, however, that women's issues concerning immigrant women must stand aside in favour of a fantasy picture of diversity. This would not be tolerated by women in mainstream society if it concerned their rights.

Multicultural society has enriched Sweden very much and will continue to do so, but it has also brought certain problems. Some of these, which all follow on the heels of women's oppression, are female circumcision, forced marriages, honour killings, and compulsory wearing of the veil. It is true that mainstream Swedish society is not free of women's oppression. But we must prevent it, regardless of how and where it is manifested.

To return to the situation in Sweden, questions concerning the collective rights of minorities have still been limited to either having to accept the entire package or nothing at all. This is of course not the case. To eliminate the risk of incorrect handling of the issues, and on the basis of a 'white, Swedish' perspective, the privilege of formulating the problem should be left to those who are mainly affected.

I want to end with the words that the Kurdish culture is, in many respects, a generous and tolerant culture. The richness of our traditions makes me happy and proud. However, improving the status of women among us remains to be done. Our culture is very much alive and possible to change.

Long-Term Measures to Combat Honour-Related Violence in Patriarchal Families

RIYADH AL-BALDAWI

INTRODUCTION

It was the murder of Fadime Şahindal that sparked off the debate on honour crimes in Sweden. Both native-born Swedes and representatives of various ethnic minorities are now seriously discussing ways and means of preventing such crimes in the future.

The government is strongly committed to this process. A number of conferences and a few training programmes have been organized in various parts of the country. The county administrative boards in the larger cities have been instructed to study needs and appropriate measures. The reports on these studies are far from exhaustive, especially when it comes to long-term measures to protect women and change patriarchal structures among the ethnic groups concerned. Immigrants' associations have now intensified their efforts to change their members' attitudes.

Several shelters for girls at risk were set up last year, especially in the larger cities. However, there is still a lack of co-ordinated long-term programmes aimed at bringing about lasting changes in attitudes. There is a need to co-ordinate efforts in this area at the local level between the social services, schools, police authorities, county councils, local authorities and voluntary organizations, and so on, in order to make the best possible use of the available resources.

The main issue is what long-term processes should be initiated to change attitudes as a complement to short-term measures, especially among ethnic groups with a more traditional orientation. It is important in this connection to identify measures and assign responsibility for implementation to various levels of society:
 1. Measures at individual level;
 2. Measures at the family and ethnic group level;
 3. Action by institutions and authorities;
 4. International contacts and exchanges of experience.

LEVEL 1: SHORT- AND LONG-TERM MEASURES TO SUPPORT WOMEN AT RISK

More attention must be paid to women at risk who seek help and to their views. Women who dare to talk about their vulnerability are only the tip of the iceberg. There are a large number of women—not included in the statistics—who are equally at risk but are afraid to ask for help. Women who elect to report their problems may help to reduce the number of cases that are never detected by encouraging others to come forward.

Women who seek help must feel that they are being taken seriously and that priority is given to measures to protect them. Their stories should be accepted at face value and efforts should be made to find out whether there are any potential resource persons in the woman's family who can help before placement outside the family is considered. This applies especially to girls under 18 and does not preclude the possibility of temporary placement in sheltered accommodation where such women can feel safe. Human support may be crucial during the crisis they are experiencing, but in any case plans should be made for the future at this stage. The woman's family situation and the relevant risk factors should be analysed with a view to deciding whether she should continue to be separated from her family or whether there are any other alternatives.

Apart from the woman's physical safety, it is important to take steps to ensure her internal safety. This involves strengthening her inborn resources, although this may not be possible during the most acute phase of the crisis. It is important to give the woman professional psychological treatment and to help her to analyse her own situation in order to build her internal safety. Sheltered accommodation and professional psychological/psychiatric care are essential elements of long-term programmes for women at risk.

While supporting the woman it is important to work with the family, especially the male members, and assess the risk factors that may affect future planning. Attention must be paid in this connection to any differences of opinion among the family members. We know from experience that opinions sometimes differ about family members who dare to challenge traditional attitudes. It is important to use such differences to try to influence attitudes. Efforts to influence the family must be based on the woman's own perception of the situation. This will help to identify the veiled messages that may be sent by family members.

The limited experience that we have gained, in particular at our multicultural clinic, Orienthälsan, shows that working with families can help to tone down the family's reactions and even prevent acts that could have disastrous consequences.

The nature and severity of the risks to which a woman is exposed can vary and murder may not necessarily be a likely outcome. She may instead be subjected to different types of physical, psychological, and mental pressure. Attention should also be paid to the other children in the family, especially as regards the potential future impact of the family's attitude. Persistent efforts to influence the parents, especially the father, should be made to ensure that the other children are not exposed to the same risks also.

We should not forget that boys may be exposed to these risks as well as girls, and it is important to take their situation into account.

In some families the loyalties of the boys are with the other male members of the family. In others, boys who try to adopt a modern, unprejudiced approach and to have a good relationship with their sisters are ostracized. It is important to support alliances between siblings in order to develop a strategy to resist the pressures exerted by the traditional patriarchal attitude.

To sum up, an integrated operational plan, describing immediate and long-term measures based on the woman's specific situation and needs, should be prepared in each case. The measures taken should be consistent with this action plan.

The health service is sometimes unprepared for women at risk who seek psychological/psychiatric help. Many county councils do not prioritize such patients and it takes a long time before professional help is provided. More resources must be provided in this area.

LEVEL 2: MEASURES AIMED AT CHANGING ATTITUDES IN FAMILIES AND ETHNIC GROUPS

Changing attitudes is a slow process. Sometimes traditions mark people for life. It is not easy to influence attitudes in a family rooted in a society where the patriarchal structures are almost sacrosanct. Consequently, we need to elaborate both short-term measures and long-term programmes for this purpose.

It is important in this connection not to consider immigrant groups exclusively in terms of their home country, region, or continent, or of their religion for that matter—that is, as Iraqis, Iranians, Turks, and so forth. There are substantial individual differences in each of these groups, depending on the members' socio-economic background, education, urban or rural origin, and degree of integration into the new society and the labour market. These factors also identify categories of potential resource persons within their ethnic group. If we succeed in identifying these individuals, they may be able to influence attitudes to gender equality, integration, and domestic violence as a result of discussions within the group rather than external pressure.

Individuals in ethnic groups who are willing to assume a role as opinion formers should therefore be identified. Nowadays, we can find such individuals in all ethnic groups. Some national immigrant organizations have made the most of such differences among their members and launched intensive internal attitude-influencing efforts. The Federation of Kurdish Associations in Sweden, the Stockholm Syrian Association, and the Democratic Iraqi Association in Rosengård, Malmö, are examples of such organizations. As I know from my own experience, they have succeeded in involving members who have a high status in their group thanks to their education and position in Swedish society in efforts to influence others. Sometimes, immigrants whose political agenda includes gender equality act as opinion formers, while in other groups it is the individual's socio-economic status in the home country that gives him/her a leading role in internal discussions.

It is important that the men in the group should take the initiative in challenging certain attitudes to child-raising and speak up against domestic violence. They are in a position to initiate discussions that also give women an opportunity to voice their views, to describe their vulnerable situation, and to wonder aloud why they should be exposed to such pressures.

Discussions about gender equality need not be confined to the national group. It is just as important to establish a dialogue between people with different ethnic backgrounds but with the same cultural attitude to patriarchal lifestyles; for example, Turkish immigrants can discuss these issues with Arab and Persian-speaking groups. The dialogue between Swedish and immigrant parents is also important.

Care should be taken not to give offence by immediately criticizing traditions, religious customs, or values, since people may 'switch off' and feel left out of the change process as a result. The people in the target group should feel accepted, not challenged. Focusing on the positive elements in the group will prepare the ground for acceptance of criticism and discussions at a later stage.

Specially trained 'moderators' can be of either sex. Their training should teach them how to conduct a discussion, as well as providing them with materials on gender equality and integration. Lectures given by speakers from different ethnic groups might be another way of encouraging debate in the group.

'Parent get-togethers', catering to all parents, should be arranged at the local level. The parents should be guaranteed anonymity and encouraged to discuss their problems to the extent they themselves want.

Schools play an important part by providing a 'neutral zone' for discussions about integration, gender equality, and family relations. Schools are already doing good work in this area, but there is a need for special measures aimed at parents from patriarchal environments in order to encourage dialogue with them. Attempts in this direction have been made in some schools, which have educated all their staff about families and family relations in patriarchal societies. Reference groups have been set up in some schools in order to stimulate debate among the pupils and their parents.

LEVEL 3: ACTION BY INSTITUTIONS AND AUTHORITIES

Swedish authorities and institutions have launched an intensive education campaign about honour crimes. Courses have been arranged with a view to raising awareness among personnel in both local government, the police, the judicial system, schools, and to some extent in county councils. These measures are commendable, but they are often short-term and there is a lack of co-ordination and collaboration. Sometimes the courses duplicate each other and they are not always followed up. Many of them last for only half a day, a day, or a few days. Theoretical knowledge is important, but is not enough when it comes to dealing with the problems that arise among people from different ethnic groups. Long-term change can only be achieved by co-ordinated training programmes that combine theoretical and practical knowledge.

One form of education that can achieve good results in the long run is special training programmes for various professional groups, who learn to analyse their work in the light of different cultural and traditional values. Such programmes could help staff to change their attitudes and improve their professional performance. The purpose is both to minimize the risk of over-reacting to events and misjudging risk factors, both of which can lead to human tragedies. We have in the past year seen many instances of women at risk not being taken seriously. We have also seen cases of over-reaction, as a result of which men, especially fathers, were hounded as criminals despite a lack of evidence.

The action taken by authorities can reinforce the prejudice against them that sometimes exists in some immigrant groups. An inappropriate response to a human tragedy may deter ethnic minorities from seeking help. On the other hand, the social services could, by exercising discretion and making sure to collect sufficient proof, resolve these problems satisfactorily. Thorough analysis and a proactive response often achieve better results than separating a woman from her family, which may sometimes even lead to adverse consequences for her.

One way for the authorities to gather and disseminate information is to set up reference groups, which in turn act as educators for other members of the profession. Groups could, for example, be made up of participants from the local police, the social services, schools, and the county council. County councils could encourage co-operation on psychiatry, including child psychiatry and the primary health service.

LEVEL 4: INTERNATIONAL EXPERIENCE AND EXCHANGES OF INFORMATION

Countries vary in the attention they pay to honour crimes. There is plenty of experience of such crimes in the world today. The United Nations has addressed the issue. The involvement of the EU's member states varies considerably. Some countries deny that honour crimes occur among their own ethnic groups and do not use this term, as a result of which such crimes are not included in their statistics. Other countries, such as the Netherlands, Belgium, and the Nordic countries, take the issue seriously. Efforts are now being made to define honour crimes and decide how they should be dealt with in the judicial system. Collaboration within the EU is extremely important, especially in view of the free mobility within the Union.

There is a great need today to discuss collaboration at the local level in the EU as well. Changes of attitude in a particular ethnic group can spread from one country to another. It is important to learn from the experience and methods established in countries with a longer history of migration and work with various ethnic groups. Exchanges of experience between public authorities are also very important.

Exchanges of experience are extremely important in other contexts too. Conferences and seminars at the national, European, and global levels are a case in point. International research on this subject should be disseminated and research in this country should also contribute. Such research will promote the development of effective methods, both in clinical and socio-cultural contexts.

To sum up: At the national level we need to improve training and achieve more effective co-ordination of measures at various levels, while at the international level exchanges of experience and research findings are the most important factors when it comes to long-term prevention of honour-related violence in patriarchal families.

The Dialogue Project to Prevent Violence: Discussions with Fathers and Sons

NIKLAS KELEMEN

The reason I am here today is to present the 'Dialogue Project' of the Save the Children organization. Our aim is *not* to prevent honour-related violence specifically but violence in general, and we also work for an increase in the level of gender sensitivity of men. Even though we quite often run into people who hold the ethics of honour, I can *not* imagine that it would be possible to *start* working with the topic of 'honour crimes' among men—in Sweden. Our approach is universal and based on the fact that about 95 per cent of all physical violence—like war, criminality and violence against women—is committed by men, which should make men aware of a specific kind of male responsibility for these issues. Factors like politics and poverty, and individual, ethnic, or religious conflicts, have their roles of course, yet all these things equally effect women also, so there is a need to reflect on the importance of male role models in the education of boys. We recognize the great Norwegian peace researcher Johan Galtung's statement that boys in all *major* cultures were and still are educated to solve conflicts by violence, and therefore we men become, all too often, conflict-illiterate.

Our team consists of three men, each with a different approach. My elderly colleague Björn talks about a father educational programme; my younger colleague Vidar raises the issue of boys' need for positive male role models; and I reflect upon violence as a part of boys' education. We visit, among others, male-dominated immigrant organizations, hold seminars and workshops, and help the organizations to start their own projects.

We also believe that the higher the level of gender equality in a society, the lower the level of violence against women. In Russia, where we do some work too, according to the official data there are around 14,000 women per year who are killed by their partners—while in Sweden the same figure is around twenty women, which *proportionally* means a thirty-times lower level of violence in Sweden. Judging purely by my impressions and experiences, the gender sensitivity of Russian men is, in general, about ten times lower than the men of Sweden and the rest of the differences are certainly due to the social, economical, and alcohol factors.

I mention Russia for another reason too. It is absurd but it is true that in the Russia of today we can talk about anything and feel free, while in Sweden we always get into a nervous and anxious mood when we talk about our experiences regarding culturally based norms and attitudes in relation to violence. In Sweden, violence is considered—on the whole rightly—as gender based, and until two years ago if somebody mentioned something about culturally based violence, the person were automatically called 'racist'. Looking at reality or the publications by the UN, Amnesty, UNICEF, or some scientists, it is really quite surprising. I'll try to explain what I mean by describing our latest seminar last week and in this way you can see a part of our fieldwork.

Our seminars usually take place in some suburb where unfortunately almost only immigrants live. The locations are sometimes very nice and spacious but this one is small and shabby with not a single picture on the naked dirty walls which make me guess that women are not frequenting the place. 'No, they have nothing to do here... they have their own association' kindly smiles our host.

About thirty-five to forty mostly young men arrive, the meeting opens and though not understanding the language we get the floor after a ten-minute introduction. People often are eager to talk and interrupt us but this time they are attentive and after fifty minutes we get into the discussion. My younger colleague Vidar is telling how hard it was with his first love affair to be a 'real man' and at the same time to have an equal relation. We describe two different family models, one traditional with male dominance, and one without hierarchy—a gender-equal model, which usually causes disagreement *among* the participants, but this time everybody prefers the hierarchical model. 'All societal units have a leader, we cannot run a family without a leader!' says someone. 'We have never had trouble in our homeland with equality, this trouble starts here in Sweden!' exclaims someone else. 'Everybody talks about women here and this country is governed by women but we men have bigger problems!' says the next one. We are familiar with the views of many immigrants who consider Sweden to be a 'dictatorship of women' wherein the children are valued highest, then next comes women, next the dogs and cats, and after that the men. One hour goes by now, debating the ups and downs of the two family models and against all the fair or unfair accusations such as: fewer children, a high number of divorces, stress, negligence of children and old people—but we still hold that a gender-equal family relation is to be preferred and the problem is not 'too much' but *too little* gender equality.

The disagreement is total but the debate is exciting, sometimes with cheerful laughs. Its time to eat but no one wants to split up so three people bring the food in and everyone gets served a paper plate with rice, meat, and salad on it. The atmosphere is joyful when a middle-aged man stands up and asks; 'You talk about women and children's rights, well what would you do if your wife deceived you or if your daughter had sex before she got married?' Vidar answers impulsively that if his wife cheated on him he would go crazy and so there will be not much talk on this. Then, he says that his daughter—who is 2 years old now—will be free to decide about boyfriends when the time comes. Then, people look at me. Vidar also looks at me as if saying, 'Well, it is your turn.' I tell them that my daughter is 18 and she just presented her first boyfriend. A heavy silence. 'And what did you do about it?' comes the question from a young man. 'Well, the boy is fine, it is all right.' The young man protests strongly, 'But, not for us, we cannot accept it!' Vidar raises his voice: 'How many of you think that a boyfriend is o.k. for your daughter before she marries?' After a few seconds of hesitation, one man lifts his hands, then another one also, and even a third one, when somebody shouts, 'Do you mean they have sex too?' 'If they want, it belongs to love', Vidar answers. All three hands fall down and the raising tension is broken by a bitter voice: 'You cannot do it to us!' 'Do what?' 'Interfere in our culture!' 'No, it is our religion that forbids it', shouts someone else, and an internal debate starts.

After a while we declare that the problem we need to solve is that there are many girls who are running away from home because of this prohibition. Vidar turns to a father of about 40 years of age: 'What would happen if your daughter tells you that she has a boyfriend?' 'It will not happen, I educate my daughter properly!' he answers confidently. Vidar insists, 'But lets say, it happens?' The man gets agitated, waves with his hands 'O.k., then she is not my daughter any more!' he says categorically. Well, then whose daughter is she? The state cannot adopt so many girls, I say it to myself—but out loud I say, 'Do you know that the Minister of Integration now puts [SEK] 120 million into shelters for runaway immigrant girls?' 'Then its wrong, they should help the girls go back to their families!' says the father. Before the air gets too hot I make a short speech on tradition and the so-called sexual revolution of the 1960s in Western Europe. A girl's virginity is an individual matter since then, and not a matter for the cultures, traditions, or the churches.

Now, people are very attentive but at the end they declare: It may go for your culture but it is nothing for us. 'O.k., what should we do about the girls who are threatened?' we ask. No answer, so Vidar asks, 'Can we have a compromise?' People get confused; 'How do you mean?' 'Well, we have to save the girls, no?' 'Yes, but do you have a compromise?' 'O.k., I have two solutions', I say:

> The first one, we were told by an immigrant woman at a previous seminar, she said: "integration is to meet half way, girls can be half virgins...," but she did not explain the way it works, so let's put away this joke. My own solution is: You educate your daughter as you wish but respect her choice even if it is different from your expectations.

Silence.... Some people talk for minutes in a smaller group, we don't understand, and then the categorical father stands up: 'It's too difficult..., we are now here for almost four hours, I suggest we break up and carry on next time.' People applaud, we get a lot of handshakes, some go, some stay asking individual questions. Someone who has been living a long time in Sweden shakes my hand and in excellent Swedish says, 'Thank you for coming, we never had this kind of honest discussion before, but I tell you there is only one solution, we will either have to accept the free ethic of this country or we will have to go home.' I don't want to say that there are many girls in his country also who want to make their own decisions—we just agree that we will meet again.

So, what did we achieve? It seems that we took a first step towards understanding each other, yet our main problem remains: How it is possible that these men are not included in the constant discussions about gender equality?

Why is it so that today all the authorities of different city and county administrations, the police, the courts, the women NGOs, everybody gets educational courses on the issues of honour-related violence except those who should be concerned in the first place: Parents who hold the ethic of chastity?

I do believe it is perfectly possible to get rid of honour crimes, but as long as we do not treat the causes, we will face these crimes. Based on our experiences, I also believe that parents who hold the ethic of honour could very well understand that it is not necessary to 'Keep their honour between the legs of their daughters'—as a Syrian-orthodox girl put it—if the politicians, community, and religious leaders would follow the appeal of the UN's Secretary General, Kofi Annan, who just recently said that these leaders should take their responsibility and work resolutely for a change of the societal attitudes regarding the ethic of honour. The reinforcement of this ethic is a violation of the human rights of the children and women, and not unusually a violation of boys' and men's rights also.

Twenty years ago the Swedish government, against the opinion of the majority of Sweden—and also in opposition to a world opinion—introduced the anti-spanking law, which prohibits giving a child a spanking. Today there are hardly any people in Sweden who disagree with this law. Another example: The absolute majority of girls in Somalia are subjected to female genital cutting, while the law in Sweden criminalizes this practice, which in combination with firm educational campaigns, gives the result that an absolute majority of these girls are not harmed in Sweden. As we can see, it is possible to change societal, collective values. It should be the same with the very specific character of honour crimes, I believe; we only have to get into existential discussions and ask the people who hold the ethic of honour some central questions like: What is life about, if not love? And what is love if it belongs to the collective and not to the individual? But avoiding the conflicts of these discussions makes things worse; not only a physical but also a spiritual segregation remains. It is as the head of a Kurdish women association said: 'Fadime would not have died if her parents and relatives were familiar with the Swedish values.' And she was right, except that its not about Swedish values, but rather the human rights of children and women.

SECTION 3

State Responses to Honour Killing

Violence in the Name of Honour Within the Context of International Regimes
YAKIN ERTÜRK

INTRODUCTION

One of the most salient and universal aspect of societies across the globe is the patriarchal nature of gender relations which systematically produces the subordination and inequality of women. This system of domination is sustained and enforced through the use of violence or its threat. At the core of patriarchal gender relations lies the interest of a social group to sustain and control socially acceptable lines of reproduction of their species. Within this context, men have used power to control women's reproductive capacity and their sexuality. The honour and prestige of a man, in many instances, became intrinsically associated with the conduct of the women related to them and paradoxically, to their ability to violate the sexuality of other women, such as in rape—in war or in peace—among others. The regulation over women's reproductive capacity and their sexuality has taken diverse forms, marriage being the most common form today.

In addition to the sexual assault and abuse of women by men, whether within or outside the home, patriarchal power manifests itself in the form of culturally approved or instigated forms of transgression against women by the wider collective group, such as the extended kinship networks. Some of the most striking cases of such violence observed across the globe are mutilation of female genitals, bride/dowry killings, and crimes committed in the name of honour, the last one being the subject matter of this expert meeting. Violence in the name of honour is one but very specific manifestation of the universal phenomenon of violence against women, which takes place from the domicile to the trans-national arena in the everyday and everynight lives of women everywhere.

The issue of honour, understood in diverse ways in different parts of the world, is important from the point of view of the integration of the individual into the group, failure of which would result in shame and loss of status. For men in some societies, this would be tantamount to a loss of their masculinity. In contrast with the often-compared crimes of passion, which is a matter involving violence against women by an intimate partner, crimes of honour embodies collective identity and action with consequences for the public reputation of all actors involved. As such, it is intimately embedded in the prevailing values and norms governing the relationships of the collective group concerned. It is this normativity and the collectivist aspect of honour crimes that makes it so complex and resistant to change. Empowerment of women, a primary goal of the international gender agenda, as a strategy to resist violence, in the case of honour crimes, may in fact result in increased violence against women. Such was the case with Fadime Şahindal who was killed by her family in Sweden in 2002 because she dared to deviate from the norms prevailing in her family and kinship environment. Therefore, efforts to employ effective strategies to deal with such violations of women's human rights require a combination of approaches employed at the level of the state, community/family and the individual women.

INTERNATIONAL AGENDA FOR GENDER EQUALITY AND WOMEN'S HUMAN RIGHTS

In the course of history, particularly with the creation of the rule of law, the public sphere came under the regulation of law, and following the Second World War this sphere increasingly became a subject of the human rights discourse, significantly altering the relations of domination to the advantage of disadvantaged groups and classes. Gender contract, on the other hand, until recently, remained marginal to the regulatory processes and the mainstream human rights agenda. However, the principle of non-discrimination on the basis of sex enshrined in the Universal Declaration of Human Rights, integrating women's rights into mainstream international human rights law, lagged behind these developments.

The evolving United Nations gender agenda,[1] which started with the norm of non-discrimination and evolved into a focus on integration of women into the development process, resulted in the First World Conference on Women in 1975. This was followed by the Decade for the Advancement of Women, during which the Convention on the Elimination of All Forms of Discrimination Against Women (CEDAW) was adopted by the General Assembly. After the Decade, the gender agenda became shaped within an empowerment discourse as defined in the Beijing Platform for Action (PfA) and finally, after the Fourth World Conference on Women in Beijing, the human rights discourse emerged as the all-encompassing approach to women's issues. This process corresponds to five periods, each encompassing key developments that successively unfolded into a new phase in the UN gender agenda (see p. 175).

---

1   For a comprehensive discussion, evaluation, and documentation of the developments in the UN gender agenda from its inception, see United Nations (n.d.).

EMERGENCE OF VIOLENCE AGAINST WOMEN AS A POLICY AND HUMAN RIGHTS ISSUE

The issue of violence against women, considered as a private matter, remained largely marginal to the early work of the UN. The First World Conference on Women in 1975, although not referring to violence as such, laid the ground for focusing on factors that inhibit or obstruct the advancement of women. It is interesting that the issue of violence could not be addressed in the drafting of CEDAW either. It was, however, addressed at the Nairobi conference in 1985 as a major concern and governments were urged to take urgent action to prevent violence. While it was acknowledged during this period that violence against women exists in various forms in everyday life, the main focus was largely on domestic violence. Thanks to the women's movement, before the end of the decade, all forms of violence against women became challenged at the cognitive, normative, and policy levels, resulting in greater sensitivity and awareness. In 1991, the Commission on the Status of Women (CSW) recommended the convening of an expert meeting to determine what international instruments were needed in confronting the problem. In 1992, the CEDAW Committee adopted General Recommendation 19 that strongly linked violence with the general framework of discrimination against women, thus making states responsible for reporting on and taking measures to eradicate violence.

The Committee's emphasis on violence as an outcome of women's inequality and subordination was further reinforced by the Vienna Declaration and Programme of Action (A/CONF.157/23) adopted at the World Conference on Human Rights in Vienna in 1993, which described women's rights as human rights. The impact of the Vienna conference within and outside the UN was astounding; within six months of the Conference, the General Assembly (GA) adopted the Declaration on the Elimination of Violence Against Women (48/104), which was followed by the creation of the post Special Rapporteur on Violence Against Women, Its Causes and Consequences by the Commission on Human Rights (CHR) in 1994

(1994/45). These developments led to an exponential growth in the engagement of mainstream human rights activists in anti-violence against women activities and stimulated action to eliminate violence at national and international levels.

The Declaration provides the normative framework for all international and national action in the field of violence against women. The preamble recognizes the urgent need for the universal application to women of the rights and principles with regard to equality, security, liberty, integrity, and dignity of all human beings. It also recognizes that violence against women constitutes a violation of the rights and fundamental freedoms of women and that violence against women is a manifestation of historically unequal power relations between men and women, which have led to domination over and discrimination against women by men. The Declaration represents a significant contribution to the international gender agenda in a number of ways:

1. It provides the first official definition of violence against women (Article 1 & 2);

2. it affirms that women are entitled to equal enjoyment and protection of human rights (Article 3); and

3. it calls upon states to condemn violence against women and not permit custom, tradition or religion to justify violent acts, and to exercise due diligence to prevent, investigate and punish acts of violence against women (Article 4).

The term 'violence against women' as defined in the Declaration was integrated into the Beijing Platform for Action as: 'any act of gender-based violence that results in, or is likely to result in, physical, sexual or psychological harm or suffering to women, including threats of such acts, coercion or arbitrary deprivation of liberty, whether occurring in public or in private life'. The Platform, by including violence against women, along with women and armed conflict and human rights of women among its twelve critical areas of concern, placed a priority on the need to respond to violence-related issues in achieving the advancement of women. Within the context of the PfA, various forms of sexual assault on women that were not specifically mentioned in the Declaration became specified. These include: systematic rape and forced pregnancy during armed conflict, sexual slavery, forced sterilization and forced abortion, female infanticide, and prenatal sex selection. The 2000 special session of the GA on the review of the implementation of the PfA, popularly referred to as Beijing + 5, clearly demonstrated that violence against women had become a priority issue on the agenda of the Member States and significant steps have been taken to address the problem, in some cases pre-dating the adoption of the Platform.[2]

The review process also revealed that violence, along with poverty, remains the most pervasive problem confronting women across the globe, with adverse consequences for other critical areas concern. On the other hand, the critical area of the Human Rights of Women, since the adoption of the Platform, emerged as an overarching goal embracing all critical areas of concern.

VIOLENCE AGAINST WOMEN COMMITTED IN THE NAME OF HONOUR

While reaffirming the strategic objectives of the PfA with regard to violence against women, the Outcome Document (OD), adopted at the special session, has gone a step further in calling for the criminalization of violence against women punishable by law (paragraphs 69c and 103b). Paragraph 69c states: 'Treat all forms of violence against women and girls of all ages as a criminal offence punishable by law including violence based on all forms of discrimination.' The OD also identified 'so-called honour crimes' as a specific form of harmful traditional practice (paragraphs 69e and 96a) in need of being eliminated by implementing law and other measures. Although honour crime was listed among harmful traditional practices much earlier[3] and addressed

---

2   For an analysis of government reports on the implementation of the PfA, see United Nations (2000).
3   The issue of harmful traditional practices was addressed by CSW as early as 1950s and then again in the 1970s, but no significant action could be taken until mid-1980s when the WHO

by the CEDAW Committee in its concluding comments on Turkey and other countries in 1997, it was not until the special session that the subject became a highly debated and at the same time contested issue in the intergovernmental forums, particularly as it gained a presumed linkage with Islam owing to the showing of the film *Crimes of Honour* prior to the circulation of a resolution on honour crimes in 2000.

Consequently, the resolution tabled by the Netherlands was received with much opposition and could only be adopted by vote with 120 in favour and twenty-five abstaining. In 2002, however, the GA was able to adopt Resolution 57/179, 'Working Towards the Elimination of Crimes Against Women Committed in the Name of Honour', by consensus. The resolution calls upon States to 'investigate thoroughly, prosecute effectively and document cases of crimes against women committed in the name of honour and punish the perpetrators' (paragraph 3c); to 'intensify efforts to raise awareness of the need to prevent and eliminate crimes against women committed in the name of honour, with the aim of changing the attitudes and behaviour that allow such crimes to be committed by involving, *inter alia*, community leaders' (paragraph 3e).

The resolution also invited the CSW to address the subject at its forty-seventh session under the priority theme, 'Women's Human Rights and the Elimination of All Forms of Violence Against Women and Girls.' As it is well known, the Commission, for the first time in its history, failed to reach a consensus on the agreed conclusion with regard to this theme. This alarming outcome can be perceived as a continuity of the difficulties encountered during Beijing + 5 in 2000, which signalled the growing trend towards political and cultural fragmentations resulting from the disparities and new polarizations unleashed by globalization and the mounting backlash in response to the progress achieved in the gender agenda. These incidents reveal that

---

and other UN entities made a strong case that traditional practices were a form of violence against women. Although crimes of honour were identified among these practices, the focus was on female genital mutilation.

consensus among Member States on critical issues concerning women's human rights are becoming increasingly difficult.

While it is important to acknowledge and seriously reflect on these trends that pose a threat to the sustenance of a common agenda for gender equality, there have also been promising developments during the same period, such as: the adoption of Security Council Resolution 1325 in 2000; the implementation, again in 2000, of the CEDAW Optional Protocol; in 2002, the GA adoption of resolution 57/179 on 'Working Towards the Elimination of Crimes Against Women Committed in the Name of Honour'; and in 2003, the renewal of the mandate of the Special Rapporteur on Violence Against Women (200/45) by the Commission on Human Rights. Furthermore, the Rome Statute of the International Criminal Court, by defining rape and other gender-based violence as war crimes, crimes against humanity, and components of the crime of genocide, has given the issue of violence against women high visibility and official acknowledgement within mainstream international law.

Although still a contested issue in multilateral dialogue, it is also encouraging that 'honour crimes' are now on the agenda of several countries as a violation of the human rights of women, which compels the state in these countries to engage in international law in reviewing and amending their penal code to ensure that sexual felonies are defined as crimes against the individual punishable by law. Reference also needs to be made to the fact that honour crimes—once a local and invisible act of transgression on women's sexuality and bodily integrity—is now a globalized problem, occurring among immigrant communities in receiving countries. In such situations it is important that, while the universality of human rights law must be observed, honour crimes should not be treated in isolation from the phenomenon of violence against women in general. This is important in order to avoid two potential risks:

1. the stigmatization of migrant communities which might result in anti-immigrant sentiments and policies; and

2. the normalization of other forms of violence in the society which might make everyday incidents of violence against women invisible or neglected.

CONCLUSION
While at the normative level the international standards are more or less adequate in addressing issues of violence against women, including crimes of honour, the challenge lies in ensuring and monitoring state compliance with existing norms and in observing respect for the human rights of women. When viewed from this perspective there are major gaps as the human rights of women fail to be universal today. Despite the international consensus on values related to human rights, existing institutional arrangements and a lack of political commitment and determination on the part of states make human rights unrealizable for most women. Women's sexuality in most parts of the world continues to be a matter of public concern, resulting in violation of their bodily integrity. Women's body is a zone for wars and the site of politics and policies as revealed in the armed conflicts around the world, recent restrictions on reproductive rights and dress codes, as well as certain immigration and refugee policies, among others. Even in situations where traditional patriarchy is ruptured, as in many of the Western countries, discrimination and violence against women continues to persist in modified, subtle, and discrete forms.

In addition, growing disparities, increased conflict, and conservative political trends worldwide make constructive dialogue among nations difficult, seriously endangering the sustenance of the progress achieved thus far. Within this context, the increased politicization of culture, especially its articulation in the form of religious fundamentalism(s) in the competition over global power, poses a major challenge to international and national governance as well as to women's human rights.

In short, the struggle to eliminate violence against women in all its forms has a long way to go. In this regard, while an inclusive, just and enabling global environment needs to be established, at the more specific level, the strategy to end violence against women in general and crimes of honour in particular must include interventions at the level of the state, community/family, and individual women, using a combination of human rights, culture, and empowerment discourses. Needless to say, the state is the main subject of international law; therefore, it is accountable and obligated to observe due diligence in protecting and promoting women's human rights and in punishing those who violate those rights. At the level of the community, on the other hand, a cultural perspective is needed to understand the causes of persisting violence and to raise awareness of the detrimental impact of violence on those who experience it as well as on the entire society by drawing on positive elements of culture. In the case of immigrant communities, it is also important to analyse the structural and policy constraints that may prevent the equal participation of individual immigrants in the wider society, a situation which may leave them dependent upon the solidarity network of their own immigrant community. Similarly, women who lack economic autonomy in their own country are also vulnerable to the pressures of their family and kinship network since their survival is dependent upon them. Finally, at the level of individual women, legal and other measures are needed to empower them in order that they might be able to resist violence and have access to justice. International women's networks can be instrumental in supporting local women's initiatives to resist violence and demand justice, while at the same time compiling good practices in this regard.

Last but not least, there is need for deconstructing hegemonic masculinity and engaging in a dialogue and alliance with alternative masculinities that are opposed to oppressive uses of power. The March 2004 session of CSW, which will address the role of men as one of its priority themes, offers an opportunity for the international community to explore these issues further and adopt effective policy guidelines without, however, deviating from the strategic objective of the Platform to achieve gender equality through the empowerment of women.

Evolving UN Agenda for Gender Equality and Women's Human Rights

1. 1945–1962: The norm of non-discrimination
- 1946 establishment of the Commission on Human Rights (CHR) and the Commission on the Status of Women (CSW)
- 1948 Universal Declaration of Human Rights
- 1952 Civil and Political Rights
- 1957 Nationality of Married Women
- 1962 Consent on Marriage, Minimum Age of Marriage

2. 1963–1975: Integration of Women into Development
- 1966 Economic, Social, Cultural Rights
- 1967 Declaration on the Elimination of Discrimination Against Women
- 1975 International Women's Year and the First World Conference on Women in Mexico City—theme: Equality, Development and Peace; adoption of 'World Plan of Action on Equality of Women and Their Contributions to Development and Peace'
- 1975 Recommendation to create INSTRAW and UNIFEM

3. 1976–1985: The Decade for the Advancement of Women
- 1979 CEDAW—Women's Bill of Rights
- 1980 Second World Conference on Women in Copenhagen (mid-term review of the Decade)—adoption of resolution of battered women in the family
- 1985 Third World Conference on Women in Nairobi—adoption of 'Nairobi Forward Looking Strategies'

4. 1986–1995: Empowerment of Women
- 1986 UN expert group meeting on Violence in the Family
- 1992 CEDAW General Recommendation 19
- 1993 The World Conference on Human Rights in Vienna—Women's Rights are Human Rights
- 1993 Declaration on the Elimination of Violence Against Women
- 1994 CHR creates the post Special Rapporteur on Violence Against Women, Its Causes and Consequences
- 1995 Fourth World Conference on Women in Beijing—adoption of Beijing Declaration and the Platform for Action (twelve critical areas of concern)

5. 1996–present: Women's Human Rights
- 1997 ECOSOC Agreed Conclusion on Gender Mainstreaming
- 1999 Optional Protocol to CEDAW
- 2000 Special Session of the General Assembly on Women 2000: Gender Equality, Development and Peace for the 21st Century (Beijing + 5)—adoption of the Political Declaration and the Outcome Document
- 2000 Security Council addresses women, peace and security and adopts resolution 1325
- 2001 CSW adopts new multi-year work programme
- 2002 GA Resolution 57/179—Working Towards the Elimination of Crimes Against Women Committed in the Name of Honour
- 2003 CHR renews mandate of Special Rapporteur on Violence Against Women—Resolution 48/104

Acting With Honour: Justice Not Excuses in Crimes of So-Called 'Honour'
CHRISTINA CURRY

INTRODUCTION

The women's rights activist, Eve Ensler, has asked us all to try to imagine a world where violence against women doesn't exist. What would that world look like? Well, I imagine that it would include a world in which men, women, and states behave honourably. There are many who argue that this word, 'honour', has been misused too long and too often for us to 'reclaim' it now. However, I believe it is useful to give words their rightful meanings—as we heard yesterday, the word 'honour' originally meant 'the rule of law'. When our objective is the eradication of violence against women, it is important to aim high. So I am going to employ a little licence and use the term 'honour' in a different way for the next twenty minutes. I see men and women 'acting with honour' when they show respect for each other and each other's choices, and do not act with violence or threats of violence towards each other. I see a state 'acting with honour' not when it take steps to protect all women in that state from violence and to prevent violence against them—because this is their obligation before the law—but when they are world leaders in doing so. Turkey has been resting on its laurels with regards to violence against women for too long, relying on its status as one of the first states to adopt the vote for women. The rest of the hard-won gains in this area have come from the women's movement. In my talk today I want to challenge the state to 'act honourably' again, and to become a world leader in the campaign to end violence against women.

We have heard many times over the course of this conference that violence against women does not occur within one religious, ethnic or socio-economic group. It is universal. Crimes of so-called 'honour' are also not the domain of a specific group. Amnesty International believes that the principles involved in the eradication of violence against women are similar regardless of the type of violence. However, the starting points and methods may vary depending on the most urgent priorities for particular states or groups.

> Violence against women is the most pervasive human rights challenge of our times. It cuts across cultural and religious boundaries, political, social and economic status. There is a call for help against domestic violence every minute in Britain. In Ciudad Juarez, more than 370 poor young women, the youngest only 11, have been abducted, brutally tortured, raped and murdered in cities on the Mexican–US border without the authorities taking proper measures to investigate and address the problem. In the USA, 700,000 women are reported raped every year. In South Africa, teenage girls are at the greatest risk of rape. Fifty per cent of all murders in Bangladesh are of women by their partners. Around the world, 120 million are genitally mutilated. According to World Bank figures, at least one in five women and girls has been beaten or sexually abused in her lifetime—that is a shameful statistic at the beginning of the 21st century.[1]

According to a Council of Europe report from 2002, in Europe every week one woman is killed by her husband or partner. The latest national survey in France has shown that in 2001, 1.35 million

---

[1] From a statement by Amnesty International on the UN Day of Elimination of Violence Against Women, <http://news.amnesty.org/mav/index/ENGPOL301125032003>.

women had been victims of domestic violence, and half of them had never before revealed the violence perpetrated against them. They found that the higher the social position of the women, the more difficult it is to denounce violence. The majority of women affected are between 20 and 34 years of age. In Norway, with a population of four million people, each year 10,000 women seek medical treatment because of physical damage due to domestic violence.

VIOLENCE AGAINST WOMEN MAY BE UNIVERSAL, BUT IT IS NOT INEVITABLE

The Secretary-General of Amnesty International has said:

> Violence against women is fed by a global culture which, despite the UDHR, despite the CEDAW, despite treaties, laws, and declarations, denies women equal rights with men. This must stop. Underlying the abuses suffered by women is a discrimination perpetuated by governments and society—and everyone has a responsibility—political leaders, corporate leaders, community leaders, the media and ordinary people. Every human rights agreement and treaty, from the UDHR onwards, has required states to ensure that discrimination of many kinds is addressed and eradicated. This should include discrimination between men and women. The UN General Assembly, the CEDAW, the Vienna and Beijing Declarations, all have confirmed that violence against women is a form of discrimination which states are required to eradicate— because it is a form of discrimination and also because it stops women from enjoying their fundamental human rights.[2]

The core human rights treaties which flow from the 1948 Universal Declaration of Human Rights (UDHR) include:
- the Convention on the Elimination of all Forms of Racial Discrimination (CERD);
- the International Covenant on Economic, Social and Cultural Rights (ICESCR);

---

2 From a speech by the Amnesty International Secretary-General on 25 November, 2003.

- the International Covenant on Civil and Political Rights (ICCPR) and its two Optional Protocols;
- the Convention on the Elimination of All Forms of Discrimination Against Women (Women's Convention) and its Optional Protocol;
- the Convention Against Torture (CAT);
- the Convention on the Rights of the Child (CRC).

In addition to being a contract between states, human rights treaties also provide a framework of rights that individuals are entitled to claim at national, and in some cases, international level. These treaties detail the obligations that the state undertakes to fulfil when it ratifies (or agrees to be bound by) the treaty in question.

Let us take the example given to me by the Purple Roof Foundation of İstanbul, an independent organization for women who have experienced violence. They told me of a shelter being closed down by the government due to suicides occurring within its walls. When shelters exist, they have the potential to be threatening because they make the problem a public problem. Opening shelters can serve to reveal the extent of hidden violence against women.

If a woman dies in the street, this may appear to relieve the government of a number of key obligations. She is not known about, she is not counted, she is not protected from violence. However, even when states are not the direct perpetrators of violence against women, they still have obligations under international law to prevent, investigate and punish violence against women. For every country, depending on what measures are already in place, this involves different steps to be taken. How many women experience violence? Unfortunately, in Turkey at present the epidemiology of this type of violence is not known. There have been no concerted efforts to learn the extent of the problem. In 1994, the office for the status of women asked questions about violence against women, and discovered that more than 40 per cent of men believed that it was acceptable to 'discipline' female family members with physical violence. In the outcry that followed, it was apparently decided that it was better not to know these types of statistics—questions about violence against women were not included in the 2000 figures. However, Amnesty International believes that the extent of the problem needs to be known, and this is seen as a step which states can take towards eradicating violence against women, no matter how bad the scenario seems at first. Potentially, the backsliding of states in steps they have taken towards ameliorating violence against women can be interpreted as a breach of their commitments to conventions, like CEDAW and its optional protocol, which they have signed.

The state may be responsible when it relies on someone or something to carry out an action that falls within the role of a state. For example, only a government can lawfully deprive a person of liberty. However, states are increasingly contracting out police and detention powers to private corporations, and many women confined by these actors have faced sexual and other forms of gender violence, or have been denied adequate mental and physical health care. In these cases, there is no doubt that the state cannot avoid its responsibilities by delegating them away.

The state may be responsible when it has 'participated' in some way, or supported abuses by others. The Convention against Torture, for example, establishes the responsibility of the state for an act of torture when 'such pain or suffering is inflicted by or at the instigation of, or with the consent or acquiescence of a public official, or other person acting in an official capacity' (Article 1).

The state may be responsible when it does not provide effective remedies. Under international law, a core obligation of the state is to provide effective remedies for human rights abuses regardless of the identity of the abuser. Broad principles set out what 'effective remedies' are, including the fact that the remedy must match the nature and severity of the harm (it must be *proportionate*); it must be accessible without discrimination to those harmed (this often means positive steps by the state to reach out to marginalized groups, such as providing legal services in rural areas or in local languages). An effective remedy has many gender-specific aspects: Do women and men have equal rights and real-life capacities to go to court to obtain redress? Does a woman's testimony have the same weight, by law and in practice, as a man's? Is the nature of the remedy sufficient and appropriate to match the gender-specific harm?[3]

In November 2003, Doğan Soyaslan, Professor of Law and advisor to the Sub-Committee Ministry of Justice working group on the Turkish Penal Code, defending an article in the Turkish Penal Code that allows sentencing to be deferred if a rapist marries his victim, stated that 'No-one would want to marry a girl who is not a virgin', and 'If I were a raped woman, I would marry the rapist. People get used to these things with time.'

The mother of a young man accused of a so-called 'honour' murder said: 'Don't hide my son's face. He did nothing to be ashamed of. He cleaned his honour.'

These statements are examples of discriminatory attitudes towards women that are supported by law and restrict women's right to choose. The right to choose their place of residence, their ability to leave their house, or their village, or their suburb. The right to choose their spouse, their place of employment, their right to political activity. These rights are denied women as a means of controlling their sexuality. Virginity is tied to the notion of so-called 'honour'. Discrimination on the basis of virginity is currently supported by law—the Turkish Penal Code (TPC).

These types of constructions diminish the legal seriousness of crimes committed against women and contribute to the invisibility of women before the law.

---

3 Taken from the Amnesty International document, 'Respect, Protect, Fulfil: Women's Human Rights. State Responsibility for Abuses by Non-State Actors'. AI INDEX: IOR 50/001/2000 (Posted: 1 September, 2000).

MAKING RIGHTS A REALITY

Action means naming violence against women as a serious human rights violation and eliminating discrimination. Change must, crucially, originate from governments. The Special Rapporteur on Violence Against Women has said,

> Perhaps the greatest cause of violence against women is government inaction with regard to crimes of violence against women... a permissive attitude, a tolerance of perpetrators of violence against women, especially when this... is expressed in the home.[4]

In Turkey, two of the urgently required reforms at present are to the Civil Code, which does not backdate property rights for divorced women, thereby severely limiting their economic rights, and to the Turkish Penal Code.

Discriminatory articles in the Turkish Penal Code include those relating to rape. International criminal law, including the Rome Statute of the International Criminal Court, identifies violence against women of many types and in many situations as crime. The Rome Statute is widely seen as 'best practice' in international criminal law. Amnesty International would simultaneously urge the Turkish government to ratify the Rome Statute and to utilize as a model of best practice the definition of rape outlined therein.[5] Other draft articles in

---

4   Special Rapporteur on Violence Against Women, Its Causes and Consequences, in her first report to the Human Rights Commission, E/CN.4/1996/53/Add.2.
5   Article 7(1)(g)–1:
    1. The perpetrator invaded the body of a person by conduct resulting in penetration however slight, of any part of the body of the victim or of the perpetrator with a sexual organ, or of the anal or genital opening of the victim with any object or any other part of the body.
    2. The invasion was committed by force, or by threat of force or coercion, such as that caused by fear of violence, duress, detention, psychological oppression, or abuse of power, against such person or another person, or by taking advantage of a coercive environment, or the invasion was committed against a person incapable of giving genuine consent. (It is understood that a person may be incapable of giving genuine consent if affected by natural, induced, or age-related incapacity).

the Turkish Penal Code in urgent need of reform include articles concerning the rape and attempted rape of a child where the sentence differs with and without the child's 'consent'.

Some articles in the TPC, for example, those relating to rape, and the exclusion of marital rape, are discriminatory before international human rights law. Turkey is a state party to the Convention on the Elimination of All Forms of Discrimination Against Women (CEDAW) and its Optional Protocol, and hence has committed itself to incorporate the principle of equality of men and women in the legal system, abolish all discriminatory laws, and adopt appropriate ones prohibiting discrimination against women. CEDAW defines 'discrimination against women' as:

> any distinction, exclusion or restriction made on the basis of sex which has the effect or purpose of impairing or nullifying the recognition, enjoyment or exercise by women, irrespective of their marital status, on a basis of equality of men and women, of human rights and fundamental freedoms in the political, economic, social, cultural, civil or any other field.

The Committee of Ministers of the Council of Europe has provided that 'member states of the Council of Europe should ensure that criminal law provides that any act of violence against a person, in particular physical or sexual violence, constitutes a violation of that person's physical, psychological and/or sexual freedom and integrity, and not solely a violation of morality, honour or decency'.[6]

Article 7(1)(g)–6:
    The perpetrators committed an act of a sexual nature against one or more persons or caused such person or persons to engage in an act of a sexual nature by force, or by threat of force or coercion, such as that caused by fear of violence, duress, detention, psychological oppression or abuse of power, against such person or persons or another person, or by taking advantage of a coercive environment or such person's or persons' incapacity to give consent.

6 Council of Europe (2002). The Protection of Women Against Violence. Recommendation Rec(2002)5 of the Committee of Ministers to Member States on the Protection of Women Against Violence, adopted on 30 April, 2002 and Explanatory Memorandum, para 34.

The judgment of the International Criminal Tribunal for the former Yugoslavia, in the case of *Furundizja*, states:

> a trend can be discerned in the national legislation of a number of States of *broadening the definition of rape* so that it now embraces acts which were previously classified as comparatively less serious offences, that is sexual or indecent assault. This trend shows that at the national level States tend to take a stricter attitude towards serious forms of sexual assault: the stigma of rape now attaches to a growing category of sexual offences, provided of course they meet certain requirements, chiefly that of *forced physical penetration*.[7]

The Court went on to say

> It is apparent from our survey of national legislation that, in spite of inevitable discrepancies, most legal systems in the common and civil law worlds consider rape to be the forcible sexual penetration of the human body by the penis or *the forcible insertion of any other object* into either the vagina or the anus.[8]

The draft Turkish Penal Code also states that marital rape does not constitute a rape offence. This directly contravenes CEDAW General Recommendation 19 (24I), which states:

> States parties should take all legal and other measures that are necessary to provide effective protection of women against gender-based violence, including, inter alia... effective legal measures, including penal sanctions, civil remedies and compensatory kinds of violence, including, inter alia, violence and abuse in the family, sexual assault and sexual harassment in the workplace,

and the Special Rapporteur on Violence Against Women's report on the framework legislation for domestic violence, which specifically

---

7   Furundzija vs. ICTY, Judgment of 10 December, 1998, paragraph 179 (italics added).
8   Furundzija vs. ICTY, Judgment of 10 December, 1998, paragraph 181 (italics added).

defines marital rape as domestic violence.⁹ By failing to define marital rape as a criminal act, Turkey would be directly in breach of its obligations under CEDAW.

The Convention on the Rights of the Child, to which Turkey is a party, states that:

> States Parties shall take all appropriate legislative, administrative, social and educational measures to protect the child from all forms of physical or mental violence, injury or abuse, neglect or negligent treatment, maltreatment or exploitation, including sexual abuse, while in the care of parent(s), legal guardian(s) or any other person who has the care of the child.¹⁰

The United Nations General Assembly in 1998 called upon

> States to criminalize all forms of sexual exploitation of children, including commercial sexual exploitation, and to condemn and penalize all those offenders involved, whether local or foreign, while ensuring that children victims of this practice are not penalized.¹¹

When the state routinely fails to respond to evidence of abduction of women and girls by allowing the rapist to either marry or avoid marrying his victim as a means of escaping prosecution, they send the message that such attacks can be committed with impunity. In so doing, they fail to take the minimum steps necessary to protect the right of women and girls to physical integrity. They may also be tolerating harmful cultural practices that perpetuate violence against women. CEDAW requires governments to:

---

9   Report of the Special Rapporteur on Violence Against Women, Its Causes and Consequences, Ms. Radhika Coomaraswamy, submitted in accordance with Commission on Human Rights Resolution 1995/85: A Framework for Model Legislation on Domestic Violence, E/CN.4/1996/53/Add.2.
10 Convention on the Rights of the Child, Article 19.
11 United Nations General Assembly, Report of the Third Committee: Promotion and Protection of the Rights of Children. A/53/621 24 November, 1998.

modify the social and cultural patterns of conduct of men and women, with a view to achieving the elimination of prejudices and customary and all other practices which are based on the idea of the inferiority or the superiority of either of the sexes or on stereotyped roles for men and women.[12]

In addition to the ground-breaking Velasquez-Rodriguez decision at the Inter-American Court of Human Rights, which found that states may be responsible for human rights violations committed by non-state actors, there have been recent decisions at the European Court of Human Rights, such as *Osman vs. United Kingdom*, in which a state's *failure* to act could be construed as that state being in breach of the European Convention, to which Turkey is a party.[13]

This area of law is evolving rapidly, and it is to be expected that states are likely to be held more accountable for the actions of non-state actors where states have demonstrated systematic failures to prevent, investigate, and punish.

There is the story of the sixteen year old 'Leyla'. Last year she became pregnant. She told her family, when it was too difficult to hide her pregnancy, that her cousin had raped her. The family was brought together, and her cousin denied it. On the basis of this denial, the girl was handed a rope by her mother and told to 'clean her honour'. Her brother was called in to make sure she did it properly. He came in and found her crying—she said the chair was not high enough and she couldn't do it. He helped her set up the chair to the right height, and when he came back an hour later she was dead.

The torturer's power derives from the silence of his victims. No one will hear you cry. No one will hear you scream. The most shocking aspect of violence against women is that, when a man batters his

---

12 CEDAW, Article 5(a).
13 For example, in *Osman v United Kingdom* (Case number 87/1997/871/1083, 28 October 1998): 'It is sufficient for an applicant to show that the authorities did not do all that could have reasonably been expected of them to avoid a real and immediate risk to life of which they have or ought to have knowledge' (para, 115–7).

wife, people hear the screams. But they don't necessarily attach any importance to them. When a woman is killed by her family, this can be seen as of little importance. Just as the torturer's aim is to destroy the victim's world, reducing that person to a mere body, so the torturer at home succeeds more completely. With society's acquiescence, he can make a woman believe she does not have the right to exist, and, when her choices are heavily restricted, she may even relieve him of the burden of a jail sentence by killing herself. The spectrum of control ranges from restricted options (which can result in suicide), to forced suicide, to murder.

Perpetrators of violence against women appear to have found the perfect crime, you could say. You can even find victims who will take responsibility for them. But states must act to prevent, investigate, and punish crimes of violence. To prevent violence means, amongst other things, collecting information about the extent of the problem in every region and providing places for women to go, including places they can access legal advice, shelter, and medical care. To investigate violence means prompt, thorough, and effective investigations. Why are so many young women apparently committing suicide in some areas of Turkey? Investigate the suicides. To punish violence means no sentence reductions for reason of 'custom' or 'tradition' and no impunity for perpetrators. It means no excuses for state authorities' failure to act. It means taking effective action to implement the Law for the Protection of the Family when women approach the authorities.

Amnesty International is also concerned that in situations where the security forces have perpetrated violence against women, it is doubly difficult for women experiencing violence in the home to access justice—and may also increase the likelihood of violence in the home. There is strong and credible research linking the availability of guns and violence against women. The risk of women being murdered by their partners increases with the availability of firearms. For example, a study in Northern Ireland showed that increased availability of firearms meant that more dangerous forms of violence were used in the home. This can be linked to conflict or post-conflict situations, and it can also be linked to a culture of violence. Amnesty International is currently conducting a 'Control Arms' campaign urging governments to sign onto treaties for non-proliferation of arms.

Women may—justifiably—fear the consequences for their husbands or families if they report violence. They may be concerned about what happens to them at the police station if they report violence perpetrated against them. In situations where many individuals have learned to fear being taken into police custody, many women may balk at the idea of reporting family violence to security forces. Some women may not be able to speak the same language as the police or court officials. These concerns make it even more important that effective, independent mechanisms exist for women to access protection, support, and shelter.

Amnesty International's Secretary-General has said:

> International treaties and mechanisms are only useful if they are carried back into a country and respected. Otherwise they are simply hot air.
> Laws only offer protection if they are implemented, otherwise they are printed documents.
> Human rights are only real if they provide real equality and equal protection.
> The shift we now need is to bring real change in the lives of many more real people.
> It is with that goal in mind that Amnesty International will launch on 8 March next year a campaign to stop violence against women. Through this campaign we will call on leaders, organizations and individuals to publicly pledge to make the Universal Declaration of Human Rights—which promised equal rights and protection for all—a reality for women.
> We will engage communities and local authorities to support programs that enable women to live free from violence.
> We will seek the solidarity of men with women. Men also suffer when the women they love are victims of violence and many of

them are part of the movement to condemn and eradicate violence against women.

Violence against women may be universal but it is not inevitable. We can end it. But for that we must be ready to listen to the voices of women and support them to organize themselves. We must be willing to challenge religious, social and cultural attitudes that belittle women. We must be ready to fight for the equal access of women to political power and economic resources. We must have the courage to confront those in authority and demand change. But most importantly, we can end it if we are ready to change ourselves—to say no: I will not do it, I will not permit others to do it and I will not rest until it has been eradicated.[14]

Amnesty International urges the Turkish government to take the necessary steps for reform—most crucially, legal reforms to the Penal and Civil codes. Not for the sake of the European Union. But so that women living in Turkey can exercise their right to be free from violence—economic, sexual, physical and psychological.

ADDENDUM

I would like to draw out some of the themes and questions arising from the conference:

- the need to emphasise what we have in common. We appear to all have the goal of the eradication of violence against women. Respect for the dignity of the person seems to be a principle that all uphold. This is a principle that can be upheld whether one utilizes a human rights framework or the lens of any of the major religions;
- the importance of the utilization of accurate information to combat prejudice and racism;
- the importance of monitoring: monitoring states, communities, and the press;
- the need for simple messages to dilute the complexity of the debate for activists, whilst continuing to develop and provide a theo-

---

14 Speech by Irene Khan, Amnesty International's Secretary-General, on 25 November, 2003.

retical 'causes and consequences' superstructure, in which to embed our activism;

• rather than involving ourselves in the traditional torture versus domestic violence debate, can we start with the experiences of the victims? The equality of pain is an important message that everyone can relate to;

• utilizing previous 'success' stories from human rights and women's global activism to ensure women's rights;

• the right to choose—this includes respect for other's religious beliefs, where those beliefs are not imposed on others with violence or threats of violence.

Swedish Government Initiatives to Help Young People at Risk of Honour-Related Violence

LISE BERGH

INTRODUCTION

I would like to start by citing some passages from the Beijing Declaration and the Beijing Platform for Action, as we, the states, have acceded and ratified these two documents.

The Declaration states that:
- we are convinced that women's rights are human rights;
- we are determined to ensure the full enjoyment by women and girls of all human rights and fundamental freedoms, and to take effective action against violations of these rights and freedoms.

The Platform for Action has designated twelve areas of concern or strategic objectives, one of which is 'Violence Against Women':
- there it is established that 'Violence Against Women' is a manifestation of the historically unequal power relations between women and men, which have led to domination over and discrimination against women by men and to the prevention of women's full advancement;'
- it is also established that 'Violence against women throughout the life cycle derives essentially from cultural patterns, in particular the

harmful effects of certain traditional or customary practices and all acts of extremism linked to race, sex, language or religion that perpetuate the lower status accorded to women in the family, the workplace, the community and society;'

• actions to be taken include to 'Adopt all appropriate measures... to modify the social and cultural patterns of conduct of men and women, and to eliminate prejudices, customary practices and all other practices based on the idea of the inferiority or superiority of either of the sexes.'

Sweden is one of the most gender-equal countries in the world. But Sweden is still a society where men dominate. What we call the gender system, the superior status of men and subordination of women, regrettably makes men's violence against women part of everyday life in Sweden. Many women are threatened, abused—sometimes even murdered—by men with whom they have a close relationship. This happens irrespective of whether the women are of Swedish or foreign origin.

In the fight against honour-related violence, we must always bear this fact in mind. Men's violence against women is a universal problem, caused by patriarchal power structures in all countries and cultures. Violence against women is the most extreme expression of the dominance of men in society.

Since the 1970s, Sweden has experienced large-scale immigration. Today more than one in ten Swedish residents were born in another country. As a result, in recent years Sweden has begun to see honour-related violence against women. This honour-related violence builds on the same patriarchal power structures as when men of Swedish origin beat women. Nevertheless, it is a special form of violence against women, which requires special action on the part of society. To be able to protect girls and women who risk being subjected to honour-related violence, it is important to see the special conditions that these girls and women live within.

HONOUR-RELATED VIOLENCE IN SWEDISH SOCIETY
Society long knew relatively little about the problem of honour-related violence. We did not see—or did not want to see—the oppression to which girls and women were subjected when they behaved in a way that was perfectly acceptable to the majority society but not to family members and fellow countrymen.

But then a number of murders were committed that forced us to realize what was happening. Over the past decade, there have been several cases in Sweden of girls and young women being murdered by male relatives for violating the rules of conduct of their families and relatives. Examples include Sara, aged 15, who was murdered by her brother and her cousin, aged 16 and 17 respectively; Pela, aged 19, who was taken to her parents' country of origin and shot by her father and uncles; and Fadime, aged 26, who was shot by her father. In all three cases, the motive for murder was that the girls had brought shame upon their families by the way in which they lived.

Even if it doesn't always go as far as murder, many young people are wronged day-to-day. Many are threatened by their relatives if they fail to follow the family's demands in every last detail. Some young people are promised in arranged marriages or married off when they are still children and should be in school. Sometimes family conflicts become so severe that young people have to run away from their families. We also hear reports about young people—girls and boys—committing suicide because of their sexual orientation.

I am sorry to say that society sometimes does too little to protect girls and women who are subjected to threats and violence or discrimination on account of their sex, not because of any lack of clarity in our laws but because many people are ignorant of the nature of the violence. There is a great need for more knowledge, and a great demand for more knowledge among personnel in the social services, the legal system, the schools, and many others. There is also a risk of people—as public employees or private individuals—hesitating to intervene when they come across violence or other problems that seem alien to them. It is therefore important to stress that honour-related violence is a human rights issue. States are bound by international law to prevent and combat this kind of violence, to investigate its occurrence and to punish the perpetrators. Culture, religion, or tradition must never be used as an excuse for evading these obligations. Human rights are universal and have been accepted by the international community as a whole.

GOVERNMENT INITIATIVES TO HELP YOUNG PEOPLE AT RISK OF HONOUR-RELATED VIOLENCE

Spreading Knowledge and Working to Change Attitudes

The Swedish government has taken a series of initiatives to tackle problems relating in particular to coercion of girls and young women. With a view to gathering knowledge, we have conducted a series of seminars bringing together representatives of public authorities, religious communities, women's shelters, immigrant organizations, other NGOs, and experts. The purpose of the seminars was to discuss ways in which public authorities and NGOs can better co-operate to improve the situation of girls and their families. The seminars have led to a number of results:

- to support them in their work, personnel in the social services now have an extensive body of information about girls living under threats and coercion, produced by the National Board of Health and Welfare;
- acting on instructions from the government, the Swedish Integration Board, in co-ordination with other government authorities, has highlighted good examples and methods for preventing conflicts between individuals and families that may be caused by ideas about honour;
- the Swedish Integration Board has provided support to projects addressing equality between women and men, so as to improve the living conditions of girls at risk. The Board has also published several documents containing concrete examples of preventive work;

- financial support has been provided to various NGOs for projects aimed at strengthening the position of girls and women.

Other measures concern, for example:

- support to Terrafem (a support network for immigrant women) for an emergency telephone service in some twenty languages that girls and young women at risk of honour-related violence can telephone for support and help;
- support for girls in families where the idea of honour plays a central role, channelled through the National Council for the Protection of Women against Violence;
- support for methods for developing reception and support for men with violent tendencies from immigrant backgrounds.

Funds for Sheltered Housing and Other Action

On commission from the government, three county administrative boards have explored the need for sheltered housing. They found that several hundred girls contact the authorities each year because they feel threatened by their relatives. There is also a severe shortage of sheltered housing where girls can be placed in emergencies.

This year the government set aside a total of SEK 20 million (USD 2,600,000/EUR 2,155,000) to encourage the municipalities in the three metropolitan counties to set up sheltered housing for girls at risk and to explore the need for sheltered housing elsewhere in the country. The government is earmarking SEK 100 million (USD 13,030,000/EUR 10,770,000) for additional action in 2004–2005.

Measures in Schools

The school system has a national responsibility for raising children to be democratic citizens. The schools are also required to work actively to break down gender stereotypes and promote equality between the sexes. Hence, much of the necessary work must be done within the school system. All children attend school, and this is where the foundation is laid for their democratic upbringing. It is within the school system that the basic values of our society are transmitted, it is here that girls and boys learn about the equal rights and responsibilities of all people.

In order to improve knowledge about the situation of young people in families where ideas about honour are prominent, a publication entitled 'Stronger than You Think' has now been distributed to all compulsory and upper secondary schools. In addition, a collection of instructive examples has been compiled illustrating the methods used by schools and municipalities, together with different organizations and public authorities, in their work on gender equality and social and ethnic diversity.

A couple of universities are now training resource staff in gender equality and gender studies. The objective is for all municipalities to have at least one gender education specialist on their staff by 2004.

Child Marriages and Forced Marriages
Currently, children between the ages of 15 and 18 who are citizens of a country that allows child marriages can also get married in Sweden without special approval. The government is now proposing a legal amendment as of 1 May next year. The effect of the amendment will be to make 18 the minimum age for marriage for all people in Sweden, irrespective of citizenship. At the same time, the legislation will clarify the fact that child marriages and forced marriages entered into in other countries are not recognized in Sweden. The minimum requirements set are that all people entering into marriage are adult and are marrying of their own free will. The same laws must apply to all members of our society.

The government also proposes that a person who does not have the right to solemnize marriages but who nevertheless conducts marriage-like ceremonies can be called to account as having committed an offence against the law. The same thing will apply to parents who force children to marry or threaten to do so.

In this context I would also like to mention the dialogue on children's and young people's rights that Mona Sahlin, the minister responsible for democracy, integration, and gender equality policies is engaged in with representatives of different religious associations and communities.

THE ROLE OF MEN
In our continued efforts to protect girls, boys, and women who are in danger, we must also put time and resources into endeavours to change the values held by the men who defend 'honour cultures' most staunchly. In various parts of Sweden work has begun on building up a dialogue between men on the subject of this violence against women. Having said this, we are aware that there are men who come from societies with honour cultures who take great responsibility for changing this way of thinking. These men are our allies in the struggle to change attitudes and perspectives on women's and men's rights.

Men must be just as involved as women in the work of creating gender equality. For twenty years, there have been working groups attached to the government whose purpose has been to engage men in gender equality work. To give two examples, there was a 'Father's group' in 1994–1995 and a 'Men and Gender Equality Project' that has worked between 1999 and 2003 on issues of masculinity from a feminist perspective.

As I have already said, there are men and women in Sweden from a wide range of cultural backgrounds. It is important that people who have recently arrived in Sweden obtain reliable and relevant information about our laws and about the rights that women, men, and children enjoy in our society. But people who have already lived in our country for a long time must also be given a chance to re-examine their values, and this can best be done by meeting other people.

We believe in meetings between men and in the value of men discussing gender equality issues with one another. For us, gender equality means that each individual woman and each individual man must have the same rights, responsibilities and opportunities in life. It is important that men who have a knowledge of our thinking on gender equality meet men who have not yet understood the advantages of a society in which women and men are equal. One approach being used in various places in Sweden today uses these types of consciousness-raising groups for men, in which Swedish-born men and men from other countries meet and engage in dialogue on our ideas about gender equality.

THE UNITED NATIONS

Honour-related violence occurs in all countries, but not all countries recognize the existence of the problem. The Swedish government considers it important that this issue be discussed internationally, that its existence is recognized by governments, and that we work together to achieve a solution. I am convinced that international co-operation is the most important tool for fighting this oppression.

As you are aware, violence committed in the name of honour has been addressed by several UN bodies, including the UN Secretary-General, the General Assembly, the Commission on Human Rights and its special rapporteurs, particularly the UN Rapporteur on Violence Against Women and the UN Rapporteur on Extrajudicial, Summary or Arbitrary Executions.

The Swedish Government welcomes the appointment of Ms Yakın Ertürk as UN Special Rapporteur on Violence Against Women. Ms Ertürk, I wish you every success in your work to combat violence against women in all its forms, including violence committed in the name of honour. I would like to ensure you of Sweden's support in these endeavours.

On 4–5 November, 2003, the Swedish government conducted an expert meeting of about fifty participants whose assignment was to prepare a major international conference to be held in Stockholm next year. It is our hope that the upcoming conference will be able to help bring about further international co-operation to overcome the violence that is exercised in the name of honour. The United Nations has a key role to play in these efforts.

FINAL COMMENTS

The Turkish women's centre KA-MER has told us the story of Ayşe (see in this volume), the woman who was harassed by a man in her home village. Although it was the man who had behaved badly—and although everyone in the village knew that Ayşe was innocent—it was Ayşe and her husband and children who were isolated and harassed in the name of honour. In the end they had to leave the village and move to the city. But the man who harassed Ayşe is still living in the village.

As long as these sorts of things happen, it is our responsibility to protest. Women who are harassed, threatened, and abused must always have the support and protection of society. Violations of women's rights must never be excused by reference to culture, tradition, or religion. We must not compromise on human rights. All people have the same right to freedom and to decide about their own lives. This is the key focus of the government's endeavours. There is no contradiction between the rights of the individual and respect for other cultures and values. Women's rights are human rights.

Confronting Honour Violence: The Swedish Police at Work
Kickis Åhré Älgamo

INTRODUCTION

I am a detective inspector at the National Criminal Investigation Department (CID) in Sweden. My tasks include violence related to honour and honour killing. I will speak about developments, my assignments, Swedish legislation, a few cases, and finally some conclusions. My hope is that we can exchange experiences as well as various strategies that work to deal with the issue of honour violence. These problems have existed in Sweden for a rather long time. Responsible individuals at a higher level—within the police, the political arena, as well as other representatives of society—have begun during the last several years to realize the existence of these problems.

A process has started in Sweden, with plans of action regarding training and development at various levels, including the authorities. Changes have started to take place, but it is a rather slow process. I have many dedicated and efficient colleagues that work hard investigating crimes committed in the belief that the honour of a family has been violated.

The individuals that I come into contact with have been subjected to assault, threats, and mental humiliation. Many of them fear the police. I maintain that this is because the police and different authorities in their native countries are perceived to be a threat to the individual or to the group. The police in Sweden do not at all have the same way of working. Methods of interrogation and investigation are not the same. It takes time to eliminate this fear and to gain the confidence of these persons. They must learn that the Swedish police are not a threat. The police are there to support them and to assist them.

MY TASKS

I am tasked by the National CID to write a report on my experiences. First of all, I am writing a manual to be used by my Swedish colleagues on how to carry out investigations concerning crimes related to honour. The manual will include all kinds of crimes of violence, for instance, assault, threats, mental humiliation, and so on, when the motive of the crime can be considered to be that family honour has been violated. I am also developing some methods regarding these kind of investigations. It is very important when you investigate a murder case to create a situation whereby it is possible to indict all actors in the chain.

I am also tasked to assist my colleagues in investigations and to teach them how to investigate the crimes that have been committed on account of honour.

The police and the social services should have the same knowledge of the problems related to honour and of how these problems appear in everyday life in Sweden; this in order to make it possible to find an acceptable solution at the societal level, and to hold the offenders responsible for their acts.

SWEDISH LAW

When a crime is committed, the legislation makes it possible to hold all involved responsible:

- the promoters, those who state that honour must be restored;
- those who plan the method by which it is restored;

- those who correct the woman by placing her in the family system again by assault, threats, or some kind of mental humiliation;
- and those who carry out the punishment.

If a serious crime—for instance, attempted murder, abduction, or an arranged accident—is committed in another country by someone that has connections to Sweden and that person:
- is a Swedish citizen, or,
- permanently or partly resides in Sweden,

then the person undertaking the action can be held responsible for the crime by Sweden. In addition, there is double liability to the penalty, such that the person can also be punished in Sweden if it appears that a sentence for a serious crime would be disproportionately low in the country where the initial punishment is to be imposed.

DOUBLE LIABILITY—AN EXAMPLE

I will briefly tell you about a case in Sweden in which double liability was used. Pela Atroshi, a Swedish girl who originated from the town of Dahok, in the north of Iraq, was murdered on 24 June, 1999 by her relatives in that town.

Pela was nineteen years old.

Pela's family was of the opinion that she had far too-Western a way of life. They thought that she should observe Kurdish rules and customs. They saw obvious signs that she had become rather Swedish. The family disliked her way of dressing, her make-up, hairstyle, and the fact that she did not go home directly after school. Pela did well in school and her intelligence was considered a threat. There were constant arguments in the family concerning her conduct. Pela wanted to be herself, and she found it hard to live up to their expectations.

Pela could no longer stand to live with this mental pressure. In January, 1999 she ran away from home. She was aware what this meant, as seen from the family's point of view: They would think that she had lost her virginity. Pela felt that she had to get away, as she was suffocating under the control of her family.

THE SEARCH FOR PELA
During the search for Pela, her sister, younger by a year, and her mother were consulted, as it was believed that they would be able to entice her out of her hiding place.

Both the women and the men of the family took part in the discussions. In this process, Pela's grandfather, who is an Australian citizen, said, 'I will not set foot in Kurdistan until she is dead.'

After some time, Pela voluntarily returned home.

After many twists and turns in the family, her mother and father decided that Pela had better marry a Kurd in the north of Iraq. Pela agreed to this. The father promised that upon this marriage, he would never hurt Pela. She thought, 'I'd rather marry a younger Kurd who perhaps will understand me than to have these constant quarrels with my father and his family.'

The preparations prior to the travel were not the usual ones of the family. The members travelled to Iraq in various groups, and on various occasions baby-sitters from Australia were engaged to take care of the younger siblings in Sweden.

In Iraq, in June, Pela's younger sister had a dispute with her father. She felt that something was wrong. One of the reasons for this dispute was that many men had proposed to Pela, but the father had declined them all. The younger sister realized that this was not in accordance with ancient tradition and was not in accordance with what had been decided in Sweden. The younger sister smelt a rat and took care of the passports of her mother and her sisters and brothers. On this occasion her father acted in a threatening way with a weapon. He could have acted, killed his daughter then, but he did not as he had promised not to hurt Pela.

Later that night, he called his brothers in Sweden and asked them to quickly travel to Dahok. He stated, 'The girls are going to run away.' In the evening of the next day, the brothers arrived in the north of Iraq. Everybody gathered at the home of their sister.

The next morning, on 24 June, most of the female relatives visited Pela, her younger sister, and their mother. When relatives make a visit, they usually do the visit in the afternoon. The female relatives took Pela, her younger sister, and their mother to various locations in the house and kept them occupied with something.

At 10h30, Pela's uncles and father entered the house in Dahok.

At the same time as they entered the house, all the female relatives left.

The youngest uncle walked directly upstairs to the room Pela was in. Two shots were heard from the room. The younger sister realized from where the shots were fired, and she rushed in that direction. On the stairs, she met her uncle with a gun in his waistband, and he said, 'Pela took her life.'

Directly after that, four men ran away from the house. On the way to their get-away car, they heard the younger sister scream, 'Mother, mother, Pela is alive, we must take her to the hospital.' The mother rushed into the house and helped the younger sister carry Pela. She was shot twice in the back. Pela couldn't see anything because of the blood in her eyes, but she could speak. She told them who had shot her and how. Pela also said, 'Mother, why have they done this to me, I have not done anything wrong.'

The screams of the younger sister made the offenders return to the house, and after a fight between the younger sister, who tried to protect Pela, and her uncles, the fatal shot was fired at Pela's head.

The offenders again ran away from the scene of the crime. They headed to the Kurdistani Democratic Party (KDP) office in Dahok, believing that they could receive help there. The younger sister managed to contact the Swedish police by telephone. The mother asked the police in Dahok to assist.

Among the Swedish police, a team was assigned to the case. I was the responsible case officer, and we worked this case for a long time. The investigators who worked on this case were dedicated and efficient.

After 9 months and a lot of hard work, we succeeded in getting the younger sister, who had witnessed the murder, back to Sweden. After another 9 months, the mother and some of the siblings were back in Sweden. The two eldest brothers who had sided with the father remained in Dahok.

In Sweden, two of Pela's uncles were convicted. The father is still the subject of an international warrant of arrest for murder. There are also two suspects who are Australian citizens, the grandfather and one uncle. The Swedish prosecutor presented this matter to the Australian administration of justice in the hope that they will act. So far, the suspects have not been held responsible for their actions with respect to the murder.

If all persons involved in the murder had had some connection to Sweden—had resided in Sweden or were Swedish citizens—we very probably would have been able to institute legal proceedings against eleven persons for the murder of Pela. Several of these are women.

In Iraq, one of the uncles and the father were convicted of the murder. The penalty was a couple of months. The reason for the mild punishment was the fact that the two families had forgiven each other and that they were uneducated villagers who did not understand what they had done. The description of these people as 'uneducated villagers' is, however, not correct in regards to the men.

THERE ARE POSSIBILITIES...

I urge you to contact the Swedish police when a crime with a connection to Sweden has been committed in another country. This can involve, for instance, the following crimes: A person has been brought to their native country against their will; someone has met with an 'accident;' someone has been the subject of attempted murder, or worse, murdered. There might be a possibility that we can act and institute legal proceedings against the offenders in Sweden.

Before Pela's sister was fetched back home to Sweden, her grandfather said to her, 'If you testify in a Swedish court, the same thing that happened to Pela will happen to you.' This statement is like a dark cloud above Sweden, and the younger sister is daily living with this deadly threat. I do everything that I can to help her. My possibilities are, however, limited. Swedish authorities have tried to reach the grandfather but we do not know if he has received this message.

HOW IS THE SITUATION IN SWEDEN TODAY?

Sweden will soon have nine million inhabitants. About one hundred murders are committed each year. On average, there are sixty-five male and thirty-five female murder victims. During the last twenty years, there have been between seventeen to twenty-one female victims of *fatal violence in a close relationship*. Each year, five to ten of the murders are not detected until the pathologist has performed an autopsy. Because of the fact that the priority as regards to autopsies is limited, pathologists maintain that about five to ten murders a year are not detected by the Swedish legal system. These murders are never investigated.

An example of such a case is the death of a young Muslim woman, wherein the family stated that she had taken her own life. Within the police, it was classified as a suicide and no further action was taken. Persons that knew the young woman contacted me after a year and asked me to look into the case.

Conducting a check-up, I found indications that a crime had been committed. A possible motive for such a crime might be that the family honour had been violated because the woman had a forbidden relationship with a Christian man. After discussions within the police, a criminal investigation involving murder was instigated. This investigation is still on-going.

An unsolved double-murder from 1986 has caught my interest by accident. At the beginning of the 1990s, the investigation had been discontinued. In the material from 1986, there were several points that I noticed; I also collected some new information. Today the double-murder is again actively investigated. The motive for the murder seems to be that family honour was violated.

At present, five to ten murder investigations are being carried out in Sweden in which honour is considered to be the motive. I can establish that in many of these cases, the mother as well as other women of the family has played an active part with respect to the crime. They are all aware of the fact that the crime was to take place. The men take care of the planning and its implementation.

CONCLUSION: THE FAMILY PYRAMID, TOOLS, AND INTERVENTIONS

My work to assist women exposed to violence can be summarized as 'an aid to helping oneself'.

First, I illustrate the case both in a visual and a mental way, together with the person who has been subjected to a threat and/or a crime. I try to figure out how her family and how the norms and rules function in the ethnic group from which she originates. I point out the measures that must be taken by the police in order to help the woman continue living as normally as possible. I try to strengthen her physical and psychological safety.

The young woman knows of course what is forbidden within her family. However, she often has difficulties understanding the roles played by the different persons in the actions of the family; I am only a tool who helps her tell what she knows.

I also advocate the importance of finding tools to moderate and prevent a dispute that is ongoing in a family concerning honour. Thus, I try to make my colleagues aware of mediation as an avenue for the purpose of preventing a crime. Unfortunately, because of ignorance and lack of time, this measure is not given priority; the reason might also be that it is difficult to make an assessment of the result of this measure. However, I am convinced that this is a strategy that will work.

Finally, I tell my colleagues that:
- we only see the tip of the iceberg;
- we must all do our share;
- you are not strong alone, but together we can go far.

Violence in the Name of Honour in Swedish Society: What Lessons can be Learnt from the Swedish Experience
Javeria Rizvi

INTRODUCTION

When I was asked to speak at this venue, I was both nervous and excited. Speaking about violence in the name of honour is a very sensitive and complex task and can be approached through many different lenses.

The debate on honour killings in Sweden relates to me on a professional as well as a personal level. As a student of Law and Development Studies at the School of Oriental and African Studies in London, I chose to write my final year dissertation on 'honour related' violence in Sweden. I was inspired by my professor in Islamic Law Dr. Lynn Welchman to get involved in the International Honour Crimes Project as I was very much interested in human rights and particularly women's rights. Getting involved in the project I also learnt about the shocking number of honour killings of young girls that took place internationally as well as in Sweden. Reading about the cases was emotionally draining and impossible to accept.

What struck me most besides the horrible acts of violence was how Swedish society reacted to the events. Being an immigrant woman of Pakistani and Muslim background myself, and having lived my entire life in Sweden, I also found it hard to digest and relate to how plural and diverse notions such as 'Muslims', 'Islam', 'immigrants', 'patriarchal families', and 'immigrant girls' were all simplified and homogenized. This was presented in the public debate and media following the killings. The idea was that there is one type of Muslim who is an immigrant because his/her Swedish is not pure, he/she comes from a patriarchal family, and the daughters are more than likely being violated of all their rights. I'm very glad to say that we have moved past the stage of what is termed *jahiliiya*, the age of ignorance. But here I would like to make a caveat: Movement does not necessarily imply progress!

Although it was a positive sign that the media was beginning to highlight the different dimensions of violence against women, I felt that the debate was not only simplistic but also stigmatizing to minority groups. It was questionable to what extent this debate was helping women and girls at risk.

All of these combined factors finalized my decision to conduct my final-year research in this subject matter. In my dissertation, I set out to examine in what ways six reported cases of honour killings have been negotiated by the Swedish courts.

Initially the aim was simply to analyse whether and how the cultural defence plea had been applied in these cases and what effects this may have on women's human rights. However, very early in the research, an examination of close to one hundred Swedish newspaper reports of these cases revealed extremely biased and stereotypical reporting in cases involving Muslims and immigrants of Middle Eastern origin. Since law cannot be studied detached from the social context in which it operates, I had to re-think the approach to this study. Astonished by the bias in the media, my investigation then focused on discerning whether biases existed in the courts' treatment of cases of honour killings, and more specifically how this informs the approach that Sweden is taking to address such violence.

I am aware that there are many girls in Sweden living under controlled circumstances, including Swedish girls who are subjected to men's violence in their homes. The focus of my study was not the actual killing but the responsibility of the courts, media, and authorities in addressing such violence.

In this chapter I present some cases of honour killings in Sweden and analyse how the courts have chosen to interpret and handle the cases, and then I examine in what ways the media has covered these cases. I finally discuss what lessons can be drawn based on my research and from the perspective of a women's NGO operating at the grassroots level.

THE LEGAL SPHERE: THE COURTS

The role of the courts is not only to interpret and apply the law but also to interpret and understand the crime in order to come to a judgment. A judgment signals what is—and is not—accepted to society and to a certain extent it also sets the tone for the debate that follows the crime.

Much development has taken place over the past ten years in the legal arena specifically in the judgments of cases involving 'honour killings'. However, on a closer examination of the cases one finds that the courts' understanding of such cases are unclear and the judgments are rather inconsistent. One could question whether the judgments are contributing to a reaffirmation of a certain level of particularization which is taking place in the public debate.

Swedish law, unlike the English legal system for instance, provides no specific place for pleading one's cultural background as a defence to a criminal charge. Yet, in the first reported case of an 'honour killing' which occurred in 1994, the question of whether cultural background may serve as a basis for reducing the severity of the charge and punishment was raised before the Swedish courts. In this case the defence presented by the father, a Christian Palestinian who claimed to have killed his daughter because of 'Arab culture', was accepted by the court as an excuse for reducing his punishment. As Eldén argues, by accepting the father's reasoning, culture was not only given a static definition but the courts also homogenized 'All of Arab Society'. Moreover, the court explicitly accepted the father's interpretation of the 'necessity' of the killing as a point of departure for its argumentation, making the woman's life as insignificant as it had been to the father (Eldén 1998). The proceedings of the courts state:

> during the legal proceedings it has become clear that the Arab culture to which (the father) belongs has significantly governed his acts.... Arab women's low status in society, compared to women's status in Swedish society, has also been clearly shown. (Eldén 1998)[1]

Although this case was appealed and the father was finally charged with murder, the initial judgement set the tone for future debates on 'honour killings.' The debates focused mainly on cultural and religious aspects of male intimate violence in immigrant families, continuing to give both 'immigrants' and 'their culture' a negative and generalized understanding.

Following the above-mentioned case, there have been more than ten reported cases of honour killings in Sweden; all of them have involved immigrants from Muslim communities.

In 1996, a sixteen-year-old Kurdish boy stabbed his seventeen-year-old sister to death. In court, he argued that the sister's behaviour had brought shame to the family, and that she had provoked his action by being disrespectful. The crime was judged as murder. In this case, the court departed from its previous stance by shifting the blame onto the boy's family (in this case, a single mother), as compared to simply his culture, although reference to culture was made. The court stated: 'the boy has infuriated himself with her [the sister's] lifestyle and dressing which is especially provoking according to their cultural and Muslim background'.[2] Although the cultural relevance in this crime is

---

1 Umeå tingsrätt. Dom 1998-05-07 b 350/98 (author's translation).
2 Eskilstuna tingsrätt. Dom 1996-10-28, Case no. B 1835-96 (author's translation).

expressly pointed out, ultimately there is no utilization of the cultural defence plea by the courts.

In 1997, the Swedish courts judged two further cases. The first of these was the high-profile 'Sara case', in which a fifteen-year-old girl of Iraqi background was strangled to death by her sixteen-year-old brother and seventeen-year-old cousin. The boys were sentenced to 2 and a half years and 4 years respectively. What was noteworthy in this case, although never brought out in the Swedish public debate, was that reference was made (although not by way of precedent) to another case, namely, the 1996 'Klippan case'. In this case, a sixteen-year-old boy, who was an activist in a neo-Nazi organization, motivated by racial hatred, had stabbed Gerard Gbeyo to death, but was sentenced to rehabilitation. When referring to this case, the court stated: 'The question before the court in this case was similar to that of the Klippan case, [and that was the choice] between a carefully regulated prison sentence or treatment of the young criminal.' It went on to state that 'as it was a district court, it could not refer to the Klippan case, and although treatment was the best option for these boys... from society's perspective, imprisonment would be the appropriate sentence for the crime the boys had made themselves guilty of.'

From the point of view of 'the law', a number of inconsistencies are apparent. First, there are clearly different facts in the 'Sarah case' (1996) and the 'Klippan case' (1996). Since there are fundamentally different motives in the two cases, such a parallel should not have been made. Even where it has been made, the court should have explained why it felt it to be necessary to raise the 'Klippan case' as well as clearly stating that it could not bind itself to its outcome. If it cannot apply the rule of precedent under Swedish law then what was the legal relevance of mentioning the 'Klippan case' in the first instance? Especially since according to the principles of Swedish law each case should be assessed *individually*, even where there is a legitimate precedent.

The third case, the 'Malmö case' (1997), involved a twenty-seven-year-old Lebanese man who murdered his twenty-one-year-old ex-wife. The main facts that appeared in the court were that the couple had an unstable marriage, and after the birth of their daughter (3 years old at the time of the crime) they had a divorce. As a result, there was an ongoing court dispute between them over the daughter's custody and according to the defendant, his ex-wife had falsely accused him of incestuous behaviour towards their daughter and was on this basis alleging that his petition for custody should be rejected by the law. Other relevant facts included evidence that the husband had problems with both alcohol and drug abuse.

The defendant claimed that his ex-wife's false accusations of him together with her not letting him see their daughter was becoming an unbearable problem in his life and that the only way he saw to deal with this problem was to kill her. He consequently pleaded for the crime to be judged as manslaughter, although the exact reasons for his plea are not outlined in the judgement. The court sentenced the defendant to life imprisonment. Although no mention of the honour/shame complex is made by either the court or the defendant in the judgement, it is relevant because it has still been viewed as such in the Swedish media debate. This particular case generated a whole article series on women's situation in the Middle East, and in reference to this case a head representative from a Muslim mosque was interviewed and references to the Qur'an were directly made, linked to the actions of the perpetrators. What was not pointed out was that the perpetrator himself officially made a statement that the killing had no relation to Islam, which interestingly enough, he did not even formally practice.

By year 2000 we see a trend wherein the Swedish courts have evolved the law to assert the message to society that honour-related violence or 'honour killings' will *not* be tolerated. This is best exemplified in the murder of a twenty-one-year-old girl named Pela Atroshi of Kurdish–Iraqi origin.

What is unique about this case, making it unlike the other cases, is that the actual crime took place in Iraq. However, according to the Swedish courts, the fact that the killing could have been potentially planned on Swedish soil was reason enough to retry the case and re-punish the offenders in Sweden.

According to paragraph 5A of the Swedish Penal Code, a person who has been tried and/or sentenced in the jurisdiction of another state cannot be tried for the same crime again in Sweden. However, in this case the Swedish courts decided that they *did* have jurisdiction, and re-opened the case on the basis of Ordinance (1993: 1467 of the Penal Code), which gave the persecutor general authorization to instigate proceedings in exceptional cases.

It does not seem that the crime committed falls under any of these subsections. The court exerted their jurisdiction and tried it irregardless. In doing so, they stretched the limits of their own law by emphasizing the fact that the murder had initially been planned on Swedish soil and thereby proved their dedication and commitment to curb such violence in the future.

It is evident that there has been a gradual exclusion of the concept of culture in outlining the distinction between murder and manslaughter, which is a major departure from the earlier approach utilizing the cultural defence as used by the court in 1994. This is a significant step forward as it is vital that effective penal sanctions are available for offenders, and that all cases of honour killings must be registered, investigated, and prosecuted effectively and properly. Despite the positive outcome of the cases discussed, certain inconsistencies are apparent. Would the court have attempted to stretch the laws in the same way if the perpetrator was of French or of American origin? It seems as if the courts are continuing to culturally stereotype the crimes as they did in the case in 1990s. This cultural stereotyping is reflected in the court of public opinion's coverage of honour killings—the media.

THE COURT OF PUBLIC OPINION: THE MEDIA

No doubt, the media has an influential and powerful role in society. The media to some extent is the court of public opinion and in media, the limits between 'good' and 'bad', 'us' and 'them', 'acceptable' and 'not acceptable', are established, challenged and at times even changed. In other words, media in certain respects sets the agenda for society and contributes to shaping a national identity. The media's coverage in reference to the debate on honour killings may also be an underlying factor for the authorities and their work, and the media also chooses the different voices in the debate.

The first failure of the media, according to the research that I have come across and in my own research, is in representation. As basic as this may seem, we will always hear about the only white cat that showed up to a party where there were 1,000 black cats. The media has generally omitted all the other girls of Middle Eastern origin who are not threatened and who do not live in a situation where they have to face violence, threats, or control from male relatives. The situation is presented as an 'either'–'or' scenario, of young women of Middle Eastern or Muslim origin as oppressed, threatened and subjected to violence. This type of coverage can further encourage misunderstanding and create a distorted image of 'Muslims' and encourage racism.[3]

This criticism is supported by media researchers at the *Quickresponse* (Red Cross) and by research conducted at Gothenburg University's Peace and Conflict department. The research maintains that the media chooses to portray immigrant women and girls primarily as victims and that this pattern has increased after the honour killings of Kurdish girls in Sweden; the media has chosen to act 'on behalf' of the immigrant women subjected to male intimate violence. There seems to be no intention to widen the horizons and give a more holistic picture.

The majority of the media coverage that has focused on patriarchal violence is generally lacking attention to all the other kinds of

---

3 Interview with anthropologist and media researcher Cecilia Englund, Expo Foundation, Stockholm, May, 2003.

violence girls can be subjected to irregardless of ethnic origin; the focus has only been 'honour killings', thereby creating a new and specific murder category and, by doing so, implying it should be viewed differently from other murders or other forms of violence against women.[4]

To a certain extent, it can be argued that this is a self-generating system wherein the participants in the debate are acting according to a set agenda on how immigrants should be discussed in Swedish society, one that maintains a black and white picture of 'us' and 'them' or 'us' versus 'them'. This may not be intended to be spiteful, rather, the contrary: It is to help people integrate into Swedish society. At the same time two typecast models are being formed—one idealizing the strongly educated immigrant who is aspiring to become Swedish, as opposed to the 'Muslim' girl who is not conforming and which situation is a problem. This whole debate also highlights the dilemma of conditional integration which in reality is experienced by minorities as forced assimilation.

At the same time it should be noted that the media response is significant in the sense that this is the first time that an issue which has not gained much attention has suddenly become a political question. In this respect it is important that the media does not sensationalize cases of honour killings and are careful in their coverage in order to avoid risking a backlash from different communities which need to be involved in the debate.

Although the debate on honour killings has significantly evolved in Sweden since the first case in 1994, it continues to be based on the assumption that 'honour killings' are symptomatic of a certain culture, and in particular a monolithic Muslim culture. It is ignorant to make the assumption that one billion of the world's population is a homogenous entity, undermining its cultural, linguistic, historic, and geographical diversity. It is also important to mention that the notion

---

[4] Interview with anthropologist and media researcher Cecilia Englund, Expo Foundation, Stockholm, May, 2003.

of an honour code is by no means specific to Islam or Muslim societies. In efforts to combat honour-related violence it is also important to clarify that Islam does not condone 'honour killings'; making this clarification is important in order to obtain the political support of ordinary Muslims and to mobilize them against the practice. This system is still deeply entrenched in most Christian Mediterranean societies, and is sadly described as an important factor in the subordination of women throughout the region. Research indicates that honour as a rationale for violence against women, including their murder, can be found in societies globally, namely, among Latin American and Mediterranean peasant societies, among nomadic people in the Middle East, South Asia, and among the various Indian castes and Chinese elites. Communities and individuals having distance from formal religiosity may also continue to practise the 'honour code'.

CONCLUSION

Honour killings and honour-related violence in Sweden have often been addressed within the integration agenda and seen as a different and worse form of violence against women. This is problematic for a number of reasons. This approach stigmatizes the immigrant family unit as well as the immigrant girls, and contributes to racism. It further polarizes 'us' and 'them', providing a simplified presentation of violence against women as an issue solely of the 'other'. As a Youth Programme Manager, my focus is on preventing abuse, empowering young girls, and educating society. The implication of the 'us' versus 'them' polarization is grave! Here the immigrant adolescent girl is faced with a double-edged sword. So, you see that this is a sensitive issue requiring a delicate balance that needs to be walked very carefully. If the answer is that a girl should repudiate the cohesion of her minority culture to become Swedish and liberated—then how does one help her maintain her particular identity and dignity? Many young girls may be critical of many aspects of their culture, but this does not necessarily imply that they want to abandon or deny their origin.

The unfortunate truth is that violence against women is a social reality in Sweden. Research shows that sixteen Swedish women are murdered yearly by their Swedish male partners in intimate violence (Lundgren 2001b). Addressing honour-related violence as a matter of integration also has implications for how immigration laws are applied which in turn can be discriminatory towards women—also for those women facing gender-based persecution and honour killings. Violence against women exists in all societies and cultures although it has different manifestations. It is not a matter of different categories but a matter of degree. Passion, honour, and alcohol use are some of the defences that men use to excuse their violence.

Female genital mutilation, dowry burnings, prostitution, rape and pornography, honour killings, crimes of passion, forced marriage—why does it happen? Why are women victims? How does one measure murder or suffering?

From the perspective of our work it also important to realize that each woman and girl has a unique story behind her and there are a number of factors involved in each case. It is therefore necessary to see each woman's situation without getting stuck in stereotypes. There are no silver bullet answers to honour killings or honour-related violence. By focusing only on honour killings, other form of violence and control against women are not highlighted. We have also come across girls who have not been taken seriously by the authorities because they do not fit into a certain category or stereotype. Giving cultural, ethnic, or religious explanations to such crimes gives a simplistic view of a complex reality and causes misinterpretations (de los Reyes 2003).

It is also significant to point out that situating this form of violence into a larger perspective of violence against women does *not* necessarily discount the severity of 'honour crimes' and the acute need for attention to and intervention in such violence. It does not mean that one is blind to the mechanism of such violence but rather that one is more aware of the structural nature of such harsh forms of violence against women. Therefore, in order to find appropriate interventions and to get to the bottom of the problem the debate must move away from particularizing the problem as 'theirs' versus 'ours'.

Terrafem, a support network for immigrant women, believes that it is important to adapt strategies and to provide support, recognizing the different dimensions of women's vulnerability and her different needs. We strongly advocate that honour-related violence be addressed within the sexual equality agenda and not the integration agenda.

Terrafem believes it is important to adapt strategies and support to the different dimensions of women's vulnerability and her different needs. We strongly advocate for honour-related violence to be addressed within the Sexual Equality Agenda and not the integration agenda.

In Sweden it seems that there continues to be a lack of coherence in the interpretation of honour crimes and the strategies that are employed to tackle such violence. There are obvious inconsistencies in the court's understanding of such crimes and, coupled with media's biased coverage, a simplistic image of the situation is portrayed. Voices in the debate have also not come to a consensus on how to conceptualize and contextualize 'honour crimes'. This scenario is not necessarily benefiting girls at risk or in need of acute help. Since the role of both courts and the media is extremely important in shaping our understanding of such violence, it is important that both spheres acknowledge and then challenge their prejudices. Journalists must strive to portray a more holistic and balanced view of violence against women and courts need to be more careful and informed in their argumentation. We need to utilize the research that is available, nationally and internationally, and provide more tools, knowledge, and education to actors in different levels of society.

It is important to realize, as An'aim states, that: 'in seeking to eliminate discrimination on grounds of sex, discrimination on grounds of race, religion, language or ethnic origin should not be encouraged' (Abdullahi 1999). Although a diversity of views is a sign of a healthy system, finding solutions to a level of conflict is not always fruitful. In reference to addressing honour crimes, it is important to have a certain level of institutional and intellectual coherence. Unless there is a common understanding of gender inequality and an awareness of racial inequality, and a common vision among authorities, institutions, organizations, and schools, we cannot get to the bottom of the problem.

At the same time it is important to state that there are many voices of contestation within minority communities and they should be heard. It is also positive that women from minority communities are organizing themselves to combat honour crimes and other forms of violence against women. It is a positive development that the media is bringing the question of honour crimes out into the open, and it is positive that judges are making judgements in favour of women. Another positive development is that both our former and current Minister of Equality have shown dedication in addressing and finding strategies to curb violence against women and violence in the name of honour. Sweden is attempting to change things, but we need to dig deeper and to be more persistent.

SECTION 4

Appendices

Recommended Resources on Women and Violence
COMPILED BY SHAHRZAD MOJAB

This resource list is organized into three sections: women and violence; theoretical debates; and reports.

WOMEN AND VIOLENCE

Abul-Husn, Randa (1994), 'Battered Women in Lebanon: Reports from Newspapers, November 1993–March 1994.' *Al-Raida* (Institute for Women's Studies in the Arab World. Beirut University College) 11(65–66).

Asmiry, Arwa (1994), 'Domestic Violence Against Women in Jordan.' *Al-Raida* (Institute for Women's Studies in the Arab World. Beirut University College) 11(65–66).

Accad, Evelyne (1994), 'Gender and Violence in Lebanon and Yugoslavia.' *Al-Raida* (Institute for Women's Studies in the Arab World. Beirut University College) 11(65–66).

Bannerji, Himani (1999), 'A Question of Silence: Reflections on Violence Against Women in Communities of Colour.' In E. Dua and A. Robertson (eds.), *Scratching the Surface: Canadian Anti-Racist Feminist Thought*. Toronto: Women's Press.

Bu Melhem, Eva (1994), 'Are Battered Women Hospitalized?' *Al-Raida* (Institute for Women's Studies in the Arab World. Beirut University College) 11(65–66).

Committee on Equal Opportunities for Women and Men (2002), 'Crimes of Honour.' Parliamentary Assembly: Council of Europe.

Canadian Council on Social Development (N.d.), 'Nowhere to Turn? Responding to Partner Violence Against Immigrant and Visible Minority Women: Voices of Frontline Workers.' Ottawa: Department of Justice, Sectoral Involvement in Departmental Policy Development.

Dasgupta, Shamita Das (1998), 'Women's Realities: Defining Violence Against Women by Immigration, Race, and Class.' In R.K. Bergen (ed.), *Issues in Intimate Violence*. Thousand Oaks, Calif.: Sage.

Ergün, Ayfer (2002), 'Against My Will.' VHS, 50 min. New York: First Run/Icarus Films.

Flynn, Clifton P. (2000), 'Woman's Best Friend: Pet Abuse and the Role of the Companion Animals in the Lives of Battered Women.' *Violence Against Women* 6(2).

Gupta, Jayoti (1990), 'Class Relations, Family Structure and Bondage of Women.' In L. Dube and R. Palriwala (eds.), *Structures and Strategies, Women Work and Family*. New Delhi: Sage.

Kurdish Human Rights Project (2003), *Turkey's Shame: Sexual Violence Without Redress—The Plight of Kurdish Women*. Trial Observation Report. N.p.

Kurz, Demie (1998), 'Old Problems and New Directions in the Study of Violence Against Women.' In R.K. Bergen (ed.), *Issues in Intimate Violence*. Thousand Oaks, Calif.: Sage Publications.

Newman, Elana (1999), 'Ethical Issues in Teaching About Violence Against Women.' *Women's Studies Quarterly* 1 and 2.

Nordstrum, Carolyn, and Antonius Robben (1995), 'The Anthropology and Ethnography of Violence and Sociopolitical Conflict.' In C. Nordstrum and A. Robben (eds.), *Fieldwork Under Fire: Contemporary Studies of Violence and Survival*. Berkeley:

University of California Press.

Ontario Association of Interval and Transition Houses (1996), 'Home Truth: Exposing the False Face of Equality and Security Rights for Abused Women in Canada.' Submission to the UN Special Rapporteur on Violence Against Women.

Rudd, Jane (2001), 'Dowry-Murder: An Example of Violence Against Women.' *Women's International Forum* 24(5).

Shell-Duncan, Bettina, and Ylva Hernlund (2000), 'Female "Circumcision" in Africa: Dimensions of the Practices and Debates.' In B. Shell-Duncan and Y. Hurnland (eds), *Female 'Circumcision' in Africa: Culture, Controversy, and Change*. Boulder, Col.: Lynne Reinner.

Youngs, Gillian (2003), 'Private Pain/Public Peace: Women's Rights as Human Rights and Amnesty International's Report on Violence against Women.' *Signs: Journal of Women in Culture and Society* 28(4).

Zaman, Habiba (1999), 'Violence Against Women in Bangladesh: Issues and Responses.' *Women's Studies International Forum* 22(1).

THEORETICAL DEBATES

Agnes, Flavia (1995), *State, Gender and the Rhetoric of Law Reform*. Bombay: Research Centre for Women's Studies, S.N.D.T. Women's University.

Andersson, Annika (2003), *Honor Killings: The Survival of Patriarchy in Different Societies*. Lund: University of Lund.

Clark, Kate (1995), 'The Right to Know: Human Rights and Access to Reproductive Rights Information.' *Women Against Fundamentalisms* 7(47).

Enloe, Cynthia (2000), 'Masculinity as Foreign Policy Issue.' *Foreign Policy in Focus* 5(36).

Feldman, Rayah (1995), 'Reply to Gayatri Chakravorty Spivak.' *Women Against Fundamentalisms* 7(47).

Hoffman, John (2001), *Gender and Soverignty: Feminism, the State and International Relations*. London: Palgrave MacMillan.
Molyneux, Maxine (1985), 'Legal Reform and Socialist Revolution in Democratic Yemen: Women and the Family.' *International Journal of the Sociology of Law* 13.
Peristiany, J.G. (ed.) (1966), *Honour and Shame: The Values of Mediterranean Society*. Chicago: University of Chicago Press.
Sangari, Kumkum, and Sudesh Vaid (1985), 'Sati in Modern India: A Report.' In K. Sangari and S. Vaid (eds.), *Women and Culture*. Mumbai: Research Centre for Women's Studies.
Shamiry, Naguib (1984), 'The Judicial System in Democratic Yemen.' In B.R. Pridham (ed.), *Contemporary Yemen: Politics and Historical Background*. London: Croom Helm.
Simsek, Sefa (2000–1), 'The Disembedded Custom: Intrafamily Murders for Sexual Honor in Turkish Metropolises.' *U.U. Fen-Edebiyat Fakultesi Sosyal Bilimler Dergisi* 2.
Spivak, Gayatri Chakravorty (1995), 'Public Hearing on Crimes Against Women.' *Women Against Fundamentalisms* 7(47).

REPORTS

Centre of Islamic and Middle Eastern Law, School of Oriental and African Studies. International Centre for the Legal Protection of Human Rights (2002), 'Initiatives to Address "Crimes of Honour."' London.
— (2003), 'Selected International Human Rights Materials Addressing "Crimes of Honour."' London.
Refugee Women's Resource Project: Asylum Aid (2002), *Refugee Women and Domestic Violence: Country Studies*. London.
The Independent Organization of Women in Sulaymaniya (2000), *Honor Killing: Catalogue of Horror in Iraq*. KurdishMedia.

Programme for the Seminar on Violence in the Name of Honour
4–6 December 2003

organized in co-operation with KA-MER, KAYA
Bilgi University and the Swedish Institute
at the Consulate General of Sweden/Swedish Research Institute
İstiklal Caddesi 497 (Tünel), Beyoğlu İstanbul

Thursday, 4 December
17.00 'Against My Will', a documentary film about women in a crisis centre in Pakistan, by Ayfer Ergün (50 min.): At the Consulate General of Sweden/Swedish Research Institute.
18.30 – 20.00 Welcome Reception hosted by the Consul General Mr Ingmar Karlsson and Mrs Margareta Karlsson at the Palais de Suède (Consulate General of Sweden).

Friday, 5 December
Introduction
Moderator: Christina Curry (U.K.)
09.30 Nebahat Akkoç (Turkey)
Namus' adına işlenen cinayetlerin kültürel dayanakları (The Cultural Base of Violence in the Name of Honour).
10.00 Dilsa Demirbag-Sten (Sweden)
Gendering Multiculturalism. The growing ethnic diversity in Swedish society has also brought growing challenges, particularly with regard to equal opportunities and human rights of women.
10.30 Lise Bergh (Sweden)
Government Initiatives to Help Young People at Risk of Honour Related Violence.

What is crime committed in the name of honour? Does the concept change with geographical, ethnic, socio-economic variables? If so, how does it change? What are the basic characteristics of these crimes in each specific context? Participants are invited to describe and discuss the basics of the issue.
The Role of Society. What is honour? What is shame? The issue of tradition, culture, gender, class. Anthropological and sociological background.

11.30	Nükhet Sirman (Turkey)
	Kinship, Politics and Love: The Social Structuring of Body and Emotions.
12.00	Nahla Abdo (Canada)
	Family, Traditional Culture and State: Understanding Violence Against Palestinian Women in Israel.
Moderator:	Yakın Ertürk (Turkey)
14.00	Shahrzad Mojab (Canada)
	The Particularity of 'Honour' and the Universality of 'Killing': From Early Warning Signs to Feminist Pedagogy.
14.30	Leylâ Pervizat (Turkey)
	A Research on Extra Judicial Executions: Honour Killings in Turkey.
15.30	Nicole Pope (Turkey)
	Honour Killings: Instruments of Patriarchal Control.
16.00	Åsa Eldén (Sweden)
	Life-and-Death Honour: Young Women's Violent Stories About Reputation, Virginity and Honour—In a Swedish Context.
16.30	Melek Taylan (Turkey) and Ulla Lemberg (Sweden)
	Presentation of a documentary currently being made in south-eastern Anatolia.

Saturday, 6 December
The Turkish Experience

Moderator:	Turgut Tarhanlı (Turkey)
09.30	Aytekin Sır (Turkey)
	Güneydoğu Anadolu'da Kadın İntiharları ve Namus Cinayetleri (Honour Killings and Women Suicides in the South-Eastern Region of Turkey).
10.00	Adem Sözüer (Turkey)
	(Turkey's legislation on honour crimes.)

The Swedish Experience

Moderator:	Åsa Eldén (Sweden)
11.00	Kickis Åhré Älgamo (Sweden)
	Survey of Honour-Related Crime in Sweden and How It is Tackled by the Swedish Police.
11.30	Javeria Rizvi (Sweden)
	Violence in the Name of Honour in Swedish Society: Lessons Learnt from the Swedish Experience.
13.30	Riyad Al-Baldawi (Sweden)
	Multidimensional and Long-Term Measures to Prevent the Violence in the Name of Honour Within the Family.
14.00	Niklas Kelemen (Sweden)
	Male Dreams of Female Chastity. Honour Crimes in 'The Dictatorship of Women'. Discussions with fathers about boy's education and gender inequalities. The Dialogue Project—Save the Children.

International and national efforts to combat honour-related crimes. What are the obstacles and challenges to recognizing crimes committed in the name of honour as a human rights violation for women? Are there any specific documents at the United Nations? If so, how can these documents be used locally and internationally?

Moderator:	Nükhet Sirman (Turkey)
15.00	Yakın Ertürk (Turkey)
	Violence Against Women Within the Context of International Regimes.
15.30	Christine Curry (U.K.)
	'Acting with Honour'. What is the State's Responsibility for Violence in the Family?
16.00	**Conclusion**

Bibliography

Abdo, Nahla (1987), *Family, Women and Social Change in the Middle East: The Palestinian Case*. Toronto: Canadian Scholars' Press.
— (1997), 'Muslim Family Law: Articulation Gender, Class and the State.' *International Review of Comparative Public Policy 9*.
— (2005), *Sexuality, Citizenship and the Nation State: Experiences of Palestinian Women*. New York: Syracuse University Press [forthcoming].
Abdo, Nahla and Ronit Lentin (eds.) (2002), *Women and the Politics of Military Confrontation: Palestinian and Israeli Gendered Narratives of Dislocation*. Oxford and New York: Berghahn.
Abdo, Nahla and Nira Yuval-Davis (1995), 'Palestine Israel and the Zionist Settler Project.' In D. Stasiulis and N. Yuval-Davis (eds.), *Unsettling Settler Societies*. London: Sage.
Abdullahi, An Na'im (1999), 'Promises We Should All Keep in Common Cause.' In S.M. Okin (ed.), *Is Multiculturalism Bad for Women?*. Princeton: Princeton University Press.
Abu-Lughod, Lila (1986), *Veiled Sentiments: Honor and Poetry in a Bedouin Society*. Los Angeles: University of California Press.
Al-Haj, Majid (2004), *Ethnic Formation in a Deeply Divided Society: The Case of the 1990s Immigrants from the Former Soviet Union in Israel*. New York: Brill.
Bannerji, Himani (2000), *The Dark Side of the Nation: Essays on Multiculturalism, Nationalism and Gender*. Toronto: Canadian Scholars' Press.
Barnard, Alan (2000), *History and Theory in Anthropology*. Cambridge: Cambridge University Press.
Bourdieu, Pierre (2001), *Masculine Domination*. Cambridge: Polity.
Bustanî, Tavge 'Ebas (2003), 'Xo sûtandinî afret le herêmî Kurdistan' [Self-immolation of Women in the Kurdistan Region]. *Govarî Shaushka 7*.
Castoriadis, Cornelius (1987), *The Imaginary Institution of Society*. Trans. Kathleen Blamey. Cambridge, Mass.: MIT Press.
Dahan-Kalev, Henriette (2003), 'The Gender Blindness of Good Theorists: An Israeli Case Study.' *Journal of International Women's Studies* (Special issue: 'Harvesting Our Strengths: Third Wave Feminism and Women's Studies') 4(3).
Delaney, Carol (1987), 'Seeds of Honour, Fields of Shame.' In David D Gilmore (ed.), *Honour and Shame and the Unity of the Mediterranean*. Washington: American Anthropological Association.

de los Reyes, Paulina & Ireen Molina (2002), 'Kalla mörkret natt! Kön, klass och ras/etnicitet i det postkoloniala Sverige.' In Paulina de los Reyes, Ireen Molina, and Diana Mulinari (eds.), *Maktens (o)lika förklädnader Kön, klass och etnicitet i det postkoloniala Sverige*. Stockholm: Atlas.

Eldén, Åsa (1998), 'The Killing Seemed to be Necessary: Arab Cultural Affiliation as an Extenuating Circumstance in a Swedish Verdict.' *NORA* 2(6).

— (2003), *Heder på liv och död. Våldsamma berättelser om rykten, oskuld och heder*. Uppsala: Uppsala universitet.

Eldén, Åsa & Jenny Westerstrand (2004), Hederns försvarare. Den rättsliga hanteringen av ett hedersmord. *Kvinnovetenskaplig tidskrift* (in press) [Also published in Eldén 2003].

Emîn, Niyan Mi°emed (2002), 'Amarêkî sûtanî afretan û amajeyekî tirsnak' [Statistics on Women's Immolation and a Fearsome Indicator]. *Hawlatî* 93.

Geertz, Clifford (1973), *The Interpretation of Cultures*. New York: Basic Books.

Hall, Stuart (1996), 'When was the "Post-Colonial"? Thinking at the Limit.' In Ian Chambers and Lydia Curti (eds.), *The Post-Colonial Question: Common Skies, Divided Horizons*, 242–60. London: Routledge.

Hegland, Mary Elaine (2001), Review of 'Crimes of Honour' and 'Our Honour and His Glory'. *Middle East Women's Study Review* 15(1–2).

Human Rights Watch (2003a), 'Climate of Fear: Sexual Violence and Abduction of Women and Girls in Baghdad.' *Human Rights Watch* 15(7).

— (2003b), 'Killing You Is a Very Easy Thing For Us: Human Rights Abuses in Southeast Afghanistan.' *Human Rights Watch* 15(5).

Joyce, Rosemary A. and Susan D. Gillespie (2000), 'Beyond Kinship. An Introduction.' In Rosemary A. Joyce and Susan D. Gillespie (eds.), *Beyond Kinship. Social and Material Reproduction in House Societies*, 1–21. Philadelphia: University of Pennsylvania Press.

Kretzmer, David (1990), *The Legal Status of the Arabs in Israel*. Boulder, Colo.: Westview.

Langer, Felitzia (1978), *In My Own Eyes: Israel and the Occupied Territories, 1967–1973*. London: Ithaca.

Lavie, Smadar (2002), 'Academic Apartheid in Israel and the Lilly White Feminism of the Upper Middle Class' [copy of an e-mail article].

Lentin, Ronit (2002), 'Writing Dislocation, Writing the Self: Bringing (Back) the Politics into Gendered Israeli-Palestinian Dialoguing.' In N. Abdo and R. Lentin (eds.), *Women and the Politics of Military Confrontation*. New York and Oxford: Berghahm.

Levene, Mark (1998), 'Creating a Modern "Zone of Genocide": The Impact of Nation- and State-Formation on Eastern Anatolia, 1878–1923.' *Holocaust and Genocide Studies* 12(3).

Lévi-Strauss, Claude (1982), *The Way of the Masks.* Trans. S. Modelski. Seattle: University of Washington Press.
Lindisfarne, Nancy (1994), 'Variant Masculinities, Variant Virginities: Rethinking "Honour and Shame."' In Andrea Cornwall and Nancy Lindisfarne (eds.), *Dislocating Masculinitiy: Comparative Ethnographies*, 82–96. London: Routledge.
Lundgren, Eva (2001a), *Ekte kvinne? Identitet på kryss og tvers.* Oslo: Pax forlag.
— (2001b), *Slagen Dam—Mäns våld mot kvinnor i jämställda Sverige.* Stockholm: Fritzes Offentliga.
Lundgren, Eva, et al. (2002), *Captured Queen: Men's Violence Against Women in Gender Equal Sweden.* Stockholm: Fritzes förlag.
Lundgren, Eva and Jenny Westerstrand (2002), 'Fadime, partiarkatet och våldet.' In *Itkua ikä kaikki.* Festskrift till Aino Nenola. Helsinki: Soumalaisen Kirjallisuuden Seura.
Marshall, Mark (1995), 'Rethinking the Palestine Question: The Apartheid Paradigm.' *Journal of Palestine Studies* 35(1).
Mellberg, Nea (2002), När det overkliga blir verklighet. Mödrars situation när deras barn utsätts för sexuella övergrepp av fäder. Umeå: Boréa förlag.
Mernissi, Fatima (1985), *Beyond the Veil: Male-Female Dynamics in Modern Muslim Society.* 2d ed. London: al-Saqi Books.
— (1991), *Women and Islam.* Oxford: Basil Blackwell.
Ministry of Women's Affairs (2004), 'Women Facing the Wall.' VHS, 35 min. Ramallah: Ministry of Women's Affairs.
Mojab, Shahrzad (1998), '"Muslim" Women and "Western" Feminists: The Debate on Particulars and Universals.' *Monthly Review* 50(7).
— (2000), "Honor Killing: Culture, Politics and Theory." *Middle East Women's Studies Review*, 18(1–2).
— (2004), 'No "Safe Haven" for Women: Violence Against Women in Iraqi Kurdistan.' In W. Giles and J. Hyndman (eds.), *Sites of Violence: Gender and Identity in Conflict Zones.* Berkeley: University of California Press.
Mojab, Shahrzad and Amir Hassanpour (2000a), 'The Politics and Culture of "Honour Killing": The Murder of Fadime Şahindal.' *Pakistan Journal of Women's Studies: Alam-e-Niswan* 9(1).
— (2000b), 'Thoughts on the Struggle Against "Honour Killing."' *The International Journal of Kurdish Studies* 16(1–2).
Motzafi-Haller, Pnina (1997), 'Writing Birthright': On Native Anthropologists and the Politics of Representation.' In D. Reed-Danahay (ed.), *Autoethnography: Rewriting the Self and the Social.* Oxford: Berg.
Muhittin, Nezihe (1931), *Türk Kadını.* İstanbul: Numune Matbaası.
Nakhleh, Khalil (1977), 'Anthropological and Sociological Studies of the Arabs in Israel: A Critique.' *Journal of Palestine Studies* 6(4).

Okin, Susan Moller (ed.) (1999), *Is Multiculturalism Bad for Women?* Princeton: Princeton University Press.
Ortaylı, İlber (1985), 'The Family in Ottoman Society.' In Türköz Erder (ed.), *Family in Turkish Society*, 93–104. Ankara: Turkish Social Science Association and Maya Press.
Pappé, Ilan (1994), *The Making of the Arab–Israeli Conflict 1947–51*. London: I.B. Taurus.
Peirce, Leslie Penn (1993), *The Imperial Harem: Women and Sovereignty in the Ottoman Empire*. Oxford: Oxford University Press.
Russell, Diana and Roberta Harmes (2001), *Femicide in Global Perspective*. Athenes Series Paper 57. New York: Teachers College Press.
Saadawi, Nawal (1980), *The Hidden Face of Eve*. London: Zed Books.
— (1997), *The Nawal Sadawi Reader*. London: Zed Books.
Sabbah, A. Fatina (1984), *Woman in the Muslim Unconscious*. New York: Pergamon.
Said, Edward (1979), *Orientalism*. New York: Vintage.
Shah, Nafisa (1998), *A Story in Black: Karo Kari Killings in Upper Sindh*. Reuters Foundation Paper, 100. Green College Oxford.
Shalhoub-Kevorkian, Nadera (2002), 'Femicide and the Palestinian Criminal Justice System: Seeds of Change in the Context of State Building.' *Law and Society Review* 36(3).
Sharoni, Simona (1993), 'Middle East Politics Through Feminist Lenses: Toward Theorizing International Relations from Women's Struggles.' *Alternatives* 18.
— (1994), 'Homefront as Battlefield: Gender, Military Occupation and Violence Against Women.' In T. Mayer (ed.), *Women and the Israeli Occupation: The Politics of Change*. London: Routledge.
Shelley, Saywell (1999), *Crimes of Honour*. VHS, 44 min. Produced by Bishari Films in association with the Canadian Broadcasting Company. New York: First Run/Icarus Films.
Shiran, Vickey (1991), 'Feminist Identity vs Oriental Identity.' In B. Swirski and M.P. Safir (eds.), *Calling the Equality Bluff: Women in Israel*. Pergamon.
Shohat, Ella (1988), 'Sephardim in Israel: Zionism from the Standpoint of Its Jewish Victims.' Social Text 19–20.
— (1996), 'Mizrahi Feminism: The Politics of Gender, Race and Multiculturalism.' *News From Within*. April.
— (2002), 'A Reluctant Eulogy: Fragments from the Memories of an Arab-Jew.' In N. Abdo and R. Lentin (eds.), *Women and the Politics of Military Confrontation*. London and New York: Berghahn.
Shohat, Ella and Robert Stam (1994), *Unthinking Eurocentrism: Multiculturalism and the Media*. New York and London: Routledge.

Shukri, Mohammad (1996), *al-Khubz el-Haafi*. London: Dar el-Saqi.
— (1998), *Jean Jeane fi Tanja; Tenissy Williams Fi Tanja*. Köln: Al-Kamel Verlag
Sirman, Nükhet (2000a), 'Gender Construction and Nationalist Discourse: Dethroning the Father in the Early Turkish Novel.' In Feride Acar and Ayşe Güneş-Ayata (eds.), *Gender and Identity Construction: Women of Central Asia, the Caucasus and Turkey*, 162–76. Leiden: Brill.
— (2000b), 'Writing the Usual Love Story: The Fashioning of Conjugal and National Subjects in Turkey.' In V.A. Goddard (ed.), *Gender, Agency and Change*, 250–72. London: Routledge.
Svalastog, Anna-Lydia (1998), Det var ikke meningen... Om konstruktionen av kjönn ved abortinngrep, et feministteoretisk bidrag. Uppsala: Teologiska institutionen, Uppsala universitet.
United Nations (2000), *From Beijing to Beijing + 5: Review and Appraisal of the Implementation of the Beijing Platform for Action*. New York: United Nations.
United Nations (N.d.), *United Nations and the Advancement of Women, 1945–1996*. New York: UN Department of Public Information.
Yasin, Bu-Ali (1996), *al-Thalouth al Muharram: Dirasa fil-Din wal-Jins wal Sira' al-Tabaqi* [The Unholy Trinity: A Study in Religion, Sex, and Class Struggle]. 6th ed. Beirut: Dar al-Kunouz al-Adabiyyah.
Yuval-Davis, Nira (1980), 'The Bearers of the Collective: Women and Religious Legislation in Israel.' *Feminist Review* 4(15).
Zeidan, Said (1995), 'Political Party, Civil Society and Democracy.' In *The Crisis in the Palestinian Political Party: Procedures of the Conference of Mouatin* (Ramalla, 24-11-95).
Zihnioğlu, Yaprak (2003), *Kadınsız İnkilap Nezihe Muhiddin, Kadınlar Halk Fırkası, Kadın Birliği*. İstanbul: Metis Yayınları.

Index

Abdalla, Heshu 5, 17, 18-20, 21, 36
Abdalla, Yones 18
Abdo, Nahla 8
abduction 205
Abeer 61
abla 43
Abu-Lughod 45
Adana 121
adultery 16
Afghanistan 1, 5
Africa 1, 144
    North 6
    South 178
Africans 69
ağabey 43
AKADER 121
Akkoç, Nebahat 9, 131, 147
Al Baldawi, Riyadh 9
al-Fanar 71
Älgamo, Kickis Åhré 10
Allah 137
Allak, Şemse 9, 115-118, 138, 137, 140, 158
Amnesty International 1, 158, 178, 181, 183, 188-190
amour passion 48
An'aim 222
Anfal 30
Ankara 134
Annan, Kofi 162
antiracist 82
    resistance 77
Apartheid Wall 85
Arab Palestinian women 88
Arab
    cultural markers 77

culture 74, 78, 213
family 73, 74
feminist movement 84
feminists 86
Jews 73, 79
media 72
mentality 68
mind 75
society 214
women 88, 92
Arab world 85, 88, 89
Arab/Islamic world 86
Arab/Muslim world 83, 88
Arab/Muslim countries 85
Arab/Palestinian family 75
Arabs 32, 68, 73
Aral, Jülide 128
arranged accident 205
arranged marriages 51, 195
Ashkenazi 69, 73, 79, 81
    Jewish 67
    Jews 79
Asia 1, 144
    South 220
    Southeast 2
Assiwar 71
Atroshi, Pela 195, 205-208
attempted murder 205
attempted rape 75, 184
Australia 206
Awlad Ali Bedouins 45
Ayşe 17, 20, 21, 128-132, 134, 201

backwardness 68, 75
Badeel 71
Bangladesh 178

barbaric culture 29
battering 75
Baywatch 103
BBC 63
Bedouins 45
Beijing Platform for Action (PfA) 167, 169, 170, 171, 174, 193
Belgium 156
Berde-nusek 30
Bergh, Lise 10
Bingöl 123
birth control 87
Björn 158
Blacks 69
blood feud 132
bride price 138
bride/dowry killings 166
Britain 17, 21, 105, 106, 178
burning witches 57

Canada 2, 24, 28
canonical law 5
capital punishment 24, 27, 139
capitalism 35, 50
capitalist market 60
capitalist state 59
CAT 180
CEDAW 37, 167, 168, 172, 179, 181, 184-186
CEDAW Committee 171
CERD 179
chastity belt 57
child marriages 198
children's rights 159, 162
Chinese elites 220
CHR 168
Christian Mediterranean societies 220
CIS 66
citizenship education 24
civil courts 71

civil society 32
clitoridectomy 27
code of honour 39
colonial order 57
colonial racist policies 78
colonial state 8
colonialism 62, 82
colonization 40
Commission on Human Rights 172, 200
Committee of Ministers of the Council of Europe 184
communists 69
conditional integration 219
Consul-General of Sweden 11
Consulate General of Sweden 7, 11, 115
contraception 87
Control Arms campaign 189
Convention against Torture 181
Convention on the Rights of the Child 186
Council of Europe 178, 184
CRC 180
crime as a practice 26
Crimes of Honour 27, 171
crimes
   against humanity 172
   customary 8, 41
   honour 29, 40, 41, 58, 62, 82, 107, 149, 155-157, 161, 162, 166, 170-174, 221-223
   honour related 39, 71, 147, 161
   of passion 57, 104, 221
   sex 64
   war 172
criminality 143
CSW 168, 171
cultural difference 6, 52
cultural diversity 26

cultural relativism 6, 24-26, 28, 88, 89, 106
cultural relativists 35
cultural taboo 71
culturalist 67
culturalist approach 63
culturalists 34
culturalization 24
culture 24-26, 28, 33, 101
cultures of honour 146, 147
Curry, Christina 10

Dahok 205, 207, 208
Decade for the Advancement of Women 167
Declaration on the Elimination of Violence Against Women 168-70
Demirel, Kadriye 9, 115-119
Democratic Iraqi Association 153
Dialogue Project 157-62
difference 25, 26
discrimination 109, 143, 144, 170, 222
    against women 168, 173, 184
    hidden 80
    institutional 80
    open 80
discriminatory attitudes 182
discriminatory practices 106
divan 123
diversity 26, 147, 219
diversity of cultures 25
divide and rule 62, 72
divided femininity 92, 95, 96
divorce 75
Diyarbakır 113, 114, 117, 123, 124, 134, 138
Diyarbakır University 121
Dobson, Stephan 12
domestic violence 50, 102, 104, 152, 179

domination 26
dowry burnings 221
dowry deaths 57
Druze 72, 73

early warning (EW) 18
Eastern Block 66
Ebdul-Qadir, Luqman 17
Egypt 45, 83, 88
Egyptian peasants 45
Egyptians 45
Elazığ 117
Eldén, Åsa 8, 214
elder neglect 27
Emergency Regulations (Israel) 80
England 105
English legal system 213
Enlightenment 28, 35
Ensler, Eva 177
equality 102, 159, 197
Ertürk, Yakın 10, 200
Ethiopian Blood 68
Ethiopian Jews 68, 73
Ethiopians 66, 68, 69
ethnic diversity 143
ethnic groups 144, 145, 150, 152, 154, 156, 210
ethnic identity 123
ethnic minorities 144, 149, 155
ethnic origin 222
ethnicity 70, 78, 144
ethnocide 70
eugenics 25, 29
Euro-imperial adventure 40
Europe 15, 17, 29, 32, 50, 178
European Court of Human Rights 187
European Parliament 24, 125
European Union (EU) 2, 7, 24, 155, 156, 190
European-ness 68

exchange of brides 102
extended family 107, 109
extrajudicial executions 139, 141
extreme right 29

family council 127, 128, 130, 131, 133, 134
family honour 58, 59, 63, 64, 66, 67, 73, 74, 77, 78, 92, 95, 209
family law 71, 72, 83
family planning 87
Father's group 199
Federation of Kurdish Associations in Sweden 153
female circumcision 148
female genital cutting 162
female genital mutilation 138, 166, 221
female infanticide 170
female political prisoners 77
female suicides 16
femicide 2, 70
feminine identity 54
feminine subjectivity 55, 56
feminism 3, 7, 23, 35
    academic 86
    activist 86
    anti- 5, 26, 29
feminist 82, 84, 96
    activism 88
    comprehensive 99
    consciousness 5
    education 36, 37
    epistemology 7
    knowledge 5, 7, 36
    movements 83, 105
    NGOs 87
    scholars 79
    struggles 4, 28
    theories 4, 22

feminists 7, 28, 40-42, 54, 79, 147
    critical antiracist 83
feudalism 35
First World Conference on Women 167, 168
forced abortion 170
forced assimilation 219
forced marriages 102, 138, 148, 198, 221,
forced pregnancy 170
forced sterilization 170
forced virginity testing 138
Fourth World Conference on Women in Beijing 167
France 178
fraternal incest 65
freedom of expression 139
French election 144
fundamentalism 58
Furundizja 185

Galtung, Johan 157
gang rape 65
Gaza 84
gaza 61
Gbeyo, Gerard 215
gender crimes 24, 29
gender equality 22, 30, 31, 89, 94, 152-154, 159, 167, 199
gender inequality 223
gender oppression 25
gender relations 47
gender violence 7, 24, 30, 181
gender-based violence 169, 172
genocide 17, 32, 70, 172
genocide studies 17
globalization 22, 62, 88
Goran, Abdullah 30
Gothenburg University 218
Gottlieb, Amy 79

governmental organizations 124
Green Line 66
Gulf Wars 30, 31

Hacı Mehmet 131
Hall, Stuart 39, 40
Hamas 61
Hamula 74-76
harassment 119, 131, 133
Hebrew University 79
Hegland, Mary Elaine 27
Help Centres 65
hierarchy 44, 46
history of origin 70
HIV/AIDS 2
Holocaust 29
honour 44, 70, 92, 140, 141, 145, 147, 148
   code 40, 220
   cultures 199
   killing 7, 8, 11, 15, 16, 18, 20-22, 24-30, 32-36, 40, 41, 57, 59-64, 71, 73, 74, 74, 82, 86, 87, 89, 91, 99, 102, 104, 105, 107-9, 137, 138, 203, 211, 213, 216-21
   killing as a practice 28
   murder 19
honour-related violence 8, 91, 92, 149, 156, 157, 194, 195, 197, 200, 203, 211, 216, 220-222
house demolitions 73
HRA 67
Human Rights of Women 170
Human Rights Watch 1
human rights 49, 54, 139, 140, 144, 167, 169, 173, 189, 193, 196, 201
   activists 169
   law 184
   violations 141

ICCPR 180
ICESCR 179
India 2, 147
Indian castes 220
Indian culture 57
Inter-American Court of Human Rights 187
International Criminal Tribunal 185
International Honour Crimes Project 211
International Seminar on Violence in the Name of Honour 7
Iran 5, 6, 147
Iranians 152
Iraq 1, 5, 31, 97, 147, 205, 206, 208
Iraqi Kurdistan 15-17, 30
Iraqi Kurds 31
Iraqis 152
Irbil 16
Ireland 105
Islam 7, 28, 33, 61, 63, 72, 137, 138, 171, 212, 220
Islamic 67
   culture 29, 62
   dowry 53
   fundamentalists 35
   Law 211
   political movements 6
   regimes 6
   Republic of Iran 6
   societies 8
   theocracies 5
   tradition 25
Islamist 6
Israel 1, 57, 60, 62, 67, 69, 70, 72-76, 78, 79, 81, 84, 85
   and racism 80
   colonial check-points 85
   colonial rule 75
   colonial state 76

Family Law 72
    feminist movement 65, 71
    Land Laws 80
    Law of Return 68, 80
    zionist racism 61, 79
Israeli discourse 69
Israeli Jews 64, 68, 78
Israeli police 74
Israelis 75

identity 25, 40, 43, 46, 48, 49
ideological chauvinism 7
imam 138
immigrant 147, 211
    communities 174
    groups 155
    organizations 153, 196
immigrants 143, 144, 159, 212, 214
    immigrants' associations 149
immigration 144
    laws 221
imperialists 89
incest 65, 75
independence 6
individualism 109
infanticide 27
integration 152, 154, 161
İstanbul 7, 114, 134
İzmir 127

jahiliiya 212
Japan 50
Jew 68
Jewish 66, 68, 72, 80
    community 78
    family 73
    feminist groups 72
    feminist movement 73
    race 73
    women 72, 81

Jewish-ness 79
Jewry 68
Jews 65, 66, 69, 80
Jihad 61
Jilani, Hina 104
Jordan 83, 85, 88
Jordanian Ministry of Education 85
Jordanian women 85
Jordanians 63
Juarez, Ciudad 178

KA-MER 9, 17, 20, 21, 113, 115-118,
    120-123, 127-134, 138, 201
kardeş 43
Karlsson, Ingmar 11
Karlsson, Margareta 11
Kelemen, Niklas 10
Khulo' law 83
kin-based societies 44-46
kinship 43, 47, 48, 50, 51
    bonds 44
    terms 44
kinship-based societies 43
Klippan case 215
Knesset 71
Koran 6
Kretzmer, David 79, 80
Kurd 206
Kurdish 93, 103, 106, 145
    culture 25, 29, 30, 32-34, 145,
        146, 148
    diasporas 15
    feminists 30
    nation 33
    nationalism 31
    nationalists 30, 31, 33
    patriarchy 34
    society 31
Kurdish Women Action Against
    Honour Killing (KWAHK) 18, 19

Kurdish Women's Organization 18
KurdishMedia 33
Kurdistan 16, 30, 31, 104, 206
Kurdistan Democratic Party of Iraq (KDP) 31, 32, 207
Kurds 29, 32, 146
    of Iran 31
    of Iraq 31
    Swedish 32

Lahore 104
language of hierarchy 44
Latin America 1, 50
Latin American and Mediterranean peasant societies 220
Laval, Amina 122
Law and Development Studies 211
law of kinship 56
Le Pen 144
Lebanon 88
legal education 23, 24
legalism 23
Lentin, Ronit 79
Levene, Mark 31
liberal (Western) societies 104, 105, 107
Lindh, Anna 113-115
Lower House 83

Maden 117
male domination 36, 50
male honour 27
male violence 15, 30, 36
Malmö 153
Malmö case 215
Mardin 137
media 11, 22, 25
Medical Faculty of Dicle University 115, 116
mehr 53

Men and Gender Equality Project 199
men's violence against women 99
mental humiliation 204, 205
Mernissi, Fatima 89
Middle East 22, 216, 220
Middle Eastern countries 78
Middle Eastern cultures 25, 28
migration 106
militarization 62, 64, 67
minorities 219
minority communities 101, 223
minority cultures 102, 220
Mizrahi 79, 81
    Jews 73, 78, 79
modern society 51
modern state 60
modernity 68
Mojab, Shahrzad 8
Muakher 83
Mukhtar 76
Mullan, Peter 105
multicultural society 148
multiculturalism 143, 144
Muslim 101
    communities 214
    culture 78, 219
    societies 220
    women 86
    world 28
Muslim Brothers 61
Muslims 32, 68, 212, 218, 220

Nairobi conference 168
namus 44, 145
nation-state 22, 46, 48, 51, 52, 54
nationalism 3, 22, 29, 31, 58, 70
nationalists 32, 34
nationalist discourses 54
nationality 78
neo-Nazi 215

neo-colonialism 26
neo-colonialist 34
Netherlands 156, 171
neutrality 27
new immigrants 66
Nigeria 122
nomadic people 220
non-governmental organizations (NGOs) 85, 116, 124, 138, 196, 197
Nordic countries 156
North America 63
North American discourses 67
Northern Ireland 188
Norway 179
nose cutting 138
nuclear family 107
Ny Demokrati 144

objectivity 27
Occident 147
Okin, Susan Moller 101
oppression of women 28
oppressive traditions 26
Orient 147
Orientalism 26
orientalists 6
Orienthälsan 151
other 70, 220
other culture 58
otherization 62
otherness 58
Ottoman Empire 6, 45
Our Honour and His Glory 27
Outcome Document (OD) 170

Pakistan 103, 104, 107, 147
Pakistani parliament 104
Palestine 11, 61, 80, 83, 85, 88
Palestinian 64, 66, 69, 71, 72, 76

Arab family 75
communities 85
family 75-77
feminist groups 71, 72
immigrants 67
land 80
Legislative Council 83
Minister of Women Affairs 83
Ministry of Women's Affairs 84
national and feminist movement 65
national identity 73
nationalism 73
Occupied Territories 61, 71
political prisoners 77
women 85
Palestinians 62, 63, 65, 68, 70, 73, 74, 77, 79-81
in Israel 66, 67
paternal incest 65
patriarchal 5, 74
attitude 152
brutality 30
communities 106, 107
control 102, 107
cultures 26, 29
families 149, 156, 212
ideology 63, 64
oppression 22, 145, 147
order 107
power 24, 165
power structures 194
societies 16, 105, 108, 154
structure 87
system 122, 125
violence 3, 5, 29, 30, 34, 36
patriarchy 3, 4, 15, 25, 26, 30, 34, 35, 57, 59, 76, 82, 102
Italian 34
Kurdish 34

Patriotic Union of Kurdistan (PUK) 18, 31, 32
Peirce, Leslie 47
Personal Status Code 83
personal status laws 71
Pervizat, Leylâ 9
Peshawar 104
philosophical agnosticism 26
physical violence 96, 97, 180, 184
political Islam 62
political rights 68
political violence 64
politics of identity 6
polygamy 138
Pope, Nicole 8
popular culture 22, 25
pornography 221
post-structuralism 6, 25
post-structuralist 26
    thinking 25, 26
post-structuralists 34
postcolonial 39, 147
    nation state 53, 54
    nationalism 52
    societies 39
postmodernism 6
poverty 2
power relations 52
practice theory 28
precapitalist 76
premarital sex 27
prenatal sex selection 170
private property 57
progressive Jews 79
Project for Killings Committed in the Name of Honour 125, 127
proper Jews 60
Prophet 137
prostitution 221
public policy 25

Purple Roof Foundation of İstanbul 180

Quickresponse 218
Qur'an 138, 139, 216

Rabbinicial courts 71
racial inequality 223
racial purification 25, 29
racial royalty 29
racism 25, 26, 29, 32, 62, 70, 79-82, 143, 146, 147, 220
    structural 144
    modernist 25
racist 145, 147, 158
    and exclusionary practices 73
    attitudes 29
    culturalization 29
    policies 78, 83
    totalitarianism 25
racists 29, 32, 34
rape 27, 65, 75, 104, 105, 118, 119, 172, 184, 185, 221
    marital 138, 184, 186
    pre-marital 75
    systematic 170
recm 115
Regional Government of Kurdistan 32
relativists 34
religion 3, 5, 22, 26, 28, 33
religious
    associations 199
    courts 71
    fundamentalism 107
    Israeli laws 71
    movements 58
    obscurantism 6
reputation 92, 93, 96, 98
respect for diversity 25
right to life 24, 37

250 index

right-wing conservatism 105
rights of minorities 148
Riksdag 144
Rizvi, Javeria 11
Rome Statute of the International Criminal Court 172, 183
Rosengard 153
rule of law 23, 24
Russia 158
Russian immigrants 66, 69
Russian Jews 68, 69
Russians 69

Saa'dawi, Nawal 90
Sabbah, Fatina A. 90
safe sex 87
Sahlin, Mona 199
Said, Edward 6
Sara 97, 98
Sarah case 215
Sarwar, Samia 104
Save the Children 157
Sawyer, Dianne 63
School of Oriental and African Studies 211
Seawell, Shelly 63
Second World War 167
second Intifada 85
Secretary-General of Amnesty International 179
self-immolation 16, 17
settler colonialism 68
settler-colonial 79
    state 70, 81
sex discrimination 117
sex education 71, 87
sexist 147
Sexual Equality Agenda 222
sexual 77, 82, 86, 87
    abuse 65

assault 105, 165, 170, 185
crimes 42, 66, 78
equality 222
harassment 65, 77, 185
revolution 160
slavery 170
torture 57
violence 8, 57, 58, 62, 68, 70, 71, 75, 77, 88, 89, 184
sexuality 48, 49, 68, 70, 71, 85, 87-89
seyis 47
Shah, Nafisa 103
shari'a 5, 6
Sharoni, Simona 79
Sheikh 74
Sheiks of the Druze 72
Shohat, Ella 6
Shukri, Muhammed 90
Sır, Dr. Aytekin 121
Silemani 17
Sirman, Nükhet 8
Siverek 117, 121
Social Services 124, 155
social taboo 71
socialism 6
Society for the Protection of Children 124
Somalia 162
Soyaslan, Doğan 182
Special Rapporteur on Violence Against Women 168, 172, 183
spousal abuse 27
starvation 2
Sten, Dilsa Demirbag 9
Stockholm 200
Stockholm Syrian Association 153
Stronger than You Think 198
subordination 26, 50
suicide 188, 195
Sulha system 75

sultan 47
Svahnström, Annika 11
Sweden 9, 17, 25, 28, 91, 94, 106,
    114, 121, 143-145, 147-149, 157-
    159, 161, 162, 194, 195, 199,
    200, 204-206, 208, 211-214, 217,
    219-223
Swedes 34, 143-145
Swedish 91, 93, 94, 99, 161, 213
    courts 212, 215, 216
    feminists 146
    government 33, 34, 162
    Integration Board 196
    Kurds 32
    law 204, 215
    legal system 209
    legislation 203
    Ministry of Justice 10
    Minister of Equality 223
    Minister of Integration 160
    National Board of Health and
    Welfare 196
    National Council for the
    Protection of Women against
    Violence 197
    National Criminal Investigation
    Department 10, 203, 204
    Parliament 94
    Penal Code 217
    police 204, 207, 208
    society 148, 153, 211, 219

Şahindal, Fadime 4, 17, 20, 25, 32-34,
    36, 91, 94, 95, 96, 145, 146, 149,
    162, 166, 195
Şahindal, Rahmi 28
Şemseddin Sami 51

tabtabeh 65, 74, 87
taciz 119

Taliban 6
Terrafem 197, 222
Tevfik Fikret 22
The Case of Ayşe 20, 21
The Magdalene Sisters 105
The Story of Ayşe 127-35
theocratic regimes 5
theorists of difference 26
theorizing the sexual 86, 87
thinking globally 82
Third World 60, 82
tolerance 25, 26
Topkapı 47
torture 57, 139
töre cinayeti 41
tradition 28
traditional societies 50
Turkey 5, 9, 11, 21, 29, 40-42, 44,
    45, 50-52, 54, 56, 107, 113, 122,
    124, 137-139, 141, 145, 147,
    171, 177, 180, 183, 187, 188, 190
Turkish
    Civil Code 1926 41, 48, 49, 52,
    55, 183, 190
    culture 140
    immigrants 153
    law 55
    Law for the Protection of the
    Family 188
    Ministry of Health 51
    nationalism 53
    Parliamentary Justice Commission
    41
    Penal Code 41, 42, 56, 139, 182-
    185, 190
    Republic 48, 52
    society 46
    Sub-Committee Ministry of Justice
    182
    Surname law 52

Turks 152

underage marriages 102
unemployment 143
UNICEF 158
United Nations (UN) 2, 10, 144, 155, 158, 162, 167, 200
United Nations General Assembly 141, 167, 168, 170, 171, 186, 200
United Nations Secretary General 200
United States 29, 82, 106, 178
Universal Declaration of Human Rights 123, 167, 179, 189
Upper House 83, 104
Upper Sindh 107
Uppsala 145
urbanization 106
Urfa 121, 123

Van 123
Velasquez-Rodriguez decision 187
Vidar 158
Vienna 168
Vienna and Beijing Declarations 179
Vienna Declaration and Programme of Action 168
violence against women 1, 2, 4, 7, 8, 15, 19, 23, 28, 29, 32, 34, 58, 82, 84, 86, 91, 92, 96, 101, 104, 105, 125, 139, 157, 166, 168, 169, 173, 174, 177, 179, 180, 181, 183, 187, 190, 193, 194, 199, 219-221, 223
virgin 92, 93, 95
virginity 39, 77, 87, 92, 93, 96, 106, 122, 123, 140, 160, 182, 205

Wales 105
wars 27
    civil 5
    neo-colonialist 5
    regional 5
Welchman, Dr. Lynn 211
West Bank 84
Western 78
    countries 106, 173
    cultural hegemony 82
    cultures 25, 33, 62, 89
    Europe 160
    liberal societies 102
    media 101
    societies 105
    society 101, 109
    states 6
Western/European tradition 57
Westerners 75
Westernized 72
Westerstrand, Jenny 97
White 69, 78
whore 92, 93, 95
Women Entrepreneurship programme 113
Women's Convention 180
Women's Street Market 113
women's activist groups 88
women's human rights 39, 55, 123, 124, 138, 139, 141, 162, 166, 167, 172, 174
women's movements 35, 83, 168, 178
women's NGOs 161, 213
women's organizations 55, 122, 124, 128, 138
women's rights 6, 35, 87, 105, 107, 116, 159, 193, 201
women's rights activist 103
women's shelters 2, 37, 67, 84, 103, 120, 124, 149, 160, 180, 196
women's studies 37
women's suicides 32
women's suppression 76

women's/gender NGO 88
World Bank 178
World Conference on Human Rights 168

Yassin, Ali 90
Yol 30

Youth Programme Manager 220
Yugoslavia 185
Yuval-Davis, Nira 79

zionist 68, 69
zionist/racist 68
zone of genocide 31